D0309468

International Political Economy Series
General Editor: Timothy M. Shaw, Professor and Director, Institute of International Relations, The University of the West Indies, Trinidad&Tobago

Titles include:

Andreas Bieler and Adam David Morton (*editors*)
SOCIAL FORCES IN THE MAKING OF THE NEW EUROPE
The Restructuring of European Social Relations in the Global Political Economy

Ian Bruff
CULTURE AND CONSENSUS IN EUROPEAN VARIETIES OF CAPITALISM
A 'Common Sense' Analysis

Steve Chan and A. Cooper Drury (*editors*)
SANCTIONS AS ECONOMIC STATECRAFT
Theory and Practice

Aldo Chircop, André Gerolymatos and John O. Iatrides
THE AEGEAN SEA AFTER THE COLD WAR
Security and Law of the Sea Issues

Chad Damro
COOPERATING ON COMPETITION IN TRANSATLANTIC ECONOMIC RELATIONS
The Politics of Dispute Prevention

Diane Ethier
ECONOMIC ADJUSTMENT IN NEW DEMOCRACIES
Lessons from Southern Europe

Jeffrey Henderson (*editor*)
INDUSTRIAL TRANSFORMATION IN EASTERN EUROPE IN THE LIGHT OF THE EAST ASIAN EXPERIENCE

Jacques Hersh and Johannes Dragsbaek Schmidt (*editors*)
THE AFTERMATH OF 'REAL EXISTING SOCIALISM' IN EASTERN EUROPE
Volume 1: Between Western Europe and East Asia

Peadar Kirby
THE CELTIC TIGER IN DISTRESS
Growth with Inequality in Ireland

Peadar Kirby
CELTIC TIGER IN COLLAPSE (*Second Edition*)
Explaining the Weaknesses of the Irish Model

Anne Lorentzen and Marianne Rostgaard (*editors*)
THE AFTERMATH OF 'REAL EXISTING SOCIALISM' IN EASTERN EUROPE
Volume 2: People and Technology in the Process of Transition

Gary McMahon (*editor*)
LESSONS IN ECONOMIC POLICY FOR EASTERN EUROPE FROM LATIN AMERICA

Árni Sverrison and Meine Pieter van Dijk (*editors*)
LOCAL ECONOMIES IN TURMOIL
The Effect of Deregulation and Globalization

International Political Economy Series
Series Standing Order ISBN 978–0–333–71708–0 hardcover
Series Standing Order ISBN 978–0–333–71110–1 paperback
(*outside North America only*)

You can receive future titles in this series as they are published by placing a standing order. Please contact your bookseller or, in case of difficulty, write to us at the address below with your name and address, the title of the series and one of the ISBNs quoted above.

Customer Services Department, Macmillan Distribution Ltd, Houndmills, Basingstoke, Hampshire RG21 6XS, England

Also by Peadar Kirby
POVERTY AMID PLENTY
THE CELTIC TIGER IN DISTRESS
INTRODUCTION TO LATIN AMERICA
VULNERABILITY AND VIOLENCE: The Impact of Globalisation

Celtic Tiger in Collapse

Explaining the Weaknesses of the Irish Model

Second Edition

Peadar Kirby
Professor of International Politics and Public Policy,
University of Limerick, Ireland

First edition published 2002 as *The Celtic Tiger in Distress.*
Second edition published 2010 by
PALGRAVE MACMILLAN

Palgrave Macmillan in the UK is an imprint of Macmillan Publishers Limited,
registered in England, company number 785998, of Houndmills, Basingstoke,
Hampshire RG21 6XS.

Palgrave Macmillan in the US is a division of St Martin's Press LLC,
175 Fifth Avenue, New York, NY 10010.

Palgrave Macmillan is the global academic imprint of the above companies
and has companies and representatives throughout the world.

Palgrave® and Macmillan® are registered trademarks in the United States,
the United Kingdom, Europe and other countries.

ISBN 978–0–230–23743–8   hardback
ISBN 978–0–230–23744–5   paperback

This book is printed on paper suitable for recycling and made from fully
managed and sustained forest sources. Logging, pulping and manufacturing
processes are expected to conform to the environmental regulations of the
country of origin.

A catalogue record for this book is available from the British Library.

A catalog record for this book is available from the Library of Congress.

10 9 8 7 6 5 4 3 2 1
19 18 17 16 15 14 13 12 11 10

Printed and bound in Great Britain by
CPI Antony Rowe, Chippenham and Eastbourne

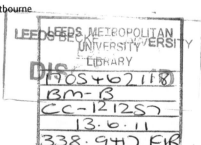

I dedicate this book to Kitty O'Shea whose constant love and support since my childhood has helped make my life's journey possible.

Contents

List of Tables

List of Boxes

Foreword

There could seldom have been as good a reason for a second edition of a book as there is for this one. Most second editions update texts, incorporating new developments and perhaps honing arguments in the light of the reception of the earlier edition and of ongoing debates on its subject. The change in the title of this edition from that of the first edition, *The Celtic Tiger in Distress*, indicates that this is much more than an updating since the sudden collapse of the Celtic Tiger in 2008 has thrown open in a dramatic way the predominant interpretations of the phenomenon. While discussions for a second edition were already underway before the collapse of 2008 – prompted by the continuing interest of the series editor, Professor Tim Shaw, in the book's subject – that collapse has not only added an urgency to the need for a new edition but has also served to vindicate the basic theoretical framework that marks the book's main contribution to social science literature. Suddenly, the benign consensus about the successful nature of the Irish model, both in academic circles and among the general public, has evaporated to be replaced by varying degrees of critical appraisal that were so lacking during the boom years. In many ways, this is virtually a new book, though the essential continuity of its framework of analysis with that of the first edition will be clear to readers of both. However, the period since it was written in 2001 was marked by an avalanche of books on the Celtic Tiger and by lively debates on key aspects of the Irish model, debates to which unfortunately both the media and policymakers paid little or no attention. This new edition therefore is able to draw on these debates substantially to refine its central argument about the nature of the interrelationship between state, market and society in the Irish case that allow for the identification of a recognisable Irish model. While the first edition was widely referenced in works on the Celtic Tiger, my frustration as author was that it became one of the two or three texts that were routinely mentioned as embodying a radical critique, without the central features of that critique being explained or engaged with. I suspect that many who referenced the book had never read it, certainly not with any care nor with a concern to understand and assess its central arguments. I hope that the more critical approach towards analysing the Celtic Tiger that is now underway may lead to such an assessment as a contribution to helping overcome the entrenched features of the Irish political, economic and social structures that the collapse so clearly reveals.

As always, the debts of gratitude mount at a time like this. The first must go to Tim Shaw who has from the beginning taken a great personal interest both in me and in the Irish case. It was a suggestion by him in April 2007 that first got me thinking about the possibility of a second edition and he has strongly supported me in bringing it to fruition, not least in championing the idea with the editorial team at Palgrave Macmillan. From our first contact, Alexandra Webster, associate director and head of social sciences at Palgrave Macmillan, strongly supported the idea and did more than anyone else to ensure that it has happened. It has been a great pleasure to deal with her and with her assistant Renée Takken who ably guided me through the practical tasks that are the necessary accompaniments of a project such as this one. I thank both of them for their support and help. The project was also warmly supported by my colleagues in the Department of Politics and Public Administration at the University of Limerick to where I moved from Dublin City University between the first and second editions. My new department has proven a very fruitful environment in which to discuss, debate and develop the key themes of this book – one where woolly thinking is quickly exposed and where high standards of rigorous analysis and careful use of evidence are upheld. To all my colleagues, most especially to my friends Dr Maura Adshead and Professor Tom Lodge, I want to say a most warm thank you. From his new home in Barcelona, my former PhD supervisor, Professor Fred Halliday, has continued to be an inspiration to me and has been a good friend through his interest in and support for my work. I greatly enjoy our occasional meetings at various points of the northern Mediterranean Spanish coast for Fred has few rivals as a committed and engaged intellectual with a rich questing mind and spirit. As well as being an inspiration, I have come to recognise that he is my role model for all that is good in academic life. As always, my greatest gratitude goes to my life partner, Toni, and our two wonderful and creative daughters, Bríd and Caoimhe, daughters of the Celtic Tiger who will hopefully help fashion a path beyond it to a better society. While I dedicated the first edition to them, my dedication this time is to Kitty O'Shea whose rejoicing in my career, success and life journey remains for me a most wonderful gift. *Go raibh fada buan í inár measc.*

The epigraph in Chapter 5 is a quotation from *Ireland and the Global Question*, Cork University Press, 2006, © Michael O'Sullivan 2006. Printed with the kind permission of Cork University Press, Youngline Industrial Estate, Pouladuff, Cork.

Peadar Kirby
Limerick
September 2009

Introduction: The Collapse of the Irish Model

The collapse of the 'Irish Model'

The year 2008 was a year of rude awakening for the citizens of Ireland. After a decade-and-a-half of high economic growth which had seen the country become the envy of many around the world and was looked to by policy-makers as a model of successful development in this globalised era, the final months of 2008 brought humiliating collapse. The Irish, who had grown used to glowing praise by foreign leaders and the international media, now had to adjust to the realities of being not only in one of the most severe economic downturns in the European Union but in a depression that was estimated by the prestigious Economic and Social Research Institute (ESRI) would see Ireland's economy contract by around 14 per cent between 2008 and 2010 which they described as being 'by historic and international standards ... a truly dramatic development' (Barrett et al., 2009: 32). European Commission figures showed a decline of 2.3 per cent in Ireland's GDP in 2008, a forecast decline of nine per cent for 2009 and a further decline of 2.6 per cent in 2010. This put Ireland just behind the three Baltic states for the depth of its economic depression over these three years but Ireland found itself in the worst position in the EU in terms of its budget deficit. After years of running a budget surplus, the country's public finances dramatically worsened in 2008 with a deficit that reached 7.1 per cent of GDP; the European Commission forecast in spring 2009 that this would reach 15.6 per cent of GDP by 2010, making it impossible to know when Ireland might return to the EU limit of three per cent of GDP. This compared to forecast deficits for 2010 of 13.6 per cent of GDP for Latvia and eight per cent for Lithuania, the two next worst cases in the EU (European Commission, 2009a). The IMF in mid-2009 predicted a GDP decline of about 13.5 per cent for Ireland between 2008 and 2010 with unemployment set to reach 15.5 per cent in 2010. It predicted a return to two per cent growth as late as 2014. It concluded that Ireland 'was perhaps the most overheated of all advanced economies' (IMF, 2009: 5) and said the Irish crisis 'matches

1

episodes of the most severe economic distress in post–World War II history' (IMF, 2009: 28).

At home the reality of economic recession hit with a force that shook the economic and political elites to the core. By mid-2009, unemployment had risen to 12 per cent, over double of what it had been a year previously, and the ESRI estimated it would reach 16.8 per cent of the labour force by 2010. The Taoiseach (Prime Minister), Brian Cowen, admitted publicly that living standards were likely to fall by between 10 and 12 per cent over the next few years. Tax revenues fell by €8 billion in 2008 and the government raised only €37 billion in tax, the same as it had raised in 2005. The current budget deficit reached €12 billion in 2008 and was predicted by the government to jump to over €20 billion in 2009. With tax receipts in freefall by early 2009, exceeding the government's worst-case forecasts in a number of that year's early months, the government slapped a levy on the salaries of all public service workers in early 2009 reducing annual salaries from three per cent for the lowest paid to just under ten per cent for the highest paid and followed that with further levies on income tax of between two and six per cent in an emergency budget. Even with these measures in place, by mid-year the exchequer deficit had widened to €10.6bn three times what it had been over the same period in 2008. As the *Irish Times* editorialised: 'The question now is how 2009 living standards can be financed on a 2003 level of tax revenue. The answer is with great difficulty, and only with a high – and unsustainable – level of borrowing' (*The Irish Times*, 4 June 2009: 17). For many Irish, this seemed a return to the grim days of the past that they had been led to believe were gone forever during the golden years of the Celtic Tiger boom.

During the 1990s, Ireland's economy grew at an annual average rate of around 7.5 per cent and in some years towards the end of the decade surpassed ten per cent growth. Not only was this more than three times the average of European countries at the time but it made Ireland one of the most economically successful countries in the world, rivalling the growth of China. Unemployment, for long a deep structural problem of the Irish economy, was virtually eliminated and a country used for over 150 years to seeing generation after generation of its young emigrating now had the new experience of becoming a country of immigrants, with Eastern Europeans, Africans, Latin Americans and Asians coming to share in the Irish boom. By the mid-2000s, over ten per cent of the population was made up of immigrants and the Irish became used to hearing Polish spoken in the pubs and on the buses, to being served by Chinese waiters and Latin American waitresses in the restaurants, and seeing shops opened for Middle Easterners, Eastern Europeans, Africans and Asians. For the Irish, this became known as the Celtic Tiger, a term taken from the legendary success of the East Asian Tigers in the 1980s and early 1990s. Political and policy discourse changed completely with attention being focused on our innovative system of partnership governance, Ireland's developmental state showing how to ride the waves of globalisation successfully, and its activist social policies that ensured the benefits of the boom were widely shared. The 'Irish model' as it became known was seen as a beacon of success for developmental late-comers in central and eastern Europe, in Latin America, in Southern Africa and even among developed states like Canada. Ireland became the poster child of the EU, proudly mentioned as proof of the Union's policy package. Ireland had become 'a showpiece of globalisation' (Smith, 2005: 2).

Box 0.1 'Reykjavik-on-Liffey'

In February 2009 the *Economist* (7 February) magazine made unflattering comparisons between Ireland and Iceland: what is the different between both countries, it asked, and answered: 'one letter and six months'. The collapse of the Icelandic economy six months previously had forced the country into the arms of the IMF; by early 2009 Ireland's plight seemed every bit as bad as Iceland's except for one four-letter word, the euro. It was, in the words of the *Economist*, Reykjavik on the Liffey.

For a number of commentators, including the former Irish EU Commissioner, Peter Sutherland, the president of the European Central Bank, Jean-Claude Trichet, and the EU Commission president, Jose Manuel Barroso, what kept Ireland afloat was its membership of the euro. The fate of the two countries was also linked by Economics Nobel prize winner, Paul Krugman (see below).

The similarities between the collapse in both countries were striking. It originated in the banking sector which had overextended itself – in the Irish case through loans to property developers, in the Icelandic case through diversifying abroad and drawing in capital by offering high interest rates. When the US subprime crisis began to affect liquidity in the international banking system, both countries' banks found it difficult to borrow and thereby to cover their liabilities which were growing by the day.

The economic impact of both crises was also similar with GDP predicted to decline by around nine per cent in both in 2009, unemployment in mid-2009 at below nine per cent in Iceland compared to 12 per cent for Ireland and a budget deficit of 14 per cent of GDP in Iceland compared to Ireland's 12 per cent. The principal difference is that Icelanders were labouring under interest rates of around 15 per cent in an attempt to prop up the krona even though it was no longer being traded openly. Most Icelandic economists do not expect the national currency to ever trade on the open market again and are hoping that Iceland can join the eurozone as soon as possible. Meanwhile most Icelanders are holidaying at home as foreign currency is difficult to obtain.

Yet while Iceland is taking the pain, the devaluation of its currency means that its exports are soaring and tourism is booming so that it hopes to return to growth in 2010; meanwhile Ireland, locked into the eurozone with no possibility of devaluation as a means to stimulate exports, was said to be experiencing one of its worst summers on record for tourism in 2009 (Burke-Kennedy, 2009) and facing a long and painful adjustment that could last years.

So what had caused things to change and with such severity? While Ireland's recession mirrored what was going on in most European states and further afield, the particular causes of the Irish economic crisis were decidedly local in origin as the Irish economy had come to be unsustainably dependent on house-building and private consumption since the dotcom crash of 2001 had undermined the key role the US information technology sector had played in creating the Tiger boom. Despite warnings from some economists and other academics, the feel-good factor generated by the boom made most politicians and much of the public believe the hype that the good years would last forever. Government subsidies fuelled a frenzy of building around the country, and banks lent recklessly to developers to buy land at grossly inflated prices and to customers to buy the houses and apartments built on this land at equally high prices. Being a member of the eurozone meant that interest rates in Ireland remained low which further added to the orgy of borrowing and consumption. Over these years, inflation rose to the highest levels in the eurozone. With state coffers awash with revenues from taxes on goods and services, and on the sale and buying of property, the state reduced income taxes and taxes on capital gains thereby seriously eroding its tax base. As long as high levels of growth continued, government tax receipts held up; as soon as growth declined tax revenues slumped disastrously. As former Taoiseach and professional economist, Garret FitzGerald, has written: 'The idea that when the boom ended our public and social services could be maintained with such a minuscule level of income tax payments was patently absurd, although clearly many people fell for it – including our economically unsophisticated business community' (FitzGerald, 2008a: 14). Economists have made a distinction between the structural deficit in Irish state finances and the cyclical deficit; the first is due to domestic policy decisions while the second is due to the international recession (O'Leary, 2009: 6). While estimates of the size of the structural deficit vary from six per cent to ten per cent of GDP, the Irish government accepted before the April 2009 budget that eight per cent of the estimated 12 per cent of GDP budget deficit was structural (Collins, 2009: 11); this means they accept that two-thirds of the Irish collapse is the result of domestic factors.

If Ireland was studied in the late 1990s and most of the 2000s to learn the lessons of how a small, peripheral country, a relative latecomer to development, could so successfully avail of the benefits of globalisation, its sudden collapse raised a new and more troubling set of questions for many. The economics Nobel prize winner, Paul Krugman, addressed them in an article in *The New York Times* in April 2006. He wrote: 'How did Ireland get into its current bind? By being just like us, only more so. Like its near-namesake Iceland, Ireland jumped with both feet into the brave new world of unsupervised global markets. ... One part of the Irish economy that became especially free was the banking sector, which used its freedom to finance a monstrous housing bubble. ... And the lesson of Ireland is that you really, really don't want to put yourself in a position where you have to punish your economy in order to save your banks' (Krugman, 2009). Yet however new the immediate reasons appear, they derive from more fundamental weaknesses in Ireland's model of development, weaknesses that were already apparnt at the height of the boom. The first edition of this book (Kirby 2002a), written in 2001, was devoted to identifying these weaknesses. It outlined three difficulties with the positive story of Ireland's success, weaknesses that can now be seen as being central to its collapse.

Three difficulties

Ireland's Celtic Tiger boom generated an extensive academic literature on economic, social, political and cultural aspects (see, for example, Ging et al., 2009; Ó Broin and Kirby, 2009; Bradley and Kennelly, 2008; Adshead et al., 2008; O'Donovan and Glavanis-Grantham, 2008; Kuhling and Keohane, 2007; Allen, 2007; Fahey et al., 2007; Bartley and Kitchen, 2007; O'Sullivan, 2006; Boyle, 2005; Paus, 2005; Smith, 2005; Taylor, 2005; Ó Riain, 2004; Clinch et al., 2002; Kirby 2002a; Allen, 2000; Nolan et al., 2000; Sweeney, 1999). While a very positive reading emphasising Ireland's achievements and the policy instruments used (see Chapter 2) became dominant in the public debates both at home and abroad (particularly through the media) and fed into a widespread mood of self-congratulation (Mac Sharry and White, 2000), many scholars identified weaknesses in the model to which more serious attention is now being devoted since the economic collapse of 2008. These can be summarised under three headings: firstly, fundamental questions have been raised about the validity of the assertions that the Irish economy was transformed into a high-tech, high-growth economy. Secondly, economic success goes hand in hand with glaring social failures which again pose questions about whether the Irish case was a story of developmental success as distinct from a narrower story of an economic boom. Finally, the assertion that the Celtic Tiger was an example of how economic latecomers could adjust to the challenges of globalisation in a way that maximised the benefits for their society rested on an inadequate understanding of the nature of globalisation and its impact on national states and societies, the limitations of which are now much more apparent. Each of these difficulties is briefly elaborated upon here and reference made in each case to later chapters where a fuller exposition of the critique is offered. This critique draws attention to the essential point of this book, namely that Ireland's economic depression owes far more to long-standing structural weaknesses of its economy, society and political system; these weaknesses were camouflaged during the boom but become apparent again amid economic decline.

Economy transformed?

The first difficulty relates to the claims that the Irish economy has been transformed. Briefly, the mainstream case runs as follows: since the late 1980s, Ireland has progressed rapidly towards average European living standards after decades of little or no convergence. This is measured in increased per capita income and a growth in numbers at work, particularly in the most modern industrial sectors (chemicals, and metals and engineering) (Barry et al., 1999: 22–3) and in middle-class employment positions (O'Connell and Russell, 2007). This has been done through an upgrading of Ireland's industrial structure particularly by means of attracting in a high share of foreign direct investment (FDI) which has 'affected every corner of the Irish economy' (Bradley, 2000: 12). 'Ireland eventually succeeded in attracting sufficient firms in the computer, instrument engineering, pharmaceutical and chemical sectors to merit a description of sector "agglomerations" or "clusters"' (ibid.: 13). Furthermore, at the height of the Celtic Tiger boom, indigenous Irish industry began to expand (in employment, output and, more erratically, exports) after decades of relative decline under the impact of free trade (O'Sullivan, 2000: 271). Thus, economists were claiming that 'the Irish economy is truly undergoing something of a renaissance' and, in belatedly catching up with the rest of its western European neighbours, it has, 'in a sense, come of age' (Fitz Gerald, 2000: 27 and 30). The critique of this reading rests fundamentally on two arguments. Firstly, as Bradley acknowledges, the 'dominance of the Irish manufacturing sector by foreign multinationals ... [is] quite unique by OECD experience' (Bradley, 2000: 13), leading one leading Irish economist to characterise the Celtic Tiger as 'the US High Tech Tiger with the Celtic face' (Murphy, 1998: 3). Thus the question was repeatedly raised as to whether the 'Irish' success was not largely a function of the boom in the US economy. As O'Sullivan wrote: 'The "miracle" part of the Irish economy seems to be driven by a relatively low number of high-technology multinationals (mostly American), while indigenous firms are pedestrian by comparison' (O'Sullivan, 2006: 76). Data on firms assisted by Ireland's industrial development agencies supports this conclusion: in 2006 foreign-owned firms employed 153,510 while indigenous firms employed 151,610. However, the value of the output of the Irish firms came to €9.7bn while that of the foreign-owned sector was €50.6bn or 83.9 per cent of the total output. Furthermore, the foreign-owned firms dominated the following sectors: chemicals and pharmaceuticals, electrical and electronic equipment, software and medical devices (Forfás 2008a). Secondly, through a more detailed empirical examination, Mary O'Sullivan has raised questions not only about the evolution of the microeconomic structure of the Irish industrial economy to more closely resemble a region of the US, but also about the concentration of indigenous success in a small number of firms and sectors (O'Sullivan, 2000: 283). And Michael O'Sullivan has drawn attention to the fact that 'the public face of Irish business abroad is represented by private airlines, the speculative activities of Irish oligarchs [and] the expansion of Irish property empires' (O'Sullivan, 2006: 82). This latter point is mirrored by the excessive role that construction began to play in the growth of the Irish economy following the bursting of the dotcom bubble in the US in the early 2000s. The claims made for Irish economic transformation, therefore, seem to rest on insufficient evidence and on a failure to appreciate the vulnerability of Ireland's increased economic dependence on the US (in terms of FDI and of exports). The nature of Ireland's Celtic Tiger economy is introduced in Chapter 2 and more fully explained in Chapter 8.

Economic success, social failure?

The second difficulty relates to the social impact of the Celtic Tiger economy. As will be detailed in Chapter 3, there is substantial social scientific evidence to show that Ireland's economic boom disproportionately benefited new groups of technical professionals and self-employed small business entrepreneurs and that 'the bulk of Irish society has ... acquiesced to [sic] the increasing gap between themselves and the rising professional and business classes' (Ó Riain and O'Connell, 2000: 339). Furthermore, across a range of issues – housing and homelessness, public transport and traffic gridlock, declining quality of care and growing inequality of access to health services, a crisis in services for young people in need – there was growing evidence that Ireland's level of social provision lagged badly behind that of many European countries. As former Taoiseach Garret FitzGerald wrote: 'Our chaotic health service and our grossly understaffed education system, together with the many serious inadequacies of our social services, reflect very badly upon a political system that has massively maldistributed the huge resources we have created. The harsh truth is we have allowed far too much of our new wealth to be creamed off by a few influential people, at the expense of the public services our people are entitled to' (FitzGerald, 2008b).

Finally, the Ireland of the Celtic Tiger has also been shown to have 'diverged from the European pattern of welfare effort' as the ratio of social security spending to GDP fell markedly in Ireland while it was maintained or increased in most European countries (Ó Riain and O'Connell, 2000: 331; Kirby, 2008a: 28). However, the mainstream reading of Ireland's transformation failed to acknowledge sufficiently this ambiguity at the heart of the Celtic Tiger, preferring to concentrate on aggregate increases in living standards and employment rather than on how these are distributed or how Ireland's levels of social provision compare with those of its European neighbours.

The Ireland of the Celtic Tiger therefore clearly gave priority to economic growth over social equity and discussion of what development might or should mean was remarkably absent from the mainstream debates at the time. Indeed, as Chapter 4 details, issues of distributional equity were largely ignored by mainstream theorists of the Celtic Tiger while, as Chapter 9 discusses, these have also largely slipped from the Irish state's policy agenda, with only rhetorical lip service being paid to them. This book argues in Chapters 3 and 6 that such neglect of issues of social and economic equality not only undermines the claims made for developmental success but also undermines the sustainability of economic growth and social cohesion. Chapter 9 introduces the concept of vulnerability, arguing that this best characterises the social impact of the Celtic Tiger model as is shown in its dramatic collapse in late 2008. This vulnerability, of which the multiple inequalities outlined in this book are one cause, undermines the claims made for Ireland as a model for other countries to follow. Overall, then, a central theme of this book is to highlight the social impact of Ireland's economic growth and, based on the empirical evidence, to map out how the economic boom exacerbated rather than resolved the country's long-standing problems of poverty and inequality.

Adjusting to globalisation? The role of the state

This links closely with the third difficulty with Ireland's growth model, namely the ways Ireland adjusted to globalisation and the lessons this holds. As the evidence of Ireland's economic boom grew in the 1990s, it quickly became linked to the emerging topic of globalisation and came to be seen as one of its great success cases. In the widely referenced globalisation index published by the US *Foreign Policy* magazine from 2001 to 2007, Ireland emerged as one of the most globalised countries in the world, coming first place three years in a row (2002–4) and always within the top six (see A.T. Kearney/Foreign Policy, 2007, 2006, 2005, 2004, 2003, 2002, 2001). However, if globalisation had earlier been widely seen as a very positive force from which Ireland benefited, by 2009 attention was being focused on its vulnerabilities amid debates about who was to bear the severe cutbacks being required to maintain some semblance of order in the national finances. It was clear that not only were many more Irish people vulnerable to the fate of the economy but that Ireland itself was experiencing the vulnerabilities that countries in Asia, Africa and Latin America had experienced in the 1990s as they were hit by severe financial and economic collapses.

In seeking to benefit from globalisation, the Irish state played a decisive role in structuring the relationship between state and market. As Krugman put it, the state facilitated the freedoms given to the banking sector, it spurred the housing boom and it put in place a light-touch regulatory system seeking to encourage the market rather than restrain it. To this extent, the Irish case was sometimes seen as being an alternative to neo-liberalism because of the active role played by the state. As Nolan et al. (2000: 1) claimed in their widely referenced book, 'the Irish growth experience and its distributional consequences is not a simple story of globalisation, forced withdrawal of the state and the promotion of neo-liberalism'. However, this overlooks the agency of the state in promoting the market freedoms that Krugman identified as being the principal cause of the depth and severity of Ireland's crisis. This, therefore, raises major questions about the nature and role of the Irish state, and the ways it has been reconstituted over the course of the Celtic Tiger boom. These questions are discussed in the chapters on state, market and society in Part III and structure the discussion of the future of the Irish model in Part IV (Chapters 7 to 10).

The three difficulties outlined in this section lie at the heart of the Irish collapse. The reliance on stimulating an unsustainable construction boom to replace the growth model based on FDI and the role of the very lightly regulated banks in facilitating this, was the proximate cause, but the vulnerabilities this has exposed in the capacity and resilience of the Irish state derive from the low-tax regime that was seen as the central policy mechanism for attracting foreign investment. Behind these lie the role of the state and the ways in which it understood the opportunities of globalisation. What has collapsed therefore is Ireland's dependent low-tax model of state-led development. This book is a contribution to focusing attention on this central and essential issue, as well as opening a discussion on how to construct a new model of development.

Outline

The principal contribution of this book to the social science literature on the Celtic Tiger and, more generally, to the literature on Ireland's development, is its theoretical approach. It is this, it is argued, which has helped to identify core structural weaknesses of the Irish growth model, offering insights not offered by other theoretical approaches, insights that have been vindicated by subsequent developments. However, before discussing theoretical approaches in the literature on Irish development and specifically on the Celtic Tiger, Part I is devoted to chapters on the pre-Tiger period (Chapter 1), to assessing the boom (Chapter 2) and to interrogating its social impact (Chapter 3). Since a central part of the book's case is to challenge the adequacy of the theoretical lens through which the Irish case is being interpreted and to outline an alternative theoretical approach, it devotes Part II to examining the ways in which the Celtic Tiger is being understood. Chapter 4 examines mainstream (neoclassical, new growth theory, modernisation theory) approaches, while Chapter 5 looks at critical explanations (Marxist and dependency theory, and political economy approaches). Chapter 6 devotes its attention to outlining a more adequate theoretical approach, namely the international political economy of development. This provides the theoretical lens for Parts III and IV. Part III maps out the international political economy of Ireland's development in the 1990s with chapters on state (Chapter 7), on market (Chapter 8) and on society (Chapter 9). Part IV asks if the Irish model has a future. Its one chapter examines the options facing Ireland following the collapse of the Celtic Tiger.

Part I The Celtic Tiger and Its Aftermath

1
Before the Tiger

> Irish economic performance has been the least impressive
> in western Europe, perhaps in all Europe, in the twentieth
> century.
>
> Professor Joe Lee (1989: 521)

The high-growth phase of Ireland's development known as the Celtic Tiger is
usually dated to the fiscal austerity programme implemented by the minority Fianna Fáil government which took office in March 1987 (for an insider
account, see Mac Sharry and White, 2000). However, the nature and extent
of economic transformation which followed cannot be fully appreciated
unless seen against the backdrop of various phases of Ireland's development
since its independence in 1922. This is the purpose of the present chapter.
Chapter 2 will describe the nature of the Celtic Tiger since its emergence in
1987 while Chapter 3 will examine its ambiguous social impacts.

In looking at the history of Ireland's development, this chapter proceeds
in four stages. It begins by highlighting the fact that, unlike most of its
near neighbours, Ireland is a Newly Industrialising Country (NIC) bearing
marked similarities to the development trajectory of East Asian and Latin
American countries. The chapter then traces in more detail various phases
of Ireland's development up to the advent of the Celtic Tiger. It next outlines some distinctive features of Irish industrialisation such as the duality
between foreign and domestic sectors, and its employment intensity. The
nature and pace of Irish industrialisation is then compared to that of some
East Asian and Latin American NICs. Finally, given the concerns of this book
with the distributional impact of economic growth, it examines the extent
of poverty and social inequality prior to the Celtic Tiger.

Ireland: A newly industrialising country

Irish economic development has followed a path very different to that of the
main capitalist economies, either large or small, geographically contiguous

to Ireland, the experiences of which tend to inform mainstream economic theories. The divergence between the Irish experience and that of the rest of western Europe can be dated back to the nineteenth century; the incipient levels of industrialisation in the late eighteenth century did not prosper and, particularly following the Great Famine (1845–49), the economy became more and more dependent on agricultural production and, within that, on pasture. The only exception was the north-east of the island which became an industrial growth pole within the British economy. As this remained part of the UK when the rest of the island became independent, the new state had an economy which approximated to that of a typical 'Third World' mono-crop type. Excluding food and drink industries, it 'was virtually without industries' (Ó Gráda, 1994: 313).

Conservative economic management for the first decade of the new state's existence made little attempt to change this situation. Only with a change of government in 1932 was a determined attempt made to foster industrialisation through a policy of import substitution industrialisation (ISI) similar to that followed by some Latin American countries such as Argentina, Brazil, Chile and Mexico (O'Malley, 1992: 32). Following initial successes, this policy ran up against the limitations of the small home market and led to balance of payments difficulties in the 1950s. This resulted in a complete change of economic policy with the liberalisation of the economy and the adoption of an export-oriented industrial strategy from the late 1950s. Foreign investment, with multinational companies setting up plants throughout the state, led to a second wave of industrialisation. On this occasion, however, it was oriented to export markets rather than to domestic needs and the requirements of the multinational sector came to dominate state policy.

This account of the political economy of Irish growth raises questions about the conventional categorisation of Ireland as a developed country. Though an original member of the Organisation for Economic Co-operation and Development (OECD), the group of the world's most industrialised countries, and classified by the World Bank as a high-income country, Ireland's distinctive development path distinguishes it from most of the other members of the OECD (with the exception of recent entrants Mexico and South Korea). This is due to its recent industrialisation and to its unique demographic profile which saw the population of the present territory of the Republic of Ireland decline from 6.5 million in 1841 to 2.9 million in 1925. It remained at this level until 1972 and began a marked increase only in the 1990s, from 3.6 million in 1996 to 4.2 million in 2006 (Maddison, 1995: 108, 109; the 1841 figure is taken from Ó Gráda, 1997: 193; the 1996 and 2006 figures are from the Central Statistics Office). This established a social pattern whereby emigration to Britain, the US and other English-speaking countries became a normal means for young Irish people to find work and the levels of emigration increased and decreased in tune with the fortunes of Ireland's economy. During periods of acute economic downturn, such as the 1950s and the 1980s, it reached about one per cent of the population in some years while in the boom years of the 1970s and the 1990s to 2000s, it gave way to net immigration. The persistence of emigration has been described as 'one of the key driving forces in the Irish economy' allowing rising living standards to go hand in hand with de-industrialisation (O'Rourke, 1995: 420).

If we allow for the fact that, due to emigration, Irish income levels have been higher than they would otherwise have been and accept that it has been a late industrialiser, it can be seen that the Republic of Ireland approximates more to the category of an NIC than to the developed countries of western Europe.[1] Furthermore, the nature of its industrialisation confirms its similarity to many (though not all) of the NICs. For Irish industrialisation has been extremely reliant on foreign direct investment (FDI) with the result that foreign-owned industry controlled 77 per cent of net manufacturing output in 1995 with 52 per cent of that coming from the high-tech sector which employed only 29,406 workers out of a manufacturing labour force of 220,578 workers (Murphy, 1998: 15).

Many scholars have recognised Ireland's resemblance to countries in what we call the developing world. Four distinctive groups can be identified – those taking a political economy or sociological approach to Irish industrialisation and poverty (O'Malley, Girvin, Jacobson, Ó Riain, Breen et al., and Curtin et al.), scholars working within variants of dependency theory (including world-systems theory) (O'Hearn, Crotty), a scholar working within International Political Economy (Jacobsen) and scholars working within development theory (Mjøset and Kirby). In addition, Barry, a neoclassical economist, has stated: 'Notwithstanding the fact that Ireland has been regarded internationally as a successful example of the application of the outward-oriented strategy, the dual nature of its economy is very marked, and it might usefully be thought of as a high-income developing country rather than a low-income industrialized country' (Barry, 1991: 86). O'Malley (1989) draws lessons for Irish industrialisation from the experiences of Japan, South Korea, Taiwan, Singapore and Hong Kong while O'Hearn sees Ireland as an NIC which is 'an exception to the exceptions' in following a more laissez-faire approach in comparison with the state-led approach of the East Asian NICs (O'Hearn, 1989). O'Hearn has also detailed the similarities between the Irish and the Singaporean industrialisation strategies (O'Hearn, 1998). Girvin and Jacobsen broaden the comparison though neither does more than mention the countries to which they consider Ireland comparable, with Girvin citing Greece, Brazil and Argentina (Girvin, 1989: 9) and Jacobsen giving a list of NICs which includes, in addition to those mentioned already, Mexico, Spain, Portugal, Yugoslavia and, possibly, Israel (Jacobsen, 1994: 10, note 25). Kirby has drawn some comparisons between the development experiences of Mexico and Ireland in the 1980s and early

1990s (Kirby, 1994). In their study of rural poverty, Curtin et al. (1996: 25) state that, 'as a whole, the Republic's development had more in common with the experience of other NICs'. We can conclude, therefore, that Ireland is best categorised as an NIC[2] and that comparison with other NICs in East Asia and Latin America can help elucidate Ireland's development trajectory and prospects.

Phases of Irish development

Ireland entered the twentieth century as a largely rural, agricultural society. Since the Great Famine in 1845–48, production patterns had changed as tillage gave way to cattle and sheep (and thus from more intensive to more extensive cultivation). Massive rural depopulation took place, especially among cottiers (tenant farmers) and labourers, while a thorough land reform at the end of the century effectively eliminated the landlord class. The economic legacy of the nineteenth century has been summarised as follows: 'By the beginning of the twentieth century the population of most rural communities had been reduced and transformed from a teeming mass of impoverished labourers, small cottiers and very small tenant farmers, into a stable, conservative, land-owning peasantry, established on family farms which, for the most part, and by modern standards, are quite small' (Breen et al., 1990: 185). The economy of the newly independent state was largely dependent on this sector which employed 670,000 in a total labour force of 1.3 million. Furthermore agriculture, food and drink products accounted for 86 per cent of exports in 1924 (Daly, 1992: 15). Three phases can be broadly distinguished up to the 1980s: comparative advantage from 1922 to 1932, protectionism from 1932 to 1959 and liberalisation from 1959 to the present.

Comparative advantage, 1922–32

This period, during which power was in the hands of the Cumann na nGaedheal party, was marked by policy continuity based on what was seen as the new state's comparative advantage, namely the production and export of dairy products, bacon, eggs and beef. The state's first agriculture minister, Patrick Hogan, emphasised in a memorandum to the cabinet in January 1924 that 'national development in Ireland for our generation at least is practically synonymous with agricultural development' (Daly, 1992: 16). Policy was based on the premise that Irish agriculture was retarded by ignorance and lack of capital (Crotty, 1966: 115). Attempts made to improve the quality of both inputs and outputs included establishing a farm advisory service, improving breeding stock, promoting agricultural education and setting up a lending institution for farmers, the Agricultural Credit Corporation (ACC). Coupled with these policies oriented to production, the Land Commission was set up to redistribute farmland more evenly and more efficiently, though the scope for such redistribution was very limited. Despite being energetically pursued, the results of this policy were disappointing with 'no significant change in the volume of agricultural output during this decade' (Crotty, 1966: 115). Or, as Daly evaluated it more sharply: 'Hogan's policy entailed an emphasis on cost cutting, education, and quality control. It offered little to those facing emigration or inadequate living standards' (Daly, 1992: 17). Industrial development was largely neglected. The one major developmental project was the establishment of the state-owned Electricity Supply Board in 1927 and the building of the Ardnacrusha hydroelectric generation plant on the River Shannon to substitute for Ireland's lack of coal. Overall the period was marked by a failure to recognise the need for the state to take an active role in fostering a more extensive process of socio-economic development. Indeed, as Lee has written, 'the role of the state was to keep out of the way of private enterprise, and keep taxation as low as possible and therefore, at least in the short term, social services, as meagre as possible. This was to be a competition-based, market-driven economy' (Lee, 2008: 36).

Developmental nationalism, 1932–59

The coming to power in 1932 of Fianna Fáil (the 'republican' party which had been defeated in the civil war) saw a major change in policy on both the economic and social fronts. Representing small farmers and rural labourers as well as the small urban proletariat, Fianna Fáil came to power with a radical policy of using the state to initiate a process of native industrialisation behind high tariff barriers. The energetic Seán Lemass built the Department of Industry and Commerce as a counterweight to the conservative Department of Finance and used it to spearhead 'a strategy of national industrialisation' (Girvin, 1989: 97). The Department built strong links with Irish industrialists who, though 'they did not acquire a veto over policy, they did receive significant rights of access and consultation' (ibid.: 98). When the financial institutions still showed their reluctance to lend to industrialists despite the government's decision to guarantee such capital, Lemass got approval to establish a state bank, the Industrial Credit Company 'which played a crucial role in ensuring that a prospective company flotation would be successful' (ibid.: 102). An extensive regime of protection of these infant industries was quickly established with the average tariff level rising from nine per cent in 1931 to 45 per cent in 1936 and with tariffs on some goods ranging between 50 and 75 per cent. Other non-tariff measures included quotas, import licences and regulations while the Control of Manufactures Acts in 1932 and 1934 sought to ensure that Irish manufacturing stayed in Irish hands. By 1937, Irish tariffs were one-and-a-half times as high as those in the UK, twice as high as those in the US, Japan, Belgium and France but one-third of those in Germany (Kennedy et al., 1988: 43). As Girvin put it: 'Whereas under Cumann na nGaedheal the state had been passive and minimalist, under Fianna Fáil it became dynamic and interventionist. Fianna Fáil also penetrated the state apparatus and moulded the institutions to reflect its concerns and objectives' (Girvin, 1989: 89).

The policy had an initial success as manufacturing output rose by 7.2 per cent between 1932 and 1936 while the number of Irish-owned industrial concerns quoted on the Dublin stock exchange trebled between 1933 and 1939 and their aggregate capital doubled. Industrial employment rose from 110,600 in 1931 to 166,100 in 1938 and emigration declined to an average of 14,000 a year over the decade 1930–40, one-third the rate of the previous period (partly due to the impact of the Great Depression on the UK and US economies). Yet labour productivity increased little and even declined in manufacturing. Overall, gross national product (GNP) at constant prices was about ten per cent higher in 1938 than in 1931, a smaller increase than in the UK over the same period (Kennedy et al., 1988: 47–8). Since the new industrial production was for the home market, the volume of merchandise exports declined by 29 per cent between 1931 and 1933 and the 1930 volume was not to be reached again until 1960. Thus Kennedy et al. conclude that, despite the benefits of establishing an industrial base that would not otherwise have existed, state policy failed to lay solid foundations for long-term industrial development: 'An infant-industry approach to industrialisation that did not encourage the infants to grow up was bound to result in an infantile industrial base. The home market was far too small to enable the generality of firms to produce on an efficient scale and the growth of the home market was retarded by the poor performance of the dominant agricultural sector' (Kennedy et al., 1988: 235).

Government attempts to shift agriculture from pasture to tillage, partly to favour small landholders and partly to increase output of goods like sugar beet, wheat and oats for consumption, had limited success. This, coupled with the effects of the Economic War with Britain (1932–38) when the UK retaliated against Irish exports in response to the Irish government's withholding of land annuities owed to the British Exchequer (payments that were the result of the state's lending to tenants to buy out landlords in the land reform in the last decades of colonial rule), hit farming output and exports. Farm output failed to register any real increase over the 1930s (Ó Gráda, 1994: 413). Despite the increase in industrial employment, unemployment remained high, peaking at 145,000 in 1936 before improving economic conditions in the UK saw Irish emigration there begin to increase again. By the end of this expansionary period (the eve of the Second World War), Daly sums up the situation that had emerged: 'What emerged in 1938 was the accommodation of two superficially contradictory sets of vested interests: export-oriented Irish farmers, especially cattle farmers, and protected industrialists. The former recovered their traditional access to the British market on the best terms available given Britain's policy of promoting domestic agriculture, while the latter were not forced to cede industrial protectionism' (Daly, 1992: 169–70).

Fianna Fáil proved equally energetic with regard to social policy, significantly expanding welfare schemes and undertaking an ambitious programme to clear Dublin's notorious slums and to build large working-class housing schemes. The number of housing units built increased from 2181 in 1932–3 to 13,253 by 1934–5 and saw a steady increase up to 17,017 by 1938–9. A sweeping programme of health reform was also introduced; according to Ferriter, these reforms left Ireland 'with hospital care of a high quality by international standards' (Ferriter, 2005: 400). Welfare spending rose from about three per cent of national income in 1931 to around five per cent in 1936 though it began to fall back throughout the 1940s (Cousins, 2005: 27). By then, the policy of ISI was already reaching the natural limits of the small home market. The years of the Second World War, known as the 'Emergency' in Ireland, were marked by an isolation resulting from the Irish decision to remain neutral. This period emphasised the continuing underdeveloped state of Irish agriculture. Despite acute shortages of raw materials, agricultural output held its own thus indicating how much it was the product of land and labour and how little it required by way of modern inputs. In the immediate post-war period, a lively debate took place within the leadership of the ruling Fianna Fáil party: Seán Lemass sought to deepen the industrialisation drive through more active state involvement but was roundly defeated by his more conservative colleagues. Without a strong policy direction, the state faced growing balance-of-payments problems and sluggish industrial productivity in the 1950s while remaining aloof from the liberal trading order emerging in western Europe. Meanwhile, unemployment increased and emigration returned to levels not seen since the 1850s with over 50,000 people emigrating a year. The workforce fell from 1,228,000 in 1946 to 1,053,000 in 1961 (CSO, 2000: 108). This period was one of stagnation and saw the ousting of Fianna Fáil from power for the first time since 1932, with inter-party governments taking over between 1948–51 and 1954–7 when Fianna Fáil returned for a further 16 years in power. With the first 'easy' stage of ISI exhausted and with manufacturing output growing by only 1.7 per cent per annum and manufacturing employment by a mere 0.2 per cent per annum between 1951 and 1958, it was clear that a fundamental change of policy was needed. It came with the liberalisation of the Irish economy in the late 1950s.

Liberalisation, 1959–present

'Ireland was one of the earliest of relatively late-industrialising countries to switch from an inward-looking to an outward-looking strategy and, in the matter of dropping protection at least, it has so far gone further than most of them,' wrote O'Malley in 1992 (34). The retirement of Eamon de Valera as Taoiseach (Prime Minister) in 1959 and his replacement by Seán Lemass marked a new opening and coincided with the *First Programme for Economic Expansion* covering the period 1959–63 and effectively written by the new young secretary of the Department of Finance, T. K. Whitaker. Lemass and

Whitaker have come to symbolise the swift liberalisation that then set in based on three elements: the use of grants and tax concessions to encourage export-oriented production, the attraction of foreign manufacturing firms and dismantling protection so as to gain greater access to markets abroad (Kennedy et al., 1988: 236). While the initial expectation was that the domestic firms protected by high tariff barriers would begin to win export markets, the policy led to a swift growth in foreign enterprises establishing in Ireland for the export market reflecting the new buoyancy in the global economy and the increase in FDI associated with it. As Ó Gráda (1997: 114) put it: 'At the outset few foresaw the rapid growth of the foreign sector, but direct foreign investment in Irish industry soon became the cornerstone of government policy. ... The remarkable transformation of the economy between the late 1950s and the early 1970s may be largely attributed to the arrival of the multinationals'.

The government also followed an expansionary fiscal policy both in productive and in social investment. State policy increasingly began to depend on this foreign-owned sector with the Industrial Development Authority (IDA), a key semi-state agency that bears some similarity to the 'insulated bureaucracies' of the East Asian developmental states, playing a key role as the 'hunter and gatherer' of foreign firms (Ó Riain and O'Connell, 2000: 315). Another essential part of the strategy was the dismantling of protection. Ireland unilaterally reduced tariffs by ten per cent on two occasions, in early 1963 and 1964, and in 1965 negotiated the Anglo-Irish Free Trade Agreement with the UK which took effect in 1966. This opened the way for membership of the European Economic Community (EEC) in 1973 under which Ireland agreed to establish free trade with member countries within a five-year period (Kennedy et al., 1988: 67–8). By 1973, overseas firms accounted for almost one-third of all employment in manufacturing (68,500 out of 219,000). By 1983, there were almost a thousand foreign firms in Ireland and they had invested well over £4 billion in the country; half of them came from the US, one-eighth from Britain, about one-tenth from Germany (Ó Gráda, 1997: 115). Between 1958 and 1973, manufacturing output grew by 6.7 per cent per annum while manufacturing employment grew by a more modest 2.4 per cent per annum (O'Malley, 1992: 34). Exports as a percentage of gross output grew even more dramatically, from 19.4 per cent in 1960 to 41 per cent in 1978 (O'Malley, 1989: 69, 92).

Recognising that agriculture alone could not generate adequate income for some rural families, measures were introduced to maintain small farmers on the land through the provision of direct income supports for them (the Smallholders Assistance Scheme) and through fostering rural industrialisation to provide off-farm employment. The Undeveloped Areas Act of 1952 allowed for grant aid for new industries in designated areas and this recognition of the need for rural industrialisation gradually evolved into a policy of regional balance through which the state sought to reduce regional disparities and provide jobs as near as practicable to job seekers (Ó Tuathaigh, 1986).

However, instead of any attempt to promote a policy of industrialisation based on local linkages through the processing of agricultural inputs, the state opted instead to encourage multinational companies to locate in rural areas. This met with a measure of success in locational terms: by 1973, 59 per cent of foreign firms, which located in Ireland following the liberalisation of the economy in the early 1960s, were established in the designated areas (Breathnach, 1985: 178). However, by the very nature of this type of industrialisation, its weak linkages to local suppliers meant that it constituted an enclave (Breathnach, 1985: 187; Smyth and Boylan, 1991). And, following heavy job losses in the large urban centres of Dublin and Cork in the 1970s (partly due to the impact of economic liberalisation on indigenous industry), policy tended to concentrate on replacing the jobs lost with the effect that larger urban centres benefited most (Breathnach, 1985: 193; Ó Tuathaigh, 1986: 127). On the positive side, these policies had a major demographic effect on rural Ireland, helping reverse over a century of decline. Between 1971 and 1981, the population of aggregate rural areas grew by ten per cent and by a further three per cent between 1981 and 1986, before falling again in the period 1986–91 (except for the eastern region) (Matthews, 1995: 351). In the period 1991–6, the aggregate population of most regions showed a slight increase though, apart from the east and the west, the regions' share of the national population continued to decline (NESC, 1997: Table 2.2, p. 17).

Meanwhile, indigenous industry fared less well. Though there had been hopes that Irish industry would expand and prosper under free trade, 'the combined effect of free trade and the upheavals caused by the oil crises was far more devastating than most people had imagined' (Kennedy et al., 1988: 241). There was no further employment growth in this sector from the mid-1960s to the end of the 1970s while in the 1980s employment fell sharply. This happened since Irish firms were confined to the domestic market and, when domestic demand slumped in the early 1980s, they were severely hit (O'Malley, 1992: 35–6). The greatest decline came in firms exposed to foreign competition, such as textiles, clothing and footwear, and chemicals and metals, with large firms being particularly badly hit (Kennedy et al., 1988: 242). More and more indigenous industry was being confined to sub-sectors involving either basic processing of local primary products such as the food industry or activities with a significant degree of natural protection, such as construction, cement making, or paper and packaging. This prompted a re-evaluation of industrial strategy which began with the publication of the Telesis Report in 1982 as a result of which 'attention was shifted to the international competitiveness of the whole industrial sector, rather than merely its export component. Thus the role of the indigenous sector was recognized, and new emphasis given to import substitution and linkage development efforts' (Tomaney, 1995: 102–3). These moves were further strengthened by the Culliton Report in 1992 the recommendations of which led to the IDA being divided into separate agencies for foreign firms and for indigenous industry; Culliton also recommended more selective grant-giving. These changes in industrial policy are identified as having played a major role in a 'remarkable turnaround' in the fortunes of indigenous industry (Ó Riain and O'Connell, 2000: 320).

Characteristics of Irish industrialisation

Foreign sector versus domestic sector

Since the early 1980s there has been an extensive and ongoing debate about Ireland's industrial policy which has highlighted some of the traditional weaknesses of its reliance on multinational companies. Among these is the practice of transfer pricing whereby the foreign-owned companies tend to inflate the value of their output in the Irish economy in order to avail of the state's low tax on manufacturing profits. This has been described by Murphy as generating 'a *soufflé* effect on Ireland's macroeconomic statistics' (Murphy, 1994: 11). The extent of capital repatriation by foreign-owned companies (made up of gross profit remittances – net of reinvested profits – and royalty and similar payments abroad) grew from 2.8 per cent of GDP in 1979 to around 20 per cent by the early 2000s. As O'Sullivan (2006: 76) put it: 'There is no other developed country where there is such a disparity between GDP and GNP'. The consequence of this is that investment funds are removed from the economy thus reducing the positive balance of payments impact of these companies' exports (McAleese and Foley, 1991: 3).

These are therefore evidence of what has sometimes been referred to as a dualistic industrial structure referred to by Barry (1991: 85) when he wrote that Ireland 'shares with developing countries a dual industrial structure'. In the 1990s the debate moved to a discussion of the significance of linkages between the dynamic foreign-owned sector and the domestic sector, this being a key mechanism through which the dynamism of the former can have a developmental impact on the latter. Though the extent of linkages varies from sector to sector, Paus found that it is constrained by the small size of most indigenous firms; she found that the average employment by Irish-owned firms remained virtually static during the height of the Celtic Tiger boom, growing from 29 employees in 1991 to 30 in 2000. She concludes that 'the increased scale requirements in some industries, such as the electronics, make it so much harder for Irish firms to compete in the future, unless they move up the value chain, specialise in niche production, and export more' (Paus, 2005: 110). However, when looking at the Irish-owned sector of high-tech industry she did find that, though the sector is small in comparison to the size of the foreign-owned sector, 'the weight of the high-tech sectors has increased considerably' when its output and exports are compared to those of the foreign sector (Paus, 2005: 121). This confirms evidence produced by O'Malley on the greater dynamism being shown by indigenous industry since 1987 (see Chapter 2); this leads to the conclusion that the degree of inferiority of indigenous industry is diminishing while O'Malley argues that one of the causes of this improvement has been the rapidly growing expenditures by foreign-owned industry on inputs produced by the Irish indigenous sector (1998: 55). The question that persists, however, is just how extensive might the transformation of the Irish-owned sector be. As O'Sullivan (2006: 77) has observed, while multinational companies have played a substantial role in contributing to the quantity and quality of the Irish workforce, most Irish firms remain small and there is a stark difference in performance, research levels and export activity between them and the more 'globalised' sectors. If the term 'dualism' may suggest too stark a division between the sectors, the evidence continues to point to a major gap between the foreign-owned and domestically owned sectors, with some exceptions.

Employment

Between the early 1980s and the mid-1990s, high unemployment was seen as a characteristic feature of Ireland's development. 'There is widespread consensus that the biggest blot on the Irish economic landscape is the unacceptably high level of unemployment,' wrote Browne and McGettigan in 1993 (1). Unemployment grew from 91,000 in 1980 (7.3 per cent of the labour force) to 226,000 in 1985 (17.3 per cent), declined to 176,000 in 1990 (13.4 per cent) but increased again to 230,000 (16.6 per cent) in 1993 before beginning a steady decline over the rest of the 1990s. This meant that, with the exception of Spain, Ireland had the worst unemployment problem in the EU for most of this period. Three features distinguish the Irish experience. One is 'its remarkable persistence' (Browne and McGettigan, 1993: 2) as it tended to hit new highs in response to economic shocks but not decline in intervening periods. 'There is not even a hint of mean-reversion in the Irish data over the 30 years period from 1960 to 1989,' wrote Browne and McGettigan (2). Only in the late 1990s did a steady and accelerating decline become evident. The second feature was the percentage of the labour force which remained unemployed for one year or more, the long-term unemployed. This hovered at between 56 and 60 per cent of the unemployed from 1992 to 1996, before falling in the later 1990s. The third feature was emigration with net emigration between 1985 and 1990 amounting to 160,000 (Tansey, 1998: 69). As O'Hagan (1995: 232–3) put it: 'In Ireland, throughout the 1980s, the labour force showed almost no growth because of almost 1 per cent per annum emigrating between 1983 and 1990. If this hadn't happened, the labour force growth would have been around 2.3 per cent or 20,000 to 25,000 per annum.' Thus Irish unemployment rates would have been far higher in the absence of emigration.

Economists linked high unemployment with structural features of Ireland's industrialisation. For example, an industrialisation strategy which has as a central element a low-tax regime on corporate profits in order to attract foreign investment has the effect of placing higher taxation on labour than on capital. Browne and McGettigan (1993: 15) concluded that this 'presented a strong incentive for firms in the traded goods sector to substitute capital for labour'. They quoted the OECD as showing (in 1986) that no other member country had a tax system as biased against the use of labour as had Ireland, a fact cited by the OECD as one of the main causes of Ireland's high unemployment rate. A second characteristic related to the employment intensity of growth in Ireland's manufacturing sector. A number of studies noted the weak link between growth in manufacturing output and growth in employment (O'Malley, 1992: 34; NESC, 1993: 30, 99). Fell found that between 1980 and 1987 industrial output increased by almost 50 per cent while industrial employment declined by about 20 per cent. This contrasted sharply with the period 1976–80 when industrial output rose by 24 per cent and employment by ten per cent (Fell, 1989: 1). In examining this phenomenon, NESC (1993) found it derived from the dual nature of Ireland's industrial growth with a gap in productivity levels between high-tech and low-tech sectors (loosely related to foreign-owned and indigenous sectors) substantially higher than in any other EU country even allowing for the effects of transfer pricing (35–53). Examining the employment intensity (the ratio of employment growth to output growth) of Irish growth, the report found it very low compared to other countries in the late 1980s (NESC, 1993, Table 9, p. 29) and it concluded: 'This unusually high rate of productivity growth in manufacturing industry has served to reduce the overall employment-intensity of economic growth in Ireland relative to that of other countries' (101).

As will be seen in Chapter 2, Ireland's employment levels increased dramatically from the early 1990s to 2007 thus overcoming these long-term problems of Ireland's development. However, as unemployment again increased dramatically in 2008, these memories from the past returned to haunt the psyche of many Irish people. As the more labour-intensive manufacturing sector increasingly finds wage levels too high in Ireland and moves abroad, the challenge of providing high quality employment in sufficient quantities is returning.

Ireland and the NICs

As was stated in the introduction to this chapter, Ireland's development trajectory in the twentieth century is closer to that of a group of East Asian and Latin American NICs than it is to Ireland's nearest neighbours. For this reason, Ireland's industrialisation is here compared to that of a group of NICs. The East Asian NICs chosen are Hong Kong, Singapore, South Korea and Taiwan as these are regarded as the four original 'tiger' economies (see the World Bank, 1993). Among the countries of Latin America, Argentina, Brazil, Chile, Costa Rica, Mexico and Uruguay are chosen as they are regarded as among the developmental success cases in that region and as most of them went through a period of strong state-led industrialisation efforts. Table 1.1 gives a range of data comparing Ireland's industrialisation with that of these East Asian and Latin American NICs.

Table 1.1 Patterns of NIC industrialisation

Country	GNP per capita annual growth		Annual average labour force growth (%)		Percentage of labour force in different sectors						Earnings per employee as percentage of annual growth	FDI (in US$m)		Gross domestic investment as percentage of GDP	
					Agriculture		Industry		Services						
	1965–80	1980–95	1980–90	1990–7	1970	1990	1970	1990	1970	1990	1980–92	1980	1996	1980	1997
Argentina	1.7	−0.4	1.3	2.1	16	12	34	32	50	55	−2.2	1836	4285	25	19
Brazil	6.3	−0.4	3.2	1.7	47	23	20	23	33	54	−2.4	989	9889	23	20
Chile		3.2	2.7	2.1	24	19	29	25	47	56	−0.3	590	4091	21	28
Costa Rica	3.3	0.7	3.8	2.5	43	26	20	27	37	47		163	410	27	24
Hong Kong	6.2	4.8	1.6	1.9	4	1	55	37	41	62	4.8			35	34
Ireland	2.8	3.0	0.4	1.6	31*	14	28*	29	41*	57	2.0	627	2456	27	15
Mexico	3.6	−0.9	3.5	2.8	44	28	24	24	32	48		2634	7619	27	21
Singapore	8.3	6.0	2.3	1.7	3	0	30	36	66	64	5.1	5,575	9440	46	37
S. Korea	7.3	7.5	2.3	1.9	49	18	20	35	31	47	8.4	788	2325	32	35
Taiwan	7.3†	6.2			37	13	28	41	35	46		465	2460		21‡
Uruguay	2.5	−0.6	1.6	1.0	19	14	29	27	52	59	−2.3	0	169	12	12

Sources: UNDP Human Development Report, various years; World Development Report, various years; Taiwan Statistical Data Book 1998.
*1965
†1969–80
‡1996
Note: Italics indicate that data are for years other than those specified; failure to specify the exact year here is because it is not specified in the original.

This shows some distinctive features of Ireland's industrialisation from the 1960s to the 1990s. Firstly, its per capita GNP annual growth rate from 1965 to 1980 was among the lowest of the NICs; in the period from 1980 to 1995, Ireland's growth rate is moderate, falling well behind the East Asian NICs but far better than the Latin American NICs for which the 1980s was a lost development decade. Ireland's labour force growth in the 1980–90 period was the lowest among the NICs, reflecting the high levels of emigration from Ireland during that period. Even in the more recent period, in which Ireland has seen net immigration, its labour force growth is the second lowest in the NICs. Comparing the sectoral composition of its labour force in 1965 and in 1990 to that of the other NICs in 1970 and 1990 shows that Ireland was less successful than most of the others in providing industrial employment for the labour force being shed by agriculture. The percentage of Ireland's labour force in industry was still relatively low in 1990 and closer to that in Latin America than in East Asia. As Barry and Hannan (1995: 3) stated, Ireland appeared under-industrialised compared to countries with a similar GDP per capita. The percentage annual growth of employee earnings in Ireland from 1980 to 1992 was better than in Latin America but worse than in East Asia. This reflected Ireland's own crisis over the first part of this period though this improved dramatically over the course of the Celtic Tiger boom. The final two columns on FDI and gross domestic investment show Ireland to be rivalled only by Singapore in its success at attracting foreign investment while gross domestic investment had declined sharply to the second lowest level among the NICs in the mid-1990s.

Table 1.1 indicates the extent of Ireland's poor industrial performance compared to that of other NICs until the mid-1990s. With low labour force growth and high levels of FDI compared to most of the other NICs, it still managed growth rates which were moderate at best compared to virtually all the NICs in the period 1965–80 and compared to the East Asian NICs in the more recent period.

Box 1.1 'Can Costa Rica become Ireland?'

'Can Costa Rica become Ireland?' is the subtitle to a book by the US-based development economist, Eva Paus (Paus, 2005). When Costa Rica was chosen by Intel as its one Latin American investment site for a microchip factory in 1996, it raised the question as to whether the small Central American state was going to emulate Ireland and become a 'Tico Tiger' through winning foreign investment, transforming its economy in the way Ireland had been transformed throughout the 1990s. This is the question examined by Paus in her comparative study of the two countries.

In concluding that Costa Rica is not going to emulate Ireland, she places a lot of emphasis on the failure of domestic institutions and policies, showing how the administration of President José Maria Figueres (1994–8), and indeed the president himself, 'played a critical role in bringing together all the necessary actors to attract Intel to Costa Rica' (ibid.: 167) but that this was never institutionalised and these efforts dissipated under subsequent administrations. Indeed, Paus is highly insightful in drawing attention to the consequences of the neoliberalisation of Costa Rica's political economy in the early 1980s as it 'dismantled the former leading coalition of the state, segments of domestic capital, and public sector trade unions by reducing the economic role of the state and weakening public sector unions, while empowering financial capital and transnational corporations' (162–3).

Paus also examines the different regional contexts of the two countries. Ireland's receipt of EU structural funds which allowed it to develop institutional capacity and linkage programmes between foreign and local industries had no equivalents in the case of Costa Rica. She draws attention to the fact that, while the Central America Free Trade Agreement (CAFTA) may make Costa Rica a more attractive location for US foreign investment, CAFTA contains no provisions for resource transfers as does the EU. The consequence of this is that Costa Rica is caught between 'a rock and a hard place' (203) in its attempts to attract high-tech FDI and raise tax revenue. The former requires a low-tax regime which, even if it succeeds in attracting transnational companies (TNCs), will not contribute to raising tax revenue as these companies contribute little apart from social security contributions and taxes paid by employees. She therefore predicts a race to the bottom will continue in respect to tax rates on TNCs undercutting the potential of governments to develop the policy and institutional capacity they need to translate FDI into domestic capacity.

She concludes that luck was also a factor. Ireland's ability to attract large inflows of FDI was based on 'a fortuitous conjuncture of TNCs' strategic needs and Ireland's location-specific assets' (189) in the early 1990s thereby opening the possibility for a surge in economic growth whereas Costa Rica won a major Intel investment just before the dot-com bubble burst which then hampered its ability to build on its success.

Sharing the benefits?

This section looks at the distributional impact of development in Ireland up to the advent of the Celtic Tiger and examines in turn trends in poverty, income distribution and wealth distribution.

Poverty

A paper presented by Séamus Ó Cinnéide at a poverty conference organised by the Catholic bishops' Council for Social Welfare in 1971 is often referred

to as the 'rediscovery of poverty' in Ireland (Nolan and Callan, 1994: 22).
Ó Cinnéide concluded that *'at least* 24 per cent of the population have a
personal income below the poverty line' which he based on social security
or income maintenance rates of payment in Ireland, North and South (Ó
Cinnéide, 1972: 397; emphasis in original). Subsequent studies for the period
1973–87, using poverty lines set at 40 per cent, 50 per cent and 60 per cent
of average income, concluded that 'the proportion of people in poverty in
Ireland is consistently seen to have risen, across a range of poverty lines
and equivalence scales' (Nolan and Callan, 1994: 313).[3] So, for example, in
1973 between 15 and 18 per cent of the population lived on half the average income whereas by 1987 this had increased to 20–23 per cent. Using a
poverty line based on half average equivalent household income in 1985,
Ireland was found to have the third worst level of poverty in the EU with
22.9 per cent of the population in poverty, better than Greece (28%) and
Portugal (24%) but worse than Spain (20%) (Nolan and Callan, 1994: 39).

Income distribution

There is no systematic information from which to estimate trends in income
distribution in Ireland for the first half-century of independence. Based on
Central Statistics Office (CSO) data in 1965–6, Geary estimated the distribution of gross weekly income among urban households. This showed that the
top eight per cent of urban households accounted for almost 23 per cent of
income while the bottom 60 per cent accounted for only 34 per cent (Geary,
1977: 173). Lack of data did not allow him to estimate trends over time. A
few years later, Ó Cinnéide compared the distribution of earnings in 1966–7
and 1971–5 drawing on a range of studies which showed the higher earners suffered decreases in their real gross earnings and even greater decreases
in their net earnings over the period while the lower earners experienced
large increases in their real gross earnings and smaller increases in their real
net earnings (Ó Cinnéide, 1980). He concludes that 'in the period under
review there was considerable redistribution of income and ... a substantial
number of poor people, if not them all, improved their relative position in
the population' (Ó Cinnéide, 1980: 151). A study by Nolan, based largely
on 1973 CSO data, identified a pattern of decreasing inequality of gross
income distribution from 1965/66 to 1974 with an increase from then until
1976 (Nolan, 1977–8: 118–19). Rottman and Hannan's research finds that
between 1973 and 1978 large proprietors and higher professionals registered
declining real household direct incomes while small proprietors, service
workers, intermediate non-manual workers and semi-skilled manual workers registered significant gains in direct income (Rottman et al., 1982: 179).
Data for the distribution of disposable household income between 1973 and
1987, taken from the CSO's seven-yearly Household Budget Surveys, shows
remarkable stability with the share of the bottom 40 per cent of the distribution increasing from 16.5 per cent in 1973 to 17.2 per cent in 1987 while

the share of the top 40 per cent declined slightly from 66.5 per cent to 66 per cent over the same period (Nolan et al., 2000: 40). When compared to a group of 16 OECD countries using 1987 Irish data, Ireland's income distribution was found to be among the most unequal. This showed that, after the US, the bottom ten per cent of adults in Ireland had a lower share of disposable income than in any of the other countries, that the bottom 40 per cent in Ireland had a lower share of income than in any country other than Switzerland, that the top 20 per cent of Irish adults had a larger share of income than in any country other than Switzerland, and that the top five per cent of Irish adults had a larger share than in any country other than Switzerland. The Gini coefficient for Ireland was higher than that for any country other than the US. According to this data, Ireland had moved from a position in which it displayed an average level of income inequality to one in which it was among the countries with the highest levels of inequality (Atkinson et al., 1995).

Wealth distribution

There is very little evidence available to examine the distribution of wealth in Ireland. Based on estate duty returns for 1966, Lyons concluded that nearly 65 per cent of the population possessed no capital, about 30 per cent possessed some 28 per cent of total capital and the remaining five per cent accounted for over 70 per cent of the total wealth in Ireland. The top one per cent of the population owned over 30 per cent of the net wealth (Lyons, 1972). A study based on the 1987 ESRI household survey found that the bottom 50 per cent of households have only 12 per cent of total reported wealth, the bottom 70 per cent have 28.5 per cent of wealth and the top 30 per cent have 71.5 per cent of wealth. In interpreting these findings, it needs to be borne in mind, the author states, that surveys of this type usually 'seriously understate total wealth and give a misleading picture of its distribution significantly underestimating its concentration at the top' (Nolan, 1991: 14).[4] In an attempt to correct the underestimation of wealth at the top of the distribution, Nolan estimated that the share of the top ten per cent could be about half of all household sector wealth while that of the top one per cent could be about 20 per cent (85).

Making international comparisons of wealth distribution is particularly hazardous due to differences in sources, definitions and accounting methods. However, using data from the mid-1960s to the mid-1970s for a range of Western European countries, the US and Canada, Kirby (2000, Table 5.3) found wealth to be more concentrated among the top ten per cent of wealth holders in Ireland than in any of the comparison countries.

Conclusions

This chapter has examined Ireland's longer-term development efforts up to the period of the Celtic Tiger boom and found its economic and social performance to have been relatively poor. Though different policies were attempted throughout the period, and they yielded some positive results (most notably in the 1930s and in the 1960s and early 1970s), it was not possible to sustain these successes over time. The most remarkable success of all was the boom that took off in the mid-1990s and lasted in various ways until 2007; however, this failed to reverse the high levels of relative poverty and inequality that were characteristics of Irish development, at least since the 1980s. Yet the sudden and deep collapse of the Irish economy since then gives a renewed relevance to the longer-term boom–bust cycles that have characterised Irish economic and social performance, raising deeper questions to be examined in Parts III and IV of this book. Before that, however, the story of the boom and its impacts needs to be told.

2
Assessing the Boom

> The reality is that we had growth too easy. Our own entre-
> preneurs couldn't go wrong in a climate of rapid growth
> and low real interest rates. Virtually any investment was
> bound to yield a good rate of return, and fortunes were
> made by the private sector. Policy-makers didn't have to
> conceive of alternative strategies or contingency plans. The
> economy was cruising on automatic pilot.
>
> Michael Casey, former chief economist of the
> Irish Central Bank (2009a: 13)

Ireland's Celtic Tiger boom took everyone by surprise. Internationally, Ireland was not looked to as a model of successful development and was classed as one of the poorer countries of the European Union (EU) up to the early 1990s. At home, the deep recession of the 1980s had sown a defeatist attitude, nowhere better captured than in the series of books published in 1988–9 that all drew similar conclusions: that the independent Irish state had become an economic laggard over the course of the twentieth century compared to a range of other European states, both capitalist and communist; that this was due to the poor quality of governance and the inability of the state to develop coherent policies adequate to the developmental challenges it faced and that the prospects for the future were grim indeed as the barriers to economic success grew ever more formidable (Girvin, 1989; Lee, 1989; O'Malley, 1989; Kennedy et al., 1988). Yet, despite having an impact at the time, these books were quickly forgotten as the severe cutbacks implemented by the incoming Fianna Fáil government in 1987 began to yield, not a deepening recession, but 'an expansionary fiscal contraction' (see Boylan, 2002: 20–1): growth quickly returned and by the mid-1990s Ireland was being recognised as a miracle economy, earning the title 'Celtic Tiger' as its high growth rates compared favourably to the success of the East Asian tigers.

31

This chapter examines the nature of this success and its causes. It begins by offering evidence of the success that attracted such international attention. It then goes on to describe the nature of the economic transformations that took place over that period and that underpinned the boom. The third section examines the key institutional innovations that contributed to Ireland's success while the final section interrogates the lessons to be learnt, particularly in the light of the dramatic collapse of the growth model in 2008.

Success and what it hides

Growth in economy, employment, living standards

The Irish economy began to emerge from its long recession in the late 1980s. Recovery was modest at first with economic growth averaging 3.6 per cent of GNP between 1987 and 1993 and by the latter year, 294,000 people were still unemployed. However, after 1993 both growth and employment showed considerable rise as shown in Table 2.1. This shows that the boom, with annual rates of GDP growth of over seven per cent, lasted from 1994 to 2000 before declining to somewhat lower levels. Despite the decline in the growth rate, growth in employment continued and unemployment remained at historically low levels. However, these aggregate figures hide a major shift in the sources of growth, making it more unsustainable and sowing the seeds of the collapse of 2008.

The period since 1987 has clearly seen immense changes in the Irish economy and Irish society. The basic changes are summarised in Table 2.2 showing the increase in GNP, in employment and in population, the decline in unemployment and the reversal of emigration. The impact of this economic growth on the labour market was perhaps its greatest contribution to welfare. While the labour force as a whole grew from 1.36 million in 1992 to 2.1 million in 2006, the decline in unemployment – for long a deeply institutionalised social problem in Irish society – marked a decisive break with the past.

The growth in employment was the greatest contribution to increasing living standards. Overall, average incomes rose by 125 per cent in real terms between 1987 and 2005. Walsh breaks this increase into three phases: 1987–94, during which average income grew by 34 per cent ; 1994–2001, during which it grew by 57 per cent and 2001–5, when incomes grew by seven per cent (Walsh, 2007: 25–6). These increases correlate neatly with Ó Riain's division of the Celtic Tiger period into three competing state projects: the first was neo-corporatist stabilisation from 1987 to 1994, the second was the developmentalist phase from 1994 to 2000 and the third was the neo-liberal tax-cutting phase from 2000 onwards (Ó Riain, 2008: 172–80). In terms of GDP per capita, Ireland moved over the course of the 1990s from a position of around 60 per cent of the EU average (which it had held since joining the EEC

Table 2.1 Irish economic and employment growth, 1993–2008

Year	GDP*	GNP*	Labour force (000s)	Employment rate among 15–64 year olds (%)	Unemployment rate (%)
1993	5.8	6.3	1386	51.7	15.6
1994	9.5	8.0	1423	53.0	14.3
1995	7.7	7.2	1452	54.4	12.3
1996	10.7	9.0	1498	55.4	11.7
1997	8.9	8.1	1560	57.5	9.9
1998	8.5	7.7	1645	60.6	7.5
1999	10.7	8.5	1713	63.3	5.6
2000	9.2	9.5	1767	65.2	4.3
2001	6.2	3.9	1810	65.8	3.8
2002	6.1	2.7	1845	65.6	4.3
2003	4.4	5.7	1882	65.1	4.6
2004	4.6	4.3	1920	65.5	4.4
2005	6.2	5.6	2015	67.1	4.2
2006	5.4	6.3	2150	63.3	4.5
2007	6.0	4.4	2219	63.8	4.4
2008	-3.0	-2.8	2247	63.7	6.4

* at constant prices.
Source: CSO National Accounts and FÁS Irish Labour Market Review 2006 and 2008.

Table 2.2 Key changes in economy and society, 1987–2005

	1987	1994	1997	2001	2003	2005	Change (%)
GNP	100	135	182	258	286	316	216
Population (000s)	3547	3586	3664	3847	3979	4131	16
Employment	1111	1221	1380	1722	1794	1929	74
Unemployment (000s)	226	211	159	65	82	86	-62
Migration (000s)	-23	-5	19	33	30	53	

Source: Walsh (2007: 25).

in 1973) to 145.4 per cent in 2006 making it the second richest country in the EU after Luxembourg. However, accepting that GDP significantly inflates real income accruing to Irish residents, gross national income (GNI) is considered a more accurate reflection of relative living standards.[1] Taking Ireland's GNI per capita lowers its place in 2006 to 125.2 per cent of that of the EU27, or fifth place after Luxembourg, the Netherlands, Austria and Denmark (CSO, 2008: Table 1.3). Table 2.3 shows Ireland's increase in living standards in comparison to the EU from 2000 to 2006. Taking GNI for Ireland, this shows that Ireland moved from below the EU average in 2000 to significantly above it in 2006; however, Luxembourg, Greece and Estonia increased their living standards in comparative terms by more than did Ireland over this period while Spain was not far behind.

Alongside these overall changes in employment and living standards was a significant increase in the participation of women in the formal labour force. As recently as 1993, there were 435,000 women in the labour force but this had increased to 787,000 in 2004 with the female employment rate increasing from 38.5 to 56.5 per cent over this period and the female share of total employment increasing from 36.4 to 42.1 per cent. By then, Ireland had surpassed the EU average of 56.3 per cent. Women accounted for two-thirds of the employment growth in services and women now make up over one-half of all service workers. However, 32 per cent of women work part-time as against around six per cent of men, and women account for over three-quarters of all part-time workers but constitute less than 35 per cent of full-time workers (O'Connell and Russell, 2007). While the gap between female and male hourly pay declined from 20 to 15 per cent between 1987 and 2000, recent evidence has seen female pay stabilise at around

Table 2.3 Per capita GDP growth, 2000–6: Ireland in the EU

Country	2000	2006
Luxembourg	200.0	279.1
Ireland (GDP)	*114.8*	*145.4*
Netherlands	110.8	130.5
Austria	115.2	127.5
Denmark	116.8	125.7
Ireland (GNI)	*99.3*	*125.2*
Sweden	106.2	124.6
Belgium	107.3	119.8
UK	102.0	117.9
Finland	102.9	116.9
Germany	106.1	114.1
France	101.1	110.9
Spain	82.0	104.9
Italy	101.9	103.3
EU27	*100*	*100*
Greece	65.3	97.3
Cyprus	75.3	91.9
Slovenia	70.1	87.8
Czech Republic	60.6	78.6
Malta	NA	76.9
Portugal	68.1	74.5
Estonia	40.0	68.4
Hungary	49.6	64.8
Slovakia	47.0	63.7
Lithuania	35.3	56.1
Latvia	30.8	53.7

Source: CSO (2003, 2008).

85 per cent of male rates, a gap that is regarded as being relatively wide compared to that in other European countries. These researchers also report a substantial difference in the times spent on caring and domestic work with women spending significantly more time on these activities than men, a difference that is higher than in many European countries (McGinnity et al., 2007: 202–8).

What the data hide

Examining the data on Ireland's growth hides a significant change that took place from 2001 onwards. Though overall growth rates indicate that Ireland weathered well the bursting of the dotcom bubble and the impact of 9/11, these events did lead to a significant change in the productive base of the Irish economy which is not apparent from the growth data. As FitzGerald wrote in 2007 before the collapse: '[S]ince 2002 our economic growth has not had a healthy basis' (FitzGerald, 2007). This was due to the fact that growth had come to depend more and more on domestic demand rather than being export-driven as it was in the previous period. Export growth declined from an annual average of 17.6 per cent between 1995 and 2000 to an average of 4.9 per cent annually between 2001 and 2006. Furthermore, the value of merchandise exports in 2006 was less than it was in 2002 and from a position of balance in 2003, the payments deficit reached 3.3 per cent of GDP by 2006. Meanwhile from 1998 to 2004, when merchandise exports grew by 16.5 per cent, service exports trebled in size so that the share of total exports accounted for by services doubled from 17 to 34 per cent over this period, mostly software, financial services and other business services. As Tansey put it, 'the Celtic Tiger economy met its end in 2001' (Tansey, 2007). This period also saw industrial employment begin to decline and a major increase in the construction sector which became the main engine of job growth, as is shown in Table 2.4. According to the OECD, most of the employment decline in manufacturing is in high-tech industries but the weakness was spread widely across the sector (OECD, 2006a: 20). Between 2002 and 2006, the numbers employed in construction increased by so much that by the end of this period they constituted 13.2 per cent of all those at work. Economists warned that this was not sustainable. As Barry wrote in 2006: 'Much of Ireland's growth in the new millennium has been driven by debt-financed domestic demand rather than by continuing export buoyancy, as reflected in the shift from surplus to deficit in the balance-of-payments current account. This type of growth is not sustainable in the long run' (Barry, 2006: 40–1). Despite this, little was done to calm the frenzy in domestic consumption, especially of housing.

In the years before the collapse, the Irish economy was characterised by growth that was 'rapid but lopsided' as the OECD described it (OECD, 2006b: 101). While growth was robust, it was largely driven by internal demand – construction activity contributed as much as 1.7 percentage points

Table 2.4   Sectoral changes in employment, 2002–6 (000s)

Sector	2002	2006	Change (%)
Agriculture	124	117	−5.6
Production industries	309	291	−5.8
Construction	187	269	+43.9
Services	1156	1362	+17.8
Total at work	1777	2039	+14.7

Source: CSO Quarterly National Household Survey, 2007.

to overall output growth in 2005. However, the greater reliance on construction and services led to a drop in productivity. Sexton found that while total labour productivity rose by 30 per cent between 1995 and 2005 (an annual average 2.6 per cent increase), growth began to slow noticeably after 2002 and remained virtually unchanged between 2004 and 2005. Sexton linked the decline in productivity to the shift from high-tech manufacturing to services and construction as the economy's main growth sectors (Sexton, 2007: 46).

A high-tech economy?

The collapse of Irish growth rates in 2008–9 should not distract from the strength of the contemporary Irish economy as indicated by the evidence in the previous section reflecting the transformation of its productive base since the 1960s. As Fitz Gerald (2000: 38) put it: '[T]he pro-active industrial strategy pursued by Irish policy makers was central to the long-term development of a strong industrial base.' As was outlined in Chapter 1, this focused on the attraction of foreign multinational firms to establish in Ireland. Only more recently has a modern, high-tech and export-oriented indigenous sector emerged. The emergence of both is treated separately here.

The foreign sector

In Ó Riain's memorable phrase, the Irish state has since the early 1960s assumed 'the role of "hunter and gatherer"' of foreign direct investment (FDI) (Ó Riain and O'Connell, 2000: 315). While this policy, led by the Industrial Development Authority (IDA), pre-dates the emergence of the Celtic Tiger, it came to fruition in the late 1980s and the early 1990s. In many ways the IDA resembles the insulated bureaucracies of the East Asian developmental states (see Campos and Root, 1996; Leftwich, 1996) in that it is a state body with, since the late 1960s, autonomy from the civil service, extensive resources and effective insulation from the political process. Indeed, in the account written by Padraic White, its managing director from 1981 to 1990, it saw itself as often making the policy which its ministerial bosses followed (Mac Sharry and White, 2000). Embued with a spirit of 'competitive nationalism' (ibid.: 239), the IDA became very successful at identifying emerging sectors in the global economy and in attracting many of the major companies in those sectors to Ireland. While this strategy had initially begun in the 1960s by attracting clothing and textile firms like Wrangler, Bluebell, Farah Jeans and Burlington Industries, in the 1970s an electronics sector was established by attracting firms like General Electric, Ecco and Core Memories. Already in 1971 the computer manufacturer Digital had been attracted to set up a plant in Galway and this marked the beginning of a strategy to develop a cluster of computer manufacturers in Ireland. In 1980 Apple was attracted to establish its European manufacturing base in Cork and in 1989 Intel was successfully lobbied to establish a major centre in Kildare, just outside Dublin. Bradley identifies the IDA's success as stemming from its ability to target firms 'at a relatively early stage in their (technological) life-cycle, immediately after the new product development stage' in the sectors of computers, related software, pharmaceuticals and chemicals. He gives the example of the IDA first lobbying computer manufacturers and their subsequent targeting of the makers of individual computer components, such as keyboards, hard discs, cables, mice, printers and software (Bradley, 2002: 41). Another key element of the IDA's armoury in attracting firms has been Ireland's low-tax regime on company profits (a ten per cent tax rate on manufacturing profits guaranteed for 20 years was introduced in the early 1970s and in 2003 this became a blanket 12.5 per cent tax on all trading companies). This has again and again been promoted by policy makers and senior company managers as the single most important reason for Ireland's success in winning high levels of FDI. For example, Barry quotes a survey of the executives of ten major US multinationals who stated that the corporation tax regime was the most important attraction to set up in Ireland, followed by the education and skill levels of the workforce (Barry, 2006: 39).

The remarkable success of this strategy, boosted by the expansion of the EU economy throughout the 1990s and by the advantages offered by Ireland as a relatively low-cost manufacturing platform with access to the EU market, is illustrated by the growth in inward FDI flows from 2.2 per cent of Ireland's GDP in 1990 to 49.2 per cent in 2000 (World Bank, 2002: Table 6.1). Bradley summarises the IDA's success in the 1990s:

> The high point of the IDA strategy came during the late 1990s, when Ireland became the front-runner for most of the sophisticated foreign investment in electronics, computers and software. A virtuous circle had been created, with electronic components and computer equipment at its core, a spillover into PC-related software development and customisation, and a further spillover into telecommunications-based marketing, customer and technical support services both for existing producers located in Ireland, as well as for the creation of a sophisticated international financial services sector.
>
> (Bradley, 2002: 52)

In many ways, Ireland was very lucky. Not only did it get its national finances in order just in time to benefit from the US boom and from the completion of the Single Market in the then European Community, but it also benefited from the new funding lines established by the EC in the late 1980s to improve the infrastructure and standard of living in its poor countries and regions, the structural and cohesion funds (Delors I 1989–93 and Delors II 1994–9). Ireland was successful in winning high levels of these funds on a per capita basis and they were spent in four main areas – upgrading infrastructure (roads, ports, communications), improving human resources (education and training), aids to the private sector (grants and subsidies to aid new industries) and income support (mostly to farmers and rural dwellers). O'Donnell estimates that Ireland's net receipts from the EU averaged over five per cent of GNP throughout the 1990s with a peak of 7.6 per cent in 1991 (O'Donnell, 2000: 185).

Over this period, services have come to replace manufacturing as the principal export sector of the Irish economy. Ireland has come to face more intense competition for FDI and, according to Forfás, the National Policy and Advisory Board for Enterprise, Trade, Science, Technology and Innovation, inward FDI flows in 2004 were €9.1 billion, the lowest since 1999 and a decline of over a half from 2003 and of two-thirds from 2002. Most of this went into companies associated with the Irish Financial Services Centre (IFSC) while only €1.5 billion went to non-IFSC companies, a fall from €15.7 billion in 2003 (Forfás, 2006: 33). Exports from the IFSC 'have been one of the main drivers of Irish services export growth' in recent years, and companies based in the IFSC account for the majority of Irish insurance and financial services exports and a considerable proportion of business service exports, including accounting and legal services. Insurance and financial exports grew by 310 per cent and 159 per cent respectively between 1999 and 2004 (ibid.: 26). In 2009, the IMF reported that Ireland had lost market share both in the global and in eurozone flows of FDI and it warned: '[R]esearch shows that FDI flows to a country are highly influenced by recent momentum – increased global competition for FDI implies that task for Ireland is increasingly harder' (IMF, 2009: 9).

Box 2.1 Ireland's economic development: Taking the soft option

'The Celtic Tiger period had little to do with government policy or a sudden upsurge of Irish entrepreneurship. It was caused in the main by sharply increasing foreign direct investment (FDI) and by a collapse in interest rates following membership of the EMU. The reason FDI had such a powerful effect on growth was because the investment, which came mainly from the US, embodied the latest technology and the fruits of research and development undertaken in Silicon Valley. We didn't have to spend money on research or marketing or devising business strategies. This was all done beforehand in the US. It cost us nothing.

'But the rapid growth did not come from within; it wasn't organic, as it is in countries like Denmark and Finland. There was always something artificial and unsustainable about our model of growth, based as it was on a preferential corporate tax regime. It was made even more artificial by lavish increases in credit and an overheated property market.

'In fact, our economic history is to some degree a story of soft options. There were lavish agricultural price subsidies for years after we joined the EEC; then there were structural funds, followed by generous cohesion funds from the EU. In the late 1970s and early 1980s we relied to an extremely high degree on "expansionary" budgets and relentless increases in foreign borrowing. It was a time when international banks had ample funds from Opec, the Organisation of Petroleum-Exporting Countries, to lend to the governments of other countries. Then we came to depend on FDI, including the jobs and tax revenues created by the International Financial Services Centre. There were also two periods when our exporters made easy gains from devaluations of the currency. But no one in government could see the artificial nature of all of these soft options. There was a belief that we could dine out on free lunches in perpetuity. There was no attempt to devise an alternative industrial model, a plan B.

'Instead, we paid ourselves as if the FDI model would continue indefinitely. That was how we lost competitiveness which, of course, ensured that the FDI model would have to end. ... The international recession and banking crisis probably account for one-third of our collapse. We are responsible for two-thirds. Growing an economy requires hard graft and honest intelligence by entrepreneurs, government, public officials, and employees. It is time to do the hard yards. There are no soft options left.'

Michael Casey, former chief economist
of the Irish Central Bank (2009a)

The indigenous sector

The emphasis on winning FDI had, for decades, marginalised indigenous industry within the overall industrialisation policy. However, as Ó Riain (2000: 181) put it: 'It took the massive social and economic crisis of the 1980s to delegitimise the IDA's role as the sole bearer of the task of Irish industrial transformation. It was into this restricted institutional space that the alliance of Irish technical professionals and the previously marginalized "science and technology" state agencies stepped to support indigenous industry.' The reorganisation of the state's industrial development agencies in 1994 resulted in an agency for the development of indigenous industry, Forbairt, (later re-named Enterprise Ireland) being established alongside the IDA as the general tenor of policy was shifting towards greater selectivity in grant giving, and a greater focus on marketing and technology and on indigenous firms (Ó Riain and O'Connell, 2000: 319).

As a result of these new approaches to industrial policy, O'Malley (1998: 35) detected signs of 'a substantial and sustained improvement in the growth performance of Irish indigenous industry' over the decade 1987–97, across a wide range of industrial sectors and indicators such as employment, output, exports, profitability and spending on R&D. Furthermore, he argued that the improvement was more than a response to stronger domestic demand conditions and indicated a genuine improvement in competitive performance. The emergence of the Irish software industry in the 1990s had been hailed as 'perhaps the most spectacular success story of the recent Irish development experience' (Breathnach, 2007a: 151). It was unique in that a substantial indigenous sector was developed, partly on outsourcing from foreign firms though it then became strongly export-oriented in its own right 'with Irish firms becoming world leaders in niche sectors such as credit card security and educational software' (ibid.). In the early 2000s, Ireland became one of the world's foremost exporters of software products. Employment in the software sector grew from 8000 in 1991 to 31,500 in 2001 but fell back to 24,000 in 2004. By that date, Enterprise Ireland estimated that there were some 900 companies in the industry, 130 of them foreign, and generating over €16 billion worth of products and services. However, of this, less than €1 billion was accounted for by Irish firms, indicating again the foreign dominance of the one sector which had seemed to show successful growth of indigenous firms (Gallen, 2005).

Though indigenous industry expanded over the course of the Celtic Tiger in absolute terms and as a share of EU production and employment (O'Malley, 2004), Barry points out that as a share of EU15 exports 'Indigenous exports declined for most sectors, indicating that much of the growth in EU production and employment shares derived from the buoyancy of the Irish home market' (Barry, 2006: 41). This indicates not only the depth of the crisis facing the indigenous sector with the collapse in domestic demand due to the severe recession that began in mid-2008, but also points out major structural weaknesses. These include the fact that indigenous enterprises export less than one-third of their output, less 'than one might expect for an economy of Ireland's size' (ibid.: 41) while some 40 per cent of these exports go to the UK market and so are more affected by changes in the euro–sterling exchange rate. Furthermore R&D expenditures by indigenous firms are low by EU standards and 'the indigenous sector has a very poor record in developing patentable processes or inventions' (ibid.: 42). As Barry writes: 'Ireland is often thought of as a high-tech economy, yet only 26 per cent of indigenous manufacturing employment is in medium- or high-tech sectors (16 per cent and 10 per cent respectively), compared to 76 per cent for the foreign-owned segment (with 20 per cent in medium-tech and 56 per cent in the high-tech sectors)' (ibid.: 42). On closer examination, therefore, the software sector turns out to have been an exception to the norm of Irish indigenous industry.

Despite the turnaround in the fortunes of indigenous industry, a marked dualism between foreign and indigenous firms continued to mark Ireland's industrial structure, even at the height of the Celtic Tiger boom. Gallagher et al. (2002: 64) concluded about this period: 'Foreign-owned industry treats Ireland as an export platform, generating 74 per cent of total Irish exports in 1998. On the other hand, while 85 per cent of local plants are Irish owned and 53 per cent of manufacturing employment is generated in these plants, they produce just 28 per cent of gross output.' A decade later, Casey (2009b: 6) could write that 'duality remains a unique feature of the industrial sector in Ireland'. Of the 5000 manufacturing companies, about 85 per cent are Irish-owned and some ten per cent US-owned, but these latter account for 65 per cent of gross output, 50 per cent of employment and 80 per cent of merchandise and ICT service exports, he wrote. The same is mirrored in the service sector, he writes. While FDI has contributed greatly to the Irish economy, 'the basic idea behind this policy was to encourage domestic entrepreneurs to learn from the multinationals and spin-off their own companies. This has happened to some extent but not on a sufficient scale to keep the economy growing should FDI slow down. There is no Irish equivalent of Nokia, for example' (ibid.).

Taking the Irish economy as whole then, Table 2.5 shows where most of the employment growth took place and how it changed from the height of the Celtic Tiger to the more domestically driven economy just before the collapse. Detailed data on sectoral changes for the years 2000, 2004 and 2008 are broken down for 11 key employment sectors:

Table 2.5 Irish sectoral employment trends, 2000–8 (000s)

Sector	2000	2004	2008	Change (%)
Agriculture, forestry and fishing	134	119	121	−10
Production industries	314	297	286	−9
Construction	160	202	255	+59
Wholesale and retail trade, hotels and restaurants	339	377	439	+29
Transport, storage and communication	101	113	119	+18
Financial and other business services	207	234	296	+43
Public administration and defence	77	90	103	+34
Education and health	227	297	366	+61
Other services	93	106	122	+31
Total	1651	1836	2109	+28

Source: Forfás (2008)

The principal trends can be highlighted. The long-term decline in the agricultural sector has continued over these years. Manufacturing employment, which had been growing over the decades since the 1930s reached its peak in 2000 and began to decline afterwards. The largest increase in employment took place in the construction sector which greatly increased its employment over these years and in 2006 employed about one-eighth of the national labour force. The other major increase took place in the financial sector, reflecting in part the growth of the International Financial Services Centre (IFSC) in Dublin. Since most of those employed in the education and health sectors are public employees, the growth in these sectors, coupled with that in public administration and defence, shows the significant contribution that continued to be made to employment growth by the public sector. On growth in the services sectors, Breathnach comments that 'about two-thirds of the growth in services occurred in sectors (public administration, education and health, financial and business services) in which education and remuneration tend to be high, as against one-third for those sectors (wholesaling and retailing, transport and communications, and recreation) where the opposite tends to apply' (Breathnach, 2007a: 148, 150).

This section has described the ambiguous transformations that created the Celtic Tiger boom but that also contained the seeds of its collapse. The next section examines the role of public institutions in creating some of the conditions for this boom and the final section goes on to draw some of the salutary lessons.

Institutions of the Celtic Tiger

Social partnership

Social partnership is widely seen as among the most innovative aspects of the Celtic Tiger and its endurance and expansion over the 20 years of economic growth from 1987 to 2007 gave a stability to policymaking and to relations between employers and trade unions. As such, it was strongly supported by successive governments and some commentators came to speak of it as the centrepiece of 'this new and developing form of governance in Ireland' (Taylor, 2005: 4). In a report for the OECD on local partnerships and social innovation in Ireland written by Professor Charles Sabel of Columbia Law School, the Irish effort 'to foster development and welfare through new forms of public and private local co-ordination ... in a way that blurs familiar distinctions between public and private, national and local, and representative and participative democracy' is held up as an example for the countries of the OECD to follow (Sabel, 1996: 9). A report for the National Economic and Social Forum (NESF) described Ireland's social partnership approach as 'one of the most significant developments in public policy in the European Union' (NESF, 1997: 9). More specifically, the social partnership approach is seen as having 'produced the much needed recovery and has underpinned a sustained period of growth since then' (O'Donnell and O'Reardon, 1996: 34).

While concertative arrangements at national level between employers and trade unions facilitated by the state had resulted in negotiated national pay agreements in the 1960s and the 1970s, this national approach was abandoned in 1980 amid the crisis of the national finances.

However, the advisory body, the National Economic and Social Council (NESC) made up of representatives of the state, employers' bodies, farmers' organisations and the trade unions, continued to elaborate an economic and social analysis agreed among the social partners and its 1986 report entitled *A Strategy for Development* became the basis for the incoming government in 1987 to bring the social partners together to negotiate a three-year Programme for National Recovery (PNR). This agreement between the social partners, not only on national pay awards, but on key elements of economic and social policy, became institutionalised as a feature of Ireland's governance structures; to date seven such agreements have succeeded one another with that signed in 2006 covering a ten-year period and entitled *Towards 2016*.[2] These agreements were innovative in that they included not just wage negotiations but consensus on a wide range of economic and social policies – including tax reform, welfare payments, social spending and numerous items of industrial, social and development policy. Each agreement was preceded by a comprehensive report on national economic and social development drawn up by the NESC, itself representative of the social partners. As economic growth resumed, the agreements began to include more ambitious commitments to social equality and inclusion. For example, *Partnership 2000* included a commitment to the National Anti-Poverty Strategy (NAPS), to further measures to address educational disadvantage and to consolidation of the local partnership approach to economic and social development (O'Donnell and Thomas, 1998: 118–22). Walsh, Craig and McCafferty define social partnership 'as the search for consensus on economic and social objectives between sectoral interests – trade unions, business, farming organisations – and government'. They added that 'social partnership has strong cross-party political support ... [and] has in effect been elevated to a shared political ideology, which infuses all aspects of public policy-making and with minimal dissent' (1998: 15–16). O'Donnell and Thomas concluded that the social partners 'have been effectively co-opted into the public policy-making domain' and that the form of social partnership that has emerged through these agreements 'has resulted in a more institutionalised, structured and regularised mode of participation, and in particular, increased involvement in policy formulation, monitoring and, to a lesser degree, implementation' (125, 126).

Furthermore, the partnership principle was extended to regional and local levels in such bodies as City and County Development Boards and the local area-based partnership bodies with a brief for economic and social development in deprived areas. In 1996, national social partnership bodies were expanded to include Community and Voluntary sector organisations as full members; these represent private, charitable and voluntary bodies working with people in poverty, people with disabilities, women, and other vulnerable and marginal groups. The principle now finds expression in a bewildering array of partnership bodies, at national, regional, local and even firm level. Among the key bodies at national level are the NESC, the NESF and the Central Review Committee (CRC), all representative of the social partners. While the NESC pre-dates the emergence of social partnership, as the key forum for policy coordination among the social partners it has played a central role in the emergence of the policy consensus underpinning the process. The NESF, established in 1993, broadened representation to the community and voluntary sector for the first time (and also included politicians who are not included in the NESC) and has a particular focus on issues of social exclusion such as unemployment and poverty. Subsequently, the membership of the NESC was broadened to include the community and voluntary sector. The CRC meets regularly to review and monitor progress in implementing the three-year-long programmes. The principle of partnership has also been extended to bodies temporarily established by government to examine particular issues such as the Expert Group on the Integration of the Tax and Welfare Systems, the Task Force on the Travelling Community, the Housing Forum, the Commission on the Status of People with Disabilities and the Commission on the Family. At regional level, such bodies as County Enterprise Boards (CEBs), the Urban Community Initiative and the Territorial Employment Pacts (TEPs) include representatives of local authorities and have responsibility for aspects of social and economic development in designated regions (such as counties, cities or towns). As part of a wide-ranging reform, partnership bodies have been integrated into the workings of local government (see Department of the Environment and Local Government, 1999) and a National Centre for Partnership has been established to help achieve these goals.

The principle of social partnership can therefore be seen to have underpinned the Irish economic boom. However, while some credit it with creating and maintaining the conditions for economic success, going so far as to speak of the 'partnership state' (O'Donnell, 2008), others are far more critical and see social partnership as having institutionalised a dominant policy paradigm that prioritises economic growth and marginalises social policy objectives (Connolly, 2007). In comparing the Irish and Danish models, Sørensen drew attention to the fact that 'the Danish model has been developed and strengthened by having to cope with several major challenges, including two world wars and the economic crisis of the 1930s' whereas 'the successful Irish model has not faced a real critical challenge so far; it's been all smooth sailing in sunshine and tailwinds' (Sørensen, 2007: 8). He was not hopeful that it would prove resilient when faced with difficulties.

The downturn of 2008 has plunged social partnership in crisis, with the trade unions refusing to back a government plan for a 'pensions levy' on public service workers, claiming it would lead to revolution. It remains to be seen if social partnership will be a victim of the collapse of the Celtic Tiger or whether it has the institutional resilience to lay the foundations for a more sustainable and equitable paradigm (see Chapter 9).

Educational expansion

One of the factors consistently identified by analysts as having made a major contribution to the Celtic Tiger boom is the state's investment in education. This goes back to a series of young and energetic Ministers for Education in the 1960s and early 1970s (Donogh O'Malley, Paddy Hillery, Jack Lynch) who oversaw a major expansion of both second and third-level education. The publication in 1966 of an OECD report on Irish education, entitled *Investment in Education*, resulted in a major increase in educational expenditure and participation though, as Wickham states, this report forms just one of a series of government moves which from the early 1960s were disturbing the quiet world of Irish education (Wickham, 1980: 329–30). Educational expenditure increased from 4.1 per cent of GNP in 1961 to slightly over eight per cent in the 1990s (Lynch, 1998: 6) and education continued to receive privileged treatment during the economic downturn of the 1980s even as many other sectors experienced severe cuts in expenditure (FitzGerald, 1998: 35), though Callan and Nolan point out that education was one of the targets of reductions in capital spending between 1986 and 1989 (1992). Paradoxically, as GDP grew, the expansion of the educational budget failed to keep pace and by the early 2000s it had dropped to around 4.5 per cent of GDP or 5.5 per cent of GNI (CSO, 2008, Table 5.3). The introduction of free secondary education in 1967 saw a large increase in the numbers of students completing secondary education. The proportion of the 14–19 age group still in education grew from 23 per cent in 1951 to 62 per cent in 1981 with an increase from 118,557 to 239,000 between 1967 and 1974 alone. The curriculum was also changed as *Investment in Education* had identified major shortcomings in the contribution of education to providing the skills necessary for economic expansion. This period also saw a major expansion of technological and vocational education. An Industrial Training Authority was established in 1967 and the 1970s saw the foundation of regional technical colleges around the country (later called Institutes of Technology), expanding greatly the curriculum of studies available for students at third level. Overall, the number of students at third level in 1970 was around 25,000 of which 18,600 were at university. By 1998 overall numbers at third level had grown to 112,200 of which 61,300 were at university and 41,900 at various technological colleges and a decade later 138,605 students were enrolled full-time in third-level colleges, 87,033 at universities and 51,572 at technological colleges. As a result, the percentage of those aged 25–34 with a third-level qualification increased from 27 per cent in 1999 to 41 per cent in 2007 which, after Cyprus, was together with Lithuania the highest in the EU27 (CSO, 2008: Table 5.7). The significance of this expansion can only be assessed by looking at trends over time. Thus, by 2007 the percentage of the population that has completed at least upper secondary education has increased from 43 per cent of the 55–64 age group to 88 per cent of the 25–34 age group. However, concern continues to be expressed that, as the National Competitiveness Council put it, 'the available international rankings indicate that while improving, Irish institutions still have considerable progress to make before they reach the demanding standards set by leading institutions overseas' (National Competitiveness Council, 2009: 14). This relates in particular to scientific and mathematical literacy in which Ireland ranks fourteenth and sixteenth, respectively, out of 30 OECD countries. Declining levels of interest in studying these subjects among second-level students are a particular cause of concern. Furthermore, despite a target (contained in the 1997 NAPS) to reduce the percentage of early school leavers (those aged 18–24 who leave school with at most lower secondary education) from 18 per cent in the mid-1990s to ten per cent by 2000 and two per cent by 2007, the figure was still 12.3 per cent in 2006 and 15.6 per cent among males.

Salutary lessons

The years of the Celtic Tiger saw much self-congratulation in Ireland as politicians, policymakers and many members of the public came to believe that they had foolproof means of surfing the waves of prosperity. Even economists came to believe that the good times could go on indefinitely. As Sweeney wrote in 1999: 'The Irish people appear to have built a launch pad for continued success, which is well constructed, has good foundations and is strong' (Sweeney, 1999: 238). While the principal explanations offered for Ireland's success and the theoretical assumptions informing them are discussed in Chapters 4 and 5, this section limits itself to summarising the main causes of the boom that are widely mentioned in the literature on the Celtic Tiger. They are divided into the institutional and the conjunctural thereby highlighting how much of the success may have been due to luck – to some extent, simply being in the right place at the right time – and how much due to factors of Ireland's own making.

Institutional factors

As is clear from this chapter, the Irish state has played a key role in putting in place some of the elements which have been among the necessary conditions for the economic boom of the 1990s. Some of these, like the expansion of education and an industrial policy focused on attracting multinational companies to establish plants in Ireland, date back to the 1960s.

What is significant about these is the consistent support given them by all governments since. White reminds us that at times of economic recession, like that of the 1980s, 'the IDA version of Ireland sounded like a fairy tale' (Mac Sharry and White, 2000: 210) and the support for educational spending even amid the cutbacks of the 1980s has already been mentioned. Of course, neither policymakers nor economists ever expected that these policies would result in the dramatic boom of the 1990s (just as they never expected the collapse of 2008) but it is clear that without them such high growth rates could not have been achieved. Two other actions of state institutions are also worthy of mention as among the factors leading to the economic success. The first of these was the fiscal stabilisation of the late 1980s achieved through an exceptional political consensus among the main parties. This stabilised the national finances and made Ireland a more attractive location for foreign investment in time to take advantage of the US boom in the early 1990s. Finally, the state was also successful through its forceful lobbying in achieving the largest per capita allocation of EU Structural Funds which allowed for structural weaknesses in the Irish economy to be remedied to an extent that would not have been possible otherwise. Among these were improvements to the country's physical infrastructure but also investment went into raising competitiveness and productivity and to improving the skills base of the workforce (Mac Sharry and White, 2000: 165–71). Furthermore, as the OECD pointed out, the Structural Funds 'raised the quality of public investment outlays by forcing the introduction of longer-term project planning, so that short-term budgetary pressures have not led to stopping an undertaking with the extra cost of subsequently re-starting it' (OECD, 1999: 44).

Conjunctural factors

As necessary as were the state's actions in creating some of the conditions for success, it is unlikely that they would have been quite so successful without the coincidence of a number of crucial conjunctural factors. Two of them relate to Ireland's geographical location and historical connections in that the creation of a single market within the EU following the passage of the Single European Act in 1987 added to Ireland's attraction for US investment since it now gave access to the whole EU market. That this coincided with the beginning of a long boom period in the US economy was a major piece of good luck which Ireland helped turn to its advantage. Yet another conjunctural factor further reinforcing these trends was the beginning of the Northern Ireland peace process and the very active support lent to this by the Clinton presidency. Thus Ireland featured prominently on the political agenda of the White House during a period in which the conditions were ideal for a major expansion of US investment. These can be described as being in the right place at the right time.

There was a second set of conjunctural features related to demography which also turned positive for Ireland at the same time. These relate to

Ireland's exceptional demographic profile, partly due to the baby boom of the 1970s and partly to the effects of high emigration in the 1950s. This had resulted in a high dependency ratio during the economic downturn of the 1980s as Ireland had a high dependent youth population in proportion to the working population. However, with the decline in fertility and in the birth rate, in the 1990s and 2000s Ireland found itself in a highly favourable situation with a declining dependency ratio (both a smaller youth population and a relatively small elderly population due to high emigration in the 1950s). Economists estimate that it will be 2015 before the rate of old-age dependency will rise rapidly as it is currently doing elsewhere in Europe thus making greater demands on social spending. Allied to the favourable demographic situation is the reversing of Ireland's traditional pattern of emigration as a tightening labour market attracted Irish skilled labour home. As Fitz Gerald (2000: 32) put it: 'Part of the recent transformation in society and the economy must be attributed to this influx of additional skilled labour with new ideas and skills, and new approaches to the many problems which Ireland faces.'

Finally, a conjunctural advantage from which Ireland benefited in the early 2000s was membership of the euro. This gave monetary stability at the height of the Celtic Tiger boom and, with the depreciation of the euro against both the pound sterling and the US dollar in the years following its creation in 1999, added to export competitiveness. However, membership of the euro can also be seen as a double-edged sword for two reasons. Firstly, by joining the euro, Ireland gave up its power to fix interest rates and joined a monetary zone with maintained relatively low interest rates to boost economic activity, exactly the opposite required by a country experiencing a boom. Secondly, when the euro began to appreciate against both the pound sterling and the US dollar from the mid-2000s onwards, Ireland was particular badly hit as a higher percentage of its exports go to both the UK and the US markets than do those of any other EU state.

Conclusions

Viewed from the vantage point of the economic collapse in 2008, Ireland's transformation seems less far-reaching and its institutional underpinnings more vulnerable. Clearly, as this chapter has described, the boom brought many benefits, not least through greater employment opportunities and higher living standards. However, the transformation was never as far-reaching as many presumed and contained many weaknesses, both in the structure of the productive economy with its high levels of dependence on foreign investment, and in the institutions underpinning it such as the cosy consensus created by social partnership. This helps draw attention to the mix of external environment and policy measures to which the OECD drew attention when cautioning that the Irish case offered 'no single, overriding policy that could be adopted elsewhere in order to emulate Irish experience'. Instead it drew attention to 'the confluence of a series of favourable changes in the environment and other exogenous factors (some of which were specific to Ireland and are unlikely to be replicated elsewhere), as well as prudent planning and a range of policy shifts that lay the foundations for the pickup in growth' (OECD, 1999: 10). This draws attention to the role of factors outside the control of Irish policymakers that are unlikely to turn as favourable again any time soon.

3
Best of Times?

If the men and women of Ireland's past could chose a time
to live, there would be a long queue for this one. It is far
from perfect but it is as good as it has ever been.

President Mary McAleese, in Charlottesville,
Virginia, May 2003

There was an unfortunate tendency during the Celtic Tiger period to consider economic growth as an end in itself rather than consider it as a means to the end of a better quality of life for all in society. Because of this, the Irish boom tended to be assessed simply on the basis of its ability to generate high growth rates in GDP/GNP rather than on its impact on people's lives. This is despite the fact that the social impact of the boom became the subject of lively debates which generated little consensus on whether this was, in the ESRI's controversial phrase, the 'best of times' (Fahey et al., 2007). Assessing this social impact is the subject of this chapter. Since the aspiration to greater equality in the distribution of the benefits of economic growth has been a traditional objective of social policy (and, indeed, a yardstick for judging the success of development policies), distribution is the common theme that links the various topics of this chapter. It begins by examining more closely the distributional impact of the boom years, examining poverty, inequality and the little we know about the distribution of wealth. The following section examines the distribution of employment, examining whether there has been a general upgrading of the occupational structure or rather a deepening polarisation, with a growth of not only high quality but also low quality jobs. The third section traces inequality in areas of social provision such as education, health and housing, and also regional and gender dimensions of inequality. Finally, the chapter examines quality of life under the Celtic Tiger.

Distribution

Poverty

The evolution of poverty and inequality over the course of the boom has elicited widespread public concern in Ireland. Up until the mid-2000s, data on poverty in Ireland was gathered under two headings – consistent poverty and relative poverty. The former is a combination of relative income lines together with deprivation measured according to a list of indicators such as having a meal with meat, chicken or fish every second day; having new rather than second-hand clothes; having a warm waterproof overcoat and two pairs of strong shoes. Absence of these for households falling below the different relative income poverty lines indicates deprivation (for a fuller explanation, see Whelan et al., 2003: 34–5). This was adopted as the key indicator for the National Anti-Poverty Strategy (NAPS) thus giving the indicator major political importance. Trends in this indicator over the course of the boom are given in Table 3.1 showing a fairly steady fall in poverty, though not among the very poorest.

Table 3.1 Evolution of households in consistent poverty, 1994–2001 (percentage in poverty)

Poverty lines	1994	1997	2000	2001
40% average income	2.4	3.1	2.7	2.5
50% average income	9.0	6.7	4.5	4.1
60% average income	15.1	9.7	5.8	5.2

Source: Whelan et al. (2003: 38).

However, trends in relative poverty, measured as the percentage of households falling below certain percentages of mean income poverty lines, give a somewhat more complex picture of what was happening to poverty. This is given in Table 3.2 which shows a steady rise in poverty except at the 60 per cent line where poverty has remained quite stable.

Table 3.2 Evolution of relative household poverty, 1994–2001 (percentage in poverty)

Poverty lines	1994	1997	2000	2001
40% average income	4.9	6.3	10.6	9.8
50% average income	18.6	22.4	23.7	23.8
60% average income	34.2	34.3	32.0	32.2

Source: Whelan et al. (2003: 11).

Since the initiation of the EU Survey on Income and Living Conditions (EU-SILC) in 2003, data on poverty in Ireland are grouped into somewhat different categories making them consistent with data across the EU.

However, this means that it is more difficult to assess longer-term trends in Ireland. Since 2003, the EU's 'at-risk-of-poverty' rate has been more centrally adopted in measuring poverty in Ireland. This is the share of persons with equivalised income below a given percentage of the national median income (note that median income is used in this measure whereas mean income had been used previously in Ireland). The percentage of income used is 60 per cent. Trends in the gini coefficient and in income distribution (the ratio of the income of those in the top income quintile to those in the bottom quintile) are also now regularly measured. Trends in these measures over the more recent period are given in Table 3.3.

Table 3.3 Trends in poverty and inequality, 2000–7

	2000	2001	2003	2005	2007
Relative at-risk-of-poverty gap	19.3	20.7	21.5	18.5	16.5
Gini coefficient	30.2	30.3	31.1	32.4	31.7
Income distribution (S80/S20)	4.7	4.8	5.0	4.9	4.9

Source: CSO (2008).

These data provide a broader distributional picture of what has been happening to poverty in Ireland and, by and large, show an increase to 2003 and then a marked fall since; however, inequality remained more or less static (see below). Before turning to examine Ireland's changing income distribution in more detail and to place it in an international context, it is important to look at the impact of poverty on different groups. Table 3.4 shows the levels of poverty experienced by different groups since 1994 and how these have changed.

Table 3.4 Households in poverty (60% of median income) by labour force status 1994–2007

Labour force status	1994	1998	2001	2005	2007
Employee	3.2	2.6	8.1	7.0	6.7
Farmer	18.6	23.9	23.0	n/a	n/a
Other self-employed	16.0	16.4	14.3	n/a	n/a
Unemployed	51.4	58.8	44.7	40.6	38.7
Ill/Disabled	29.5	54.5	66.5	40.6	37.0
Retired	8.2	18.4	36.9	20.5	17.6
Home duties	20.9	46.8	46.9	27.6	25.3

Source: Murphy (2006: 97), EU-SILC (2006, 2008).

These data illustrate the emergence of a category of employees whose income is not sufficient to lift them out of poverty, a category that almost tripled over the course of the boom. Farmers continued to experience significant levels of poverty and so did the self-employed other than farmers (unfortunately, these categories have been dropped from more recent surveys). This illustrates that some categories of households have not been able to avail of the opportunities offered by the booming market to lift themselves out of poverty. The other categories on this list depend by and large on state transfers to lift them out of poverty and here the growth in the percentages of households headed by ill or disabled people, by the retired and by those on home duties who fell into poverty over the course of the boom relates directly to the inadequacy of state transfers to prevent this. The significant improvement in the situation of these groups reflects the increases in welfare payments since 2002 though their levels of poverty still remain substantially above what they were before the boom. It is also important to note that, as Collins and Kavanagh (2006: 140) put it, 'consistently, the results of income surveys indicate that among all adults, women in Ireland experience a greater risk of poverty than men'. Between 2005 and 2007, the 'at-risk-of-poverty' rate for women fell from 18.5 to 17.0 per cent and that for men from 18.4 to 16.0 per cent (CSO, 2006, 2008a).

It is also important to know how Ireland fares in comparison to other countries. Were levels of poverty and inequality in Ireland found to be relatively low by international standards, then the social impact of its economic growth might have be judged somewhat less harshly than would otherwise have been the case. The Human Poverty Index for a range of industrialised

Table 3.5 UNDP Human Poverty Index (HPI) for industrialised countries 2007–8

Country	Survival	Literacy	Poverty	Exclusion	HPI value (%)	HPI rank
Sweden	6.7	7.5	6.5	1.1	6.3	1
Norway	7.9	7.9	6.4	0.5	6.8	2
Netherlands	8.3	10.5	7.3	1.8	8.1	3
Finland	9.4	10.4	5.4	1.8	8.1	4
Denmark	10.3	9.6	5.6	0.8	8.2	5
Germany	8.6	14.4	8.4	5.8	10.3	6
Switzerland	7.2	15.9	7.6	1.5	10.7	7
Canada	8.1	14.6	11.4	0.5	10.9	8
Luxembourg	9.2	n/a	6.0	1.2	11.1	9
Austria	8.8	n/a	7.7	1.3	11.1	10
France	8.9	n/a	7.3	4.1	11.2	11
Japan	6.9	n/a	11.8	1.3	11.7	12
Australia	7.3	17.0	12.2	0.9	12.1	13
Belgium	9.3	18.4	8.0	4.6	12.4	14
Spain	7.7	n/a	14.2	2.2	12.5	15
United Kingdom	8.7	21.8	12.5	1.2	14.8	16
United States	11.6	20.0	17.0	0.5	15.4	17
Ireland	*8.7*	*22.6*	*16.2*	*1.5*	*16.0*	*18*
Italy	7.7	47.0	12.7	3.4	29.8	19

Source: UNDP (2007–8).

countries allows such comparisons to be made. Published for the first time in the UNDP's 1998 *Human Development Report*, Ireland's position on this index allows us to trace comparative trends over the course of the Celtic Tiger boom. The index combines four elements – longevity (the percentage of people not expected to survive till the age of 60), knowledge (the percentage of people who are functionally illiterate), living standards (the percentage of people living below the income poverty line set at 50 per cent of the median disposable income) and exclusion (the percentage of the labour force who are unemployed for 12 months or more). It thus constitutes a more multifaceted measure of poverty than do measures based on income poverty alone. In 1998, Ireland was in second lowest position on this index and it held a similar position in 2007–8 without any significant shift in the intervening period; the data in Table 3.5 are taken from the 2007–8 report.

Inequality

Table 3.3 gives some data on income distribution at the end of the boom but for trends over the course of the boom, we need to look further. First of all, it is interesting to note that the evidence on the distribution of earnings (market income) over the period 1994–2000 shows a modest decline in earnings dispersion over this period as the ratio of the earnings of the top and bottom deciles both moved closer to the median. As a result, the ratio of the earnings of the top decile to those of the bottom decile fell from 4.70 in 1994 to 3.65 in 2000 (O'Connell and Russell, 2007: 53). The picture of overall income distribution is complicated by the fact that different sources offer different pictures of what has been happening. The Household Budget Surveys of the CSO show a marked increase at the top of the distribution and a marked decline at the bottom (see Collins and Kavanagh, 2006: 154–7) whereas EU data shows inequality to have fallen sharply in Ireland (see Nolan and Maitre, 2007: 29–33). In seeking to account for these differences, Nolan and Maitre find fault with both datasets, the former as it uses the household rather than the person as the unit of analysis and the latter because it is a longitudinal survey and some of the households inevitably drop out over time thus affecting the results. Controlling for these factors, they conclude that the evidence shows modest declines in the share of the bottom decile, modest increases among deciles in the middle of the distribution and declines in the top three deciles. However, in examining trends in the share of the top income earners over the period 1989–2000 through using tax returns, they find a substantial increase in the share of the top decile, from 33 to 38 per cent. The top one per cent saw its share rise sharply in the second half of the decade with all the growth in the share of the top decile being concentrated among this one per cent. They conclude: 'It means that by the end of the 1990s, the share of the top 1 per cent was more than twice the level prevailing through the 1970s and 1980s. As it happens, most of this growth in turn was concentrated in the top 0.5 per cent'

(Nolan and Maitre, 2007: 33–4).[1] The salary levels of some of these are illustrated by data in an ICTU publication which lists the remuneration of some top Irish executives in 2006 – this includes Brian Goggin of Bank of Ireland on an annual remuneration of €4m, Paul Walsh of Diageo on €3.75m, Liam O'Mahoney of CRH on €2.65m, Eugene Sheehy of AIB on €2.4m, Aidan Heavey of Tullow Oil on €1.6m, Hugh Friel of Kerry Foods on €1.2m, Michael O'Leary of Ryanair on €992,000 and John Maloney of Glanbia on €927,000. Keena estimates that in the year 2008, 9129 people or 0.3 per cent of earners, between them earned €6.7 billion, or 6.6 per cent of all income (Keena, 2009a). Meanwhile, 1.5 million workers or 71 per cent of those in employment were earning an average of €38,000 a year (ICTU, 2008: Table 2.3, p. 43).

Comparing Ireland's income distribution with EU and OECD countries shows that, even if the impact of the boom on distribution is somewhat disputed, it remains something of an outlier for its level of economic development. Comparing it to 30 countries using data from around 2000, Smeeding and Nolan write that 'Ireland is indeed an outlier among rich nations. Only the United States, Russia, and Mexico have higher levels of inequality. ... Among the richest OECD nations Ireland has the second highest level of inequality' (Smeeding and Nolan, 2004: 9). They find that low-income Irish people in the bottom decile in 2000 had an income that was only 41 per cent of median income making them among the least well-off of the whole sample whereas a high-income compatriot in the top decile had an income that is 189 per cent of the median, a little below the average. Ireland's gini coefficient was the fifth highest in the EU25 in 2003–4.

A final indicator of Ireland's comparable distributional position in Europe and how it has changed over the course of the boom is given by data on functional distribution rather than personal distribution. Table 3.6 compares Ireland's adjusted wage share of the total economy as a percentage of GDP at total factor cost with that of the EU12 from 1960 to 2010.[2] This shows that in Ireland the wage share was higher than that for the EU12 up to the 1990s but that it has fallen badly behind over the course of the boom.

Table 3.6 Wage share of total economy, Ireland and EU12, 1960–2010 (percentage of GDP)

Period	Ireland	EU12
1960–70	78	70
1971–80	76	72.5
1981–90	71.3	69.5
1991–2000	62.4	66.7
2001–10	55.4	64.2

Source: Statistical Annex of European Economy (Spring 2009).

The economic boom of the 1990s has greatly increased living standards in Ireland; in this context, the decline in constant poverty is no surprise. However, there is evidence of a deeply entrenched core of extreme poverty that the boom bypassed. Turning to relative poverty, the evidence is clear that the economic boom had the paradoxical effect of increasing this measure significantly; only since growth rates decreased did relative poverty show a steady decline. With the swift increase in unemployment in 2008 and 2009, these rates of poverty are almost certain to increase also. Measures of income distribution paint a somewhat more complex picture but the weight of evidence points to a deepening polarisation with evidence indicating that the top one per cent or even 0.5 per cent of the distribution has benefited greatly. The swift decline in the wage share of national income would also confirm that an ever larger share is going to profits. There is an urgent need for more systematic research to identify the levels of concentration of income among a small elite.

Wealth

Even less is known about the distribution of wealth in Ireland. Yet wealth is always far more unequally distributed than is income since those who hold wealth (in the form of assets such as property, company shares or luxury goods of many different kinds) can pass it on as an inheritance and can find numerous ways to avoid taxation. Almost no research has been done into wealth inequality in Ireland and what has been done is quite dated. Journalistic accounts and impressionistic evidence highlight the extent to which an extremely wealthy elite emerged as the main beneficiary of the Irish boom, most of whom made their money not from productive entrepreneurship but from property speculation and as building developers. The levels of debts they carry at the end of the boom (see details in Chapter 8) are one indication of just how wealthy they became. At the height of the boom Pat O'Sullivan estimated that the top one per cent of the population held 20 per cent of the wealth, the top two per cent held 30 per cent and the top five per cent held 40 per cent of the wealth (O'Sullivan, 2006: 16). When the value of housing is excluded, then the concentration of wealth is even greater with one per cent of the population accounting for around 34 per cent of the wealth.

According to O'Sullivan, Ireland was second only to Japan in the OECD for wealth per capita, with €150,000 per head in 2005, though this was very largely due to the boom in property prices which have subsequently collapsed. In mid-2009, it was estimated that the net financial assets (including deposits, shares, life insurance and pension funds) of Irish households had fallen 42 per cent since peaking at almost €140 billion in 2006. In 2008 alone, net financial assets fell by 31 per cent with the average per household falling from €209,000 at the end of 2006 to €179,000 at the end of 2008. The level of household debt continued to rise, to reach €128,000 in 2008

(Madden, 2009a). Yet these average levels fail to distinguish between the prospects for the very rich and for those on more average incomes; despite significant falls in asset prices it is likely that the very rich will be able to shield themselves better from the downturn than can those on average incomes dependent on a small quantity of assets (such as modest property or share holdings).

Employment

There has been a lively debate over the course of the Celtic Tiger about trends in employment. The influential commentator and economist David McWilliams has proclaimed that 'We are all middle class now' (quoted in Tasc, 2009: 1); if the boom had indeed moved most occupations into a middle class position (judged either in terms of income or skill levels), that would indicate a major achievement and would influence judgements of the distributional impact of the boom years. Some evidence for this is given in the work of ESRI researchers, O'Connell and Russell, who argue that the data points to a steady professionalisation of the Irish occupational structure, with a growth in higher income and higher skill job positions and a decline in lower ones. They conclude that economic development in Ireland 'gave rise to a sustained long-term trend of occupational upgrading, which entailed the expansion of professional, technical and managerial occupations and increased the importance of education and skills' (O'Connell and Russell, 2007: 64). While acknowledging 'some expansion' in lower-skilled occupations, they conclude that the impact of the boom on employment has been largely positive.

Breathnach examines the data in a more thorough way to find out what evidence there may be in the Irish case for the polarisation thesis, namely that economic and technological changes associated with the end of Fordism are generating a rapid growth in professional employment but alongside a corresponding increase in poorly paid employment such as catering, retailing, cleaning, leisure, personal care and retailing. And, as both extremes of the jobs spectrum have been growing, middle-income groups have seen their positions being eroded by a combination of technological change and public sector cutbacks (Breathnach, 2007b: 23). If these changes were found in Ireland then it would complicate any easy conclusion that the boom years had created a largely middle-class society. While his first examination of the data tends to confirm the professionalisation thesis, he finds the broad job categories used by the Central Statistics Office unsatisfactory as a way of assessing the polarisation thesis since it combines within the same categories workers with high skills levels and with low skills levels and with very varied incomes. An example is the personal and protective services category which combines such groups as members of the defence forces and of the police with care assistants, nurses' aides, waitresses and bar staff; the wide range of weekly earnings for these categories make the average given quite useless as a guide to tracking occupational change, he argues (ibid.: 27). Instead, he divides the labour forces into a set of occupational groups which are internally homogenous in terms of skill levels and remuneration. His revised analysis of trends in occupational change in Ireland from 1991 to 2002, covering the years of the Celtic Tiger boom, finds 'many features which comply with key tenets of social polarisation theory' (ibid.: 37). While higher-level employer, managerial, professional and technical occupations have shown strong growth, moving from 33.8 to 40.4 per cent of the labour force, there was also a growth in unskilled occupations such as personal service and sales, though the growth was not as strong as for the high-skills occupations. However, he finds that the main loss of employment share was experienced by the intermediate clerical and blue-collar groups, whose share fell from 35.7 to 29.8 per cent. He also finds that trends in public service employment provide additional evidence for the polarisation thesis as it has experienced a significant contraction in its employment position relative to the high-skilled groups. Examining female employment, he finds a notable growth in high-skilled occupations but also in unskilled occupations. Overall, he finds 'that the profound occupational restructuring which has been going on in Ireland at least since the beginning of the 1990s has involved both an increasing professionalisation and polarisation of the Irish workforce, with the growth of female employment playing a key role in driving both these processes' (ibid.: 40).

Inequalities

The evidence in the previous section indicates that a characteristic of Irish economic growth is that its impact on society is markedly inegalitarian, namely that it benefits some sectors far more than it does others. In this section we examine various aspects of Irish society to identify how institutions and policy are contributing to greater inequality.

Health

Ireland's health service has long been two-tier with the middle classes resisting attempts to introduce a more comprehensive system. What evolved was a system of means-tested eligibility for public hospitals and health services. As Kelleher has put it: 'Rather than introducing a comprehensive system of care, the notion of means testing and the partial subsidy of health insurance for the more affluent taxpayer became the norm' (Kelleher, 2007: 205). The Mother and Child controversy of 1951 'set a principle of non-state interference in family healthcare which remains at the heart of public policy debate today' (ibid.: 205). Describing this 'long-standing two-tier healthcare system', she concludes that 'most people in Ireland today are not entitled to comprehensive healthcare, and the one-half of the population that holds private insurance currently receives hospital care predominantly in the public setting' (ibid.: 202). Wren documented how the percentage of the population with access to free primary care due to low income declined from nearly 28 per cent in 2003 to 25 per cent at the end of 2005 (Wren, 2003, 2006).

One high profile issue that illustrates the inequity in the Irish health care system is outpatient waiting, namely the length of time public patients (patients without the ability to pay through, most commonly, health insurance) are waiting to be seen by a specialist, many of them with serious complaints. Figures published in late 2007 showed patients having to wait between two and four years in many leading hospitals (Donnellan, 2007). Indeed, in a 2006 Euro Health Consumer Index, Ireland ranked second last out of 26 European countries on consumer health care, citing long waiting times for treatment, bleak medical outcomes and widespread MRSA infections (*The Irish Times*, 27 June 2006). So, Kelleher (2007: 223) concludes, as Ireland became richer during the Celtic Tiger boom, 'we have replaced a traditional pattern of fairly universal disadvantage with a widening health inequality'. She found that 'Ireland straddles the gap between the newer accession states in the expanded EU-25 and the older EU countries' with life expectancy lower and expectancy from the age of 65 also lower than average; she adds that the health gain in this age group has been negligible in recent years (Kelleher, 2007: 206). Compared to its neighbours, Ireland has high mortality from cardiovascular diseases, particularly for coronary heart disease while the rates of some of the common cancers, particularly colon and bowel in both sexes and breast cancer in women, are also high. Despite the growth in state funding for cancer cure and treatment, which is now around the average spent by OECD states, the Irish health system tends to mirror the deep inequalities of Irish life. As Burke (2009: 4) put it, 'we have an apartheid system of healthcare. ... This has always been the case, but, in the past decade, the two-tier system of healthcare has been accentuated, with increasing numbers of people incentivised to take out private insurance, privileging them over those who cannot afford to skip the queue'.

Education

Ireland has long prided itself on a high-quality education system yet, for all its successes, there remain major challenges that were not sufficiently addressed during the boom years. Foremost among these is early childhood education for which, according to EU figures, Irish parents pay more than most other Europeans with childcare costs consuming 29.2 per cent of family income (Smyth, 2008). Despite this, Ireland found itself at the bottom of a UNICEF league table of 25 countries on services for early childhood education. It found that Ireland's public expenditure on childcare is one-fifth the recommended international minimum of one per cent of GDP and Ireland ranked joint lowest on the table with South Korea (UNICEF, 2008).

While, as detailed in Chapter 2, educational participation has steadily increased over recent decades, Smyth and Hannan found 'a notable persistence in educational inequalities by social background' at the height of the Celtic Tiger boom (Smyth and Hannan, 2000: 117). They pointed out that, at second-level, participation tends to be higher among those whose parents have higher levels of education while educational under-performance is more evident among pupils from working-class backgrounds, whose parents are unemployed or have lower levels of education or who come from larger families. They find a widening gap between the professional and unskilled manual groups in their access to full-time third-level education over the past two decades. Systematic details of this gap only became available in 2008 when the Higher Education Authority (HEA) asked third-level institutions to gather such data on a basis that was comparable across the sector. This showed that, in the university sector, 20 per cent of its student cohort was from the employer and manager socio-economic group making up the largest group while only 2.5 per cent came from the unskilled group and 0.3 per cent from the agricultural workers group; in the Institute of Technology sector, the figures for the same socio-economic groups were 18 per cent, 5.3 per cent and 0.6 per cent, respectively (HEA, 2008a: Table 7.2). These data confirm the socio-economic inequalities that persist in higher education and offer a basis for surveying how they develop over future years.

Furthermore Archer found public spending on education to be regressive as the state spends more on the education of better-off young people who tend to remain in the system longer than it does on young people from poorer backgrounds who tend to leave the system earlier. Examining the significant expansion of special measures to tackle educational disadvantage, he found that it was not possible to say to what extent it has made a difference to the relative position of disadvantaged schools (Archer, 2001). Thus, the available evidence pointed to the fact that education tends to further marginalise those who come from more disadvantaged backgrounds since, as Smyth and Hannan (2000: 125) put it, 'young people in Ireland who do not achieve educational qualifications are disproportionately likely to experience labour market marginalisation in terms of unemployment, insecure jobs and/or low pay'. They concluded on a pessimistic note: 'In the absence of a fundamental reduction in inequalities in life-chances, it is difficult to see how these inequalities will diminish radically in the future' (ibid.: 125).

Housing and homelessness

Housing presents different features than do health and education. For, while the former are still largely state-provided services, the state has progressively extricated itself from responsibility for housing provision, leaving it instead to market forces. An extensive programme of public authority housing characterised the Fianna Fáil governments of the 1930s and early 1940s so that public authorities built 49,000 units which represented 60 per cent of total housing output and, up to the mid-1950s, public provision of housing always exceeded 50 per cent of total housing built. Then began a steady move towards private provision, assisted by both state subsidies and general tax reliefs. Over the period from 1961 to 2002, this grew from 59.8 per cent of housing tenure to 77.4 per cent, one of the highest rates in Western Europe. Meanwhile, the public provision of housing has steadily declined, from 18.4 to 6.9 per cent of all the housing stock in 2002, reflecting a steady decline in the number of housing units being built by local authorities (Fahey et al., 2004). The Celtic Tiger boom saw a huge jump in house prices, making it more difficult for people on average incomes to access the market and increasing reliance on the private rented sector. The total number of households in housing need increased from 28,624 in 1993 to 43,700 in 2005 though Drudy argues that this is an underestimate and may have been as high as 101,200 households that year; furthermore, homelessness doubled between 1993 and 2005 (Drudy, 2006: 262–3). In the latter year, 2399 households were officially categorised as homeless, with 1725 households living in unfit accommodation, 4112 in overcrowded accommodation and 3375 involuntarily sharing. However, the Simon Community which works with the homeless considered the official figure to be an underestimate (Simon Community website) (see Box 3.1). A further result of the greater reliance on the market is that many younger people have been forced to buy far from where they work thereby incurring long commuting times. Concern has been expressed at the impact on the quality of life of these people and their families, as well as on that of the communities and housing estates to which they move. As the economy entered into severe recession, a new threat loomed for many – inability to service the high mortgages with which they were burdened.

Box 3.1 Sr Stan on the state turning away from people in need

Anti-poverty campaigner, Sr Stanislaus Kennedy, is widely known among the general public simply as Sr Stan. In 1985 she founded Focus Ireland to help house the many homeless in Ireland. In September 2008, on the 23rd anniversary of its founding, she reflected on how the problem had evolved over the Celtic Tiger boom.

'In 1985, it was estimated that up to 1,000 people were homeless at any one time. There are now up to 5,000 people who are homeless at any one time. This figure is not static as people enter and leave homelessness all the time, but it is worrying that the *Counted In* report found up to 1,800 become homeless in Dublin each year. In 1984, it was found that 37 women and 93 children were homeless in Dublin. The most recent official figures available show that 463 dependent children who are part of 1,361 households are homeless in Dublin. These figures are an indictment of how successive governments have failed to tackle homelessness and housing need.

'It is shocking to see the level of shortfall in delivery of social housing during the boom years. This is largely a direct result of a conscious decision by successive governments to, in effect, cut back on provision of social housing while the level of need was rising year on year. In the 1970s and 1980s, social housing as a percentage of total housing output in the country ranged from 20 to 33 per cent. There was a shift in 1987 when it dropped to 16 per cent and in subsequent years it dropped as low as 4 per cent.

'This shift of State policy continued during the 1990s as general housing output rose significantly but social housing output did not follow suit. In 1993, social housing was 9.8 per cent of total housing output, in 1999 it was 7.5 per cent and in 2004 it fell as low as 6.6 per cent. These figures support the view that year on year, the State was turning away from its commitment to provide social housing for people in need. I believe that this was a conscious decision by the State to transfer the responsibility for meeting social needs, namely housing, to the private sector and massively subsidising them in this role. This strategy has now backfired spectacularly.

'It is incumbent on the Government, when considering its budgetary options, to ensure that those who have benefited the least during the boom years are not made pay the price during any downturn. Any continuing failure to deliver on social housing targets makes a mockery of the Government's commitment to meet its own target to end long-term homelessness by 2010. Official figures show over 43,000 households on local authority housing waiting lists today compared to 23,000 in 1991. When Focus Ireland was founded people were generally housed in under six months. Now families and single people can languish on the waiting lists for two years and more. This housing shortfall must be addressed as a home is the very foundation stone of any attempt to create a more equal society.'

Sr Stanislaus Kennedy, founder of Focus Ireland (Kennedy, 2008)

Taxation

While taxation and welfare systems are key instruments through which governments can redistribute income and wealth, studies of the redistributive effects of the Irish tax and welfare systems point to their inequities.

Despite the high levels of economic growth over the course of the Celtic Tiger boom which gave the state greater scope for such reform in the 1990s, the income tax system was found to be less progressive in the late 1990s than it had been in 1980. Employees on 50 per cent of the average industrial wage saw their average tax rate increase from 14.4 per cent in 1980 to 17.4 per cent in 1995 and those on the average industrial wage saw an increase from 26.9 per cent in 1980 to 30 per cent in 1995. Those on five times the average industrial wage, however, saw their tax level decrease from 50.6 per cent in 1980 to 46.8 per cent in 1995. When various allowances are added, such as tax relief for pension or health insurance contributions, or mortgage interest relief, higher income earners benefit even more (O'Toole, 1997: 8–13). As Cahill and O'Toole (1998: 226) conclude about the effects of changes between 1987 and 1998: 'Changes in the tax and social insurance system have reduced everyone's tax 'burden', but these reductions have benefited those with the highest incomes most; reductions in tax and social insurance contributions are almost inevitably biased towards those on higher pre-tax incomes.' The National Economic and Social Council (NESC) found that these trends continued into the 2000s as 'from 1995 to 2002, a regressive pattern was dominant with Budgets improving the disposable income of the top three quintiles by significantly more than for the bottom two quintiles' (NESC, 2005: 81).

Examining the overall composition of the tax system shows that Ireland relies significantly more than do other EU countries on taxes on goods and services as a source of revenue, which is widely regarded as a regressive tax. The trade-off associated with the boom years of the mid-1990s when government negotiated moderate wage increases for reductions in personal income taxes is reflected in a reduction in the share of income taxes from 30.7 per cent of all tax revenue in 1997 to 26.5 per cent in 2003. Alongside this there was a comparatively larger tax take from corporation tax and property taxes with the former increasing from 8.5 to 12.9 per cent over this period and the latter from 4.5 to 6.5 per cent, a function of the booming economy (O'Toole and Cahill, 2006: 206). Though the corporation tax rate is comparatively low at 12.5 per cent, the tax base is wide and corporations declare large profits in Ireland (some of which, it is suspected, are due to transfer pricing). For example, Allen argues that the doubling of profits from US corporations declared in Ireland – from $13.4bn in 1999 to $26.8bn in 2002 – derives not from a surge in profitable investment but from the 1997 double taxation agreement between both countries that widened opportunities for corporations to avoid being taxed in the US (Allen, 2007: 83). While there are no taxes on owner-occupied private dwellings, tax is paid on their sale or purchase and the growth in tax revenue from this source over the boom reflects the large increase in property prices that took place. However, as O'Toole and Cahill commented on these data, reliance on corporation tax and property tax (stamp duty) 'leaves the Irish economy particularly vulnerable to an economic shock' as flows of FDI and property prices begin to fall (O'Toole and Cahill, 2006: 207). This is precisely what happened when recession hit in late 2008 and the state's revenue stream collapsed. Other aspects of the Irish tax system are questionable from the point of view of equity as they benefit the better off. These relate to tax exemptions and incentives. Among these are benefits for health expenses and for private pensions which are of far greater value to higher rate taxpayers. For example, Hughes estimates that two-thirds of tax reliefs for private pensions in 2000 went to highest paid employees in the top quintile while only one per cent went to lowest paid employees in the bottom quintile (Hughes, 2005: 143) while O'Shea and Kennelly report that tax relief on approved pension schemes is equivalent to approximately one-fifth of total social expenditure on pensions (O'Shea and Kennelly, 2002: 64). Investors in property get tax relief on mortgage payments and also on rent paid by private tenants. Finally, illustrating the extent of tax breaks available to the wealthy in Ireland, attention has been drawn to the fact that, of the top 400 income earners in Ireland, 73 paid less than 15 per cent of their income in tax in 1999–2000, a figure that dropped to 58 a year later. However, in 2001, 41 people earning over €500,000 a year paid no income tax while 242 earning over €100,000 paid none. This was done legally through availing of various tax breaks. As Timonen summed up the cumulative impact of these characteristics: 'The tax system in Ireland is favourable to households that live in owner-occupied accommodation and take private insurances against social risks such as illness and old age' (Timonen, 2003: 49).

Regional inequalities

In the early Celtic Tiger period, there were fears that economic growth was exacerbating regional inequalities. For example, research for the Western Development Commission shows that between 1991 and 1996 the average annual growth in net industrial output in the seven western counties[3] was 3.7 per cent compared to a national rate of 12.7 per cent. Over the same period, these counties' share of national industrial output dropped from 14.6 to 9.6 per cent (WDC, 1999: 11). Furthermore, between 1993 and 1997 employment in IDA-backed companies in these western counties increased by 22.8 per cent as against an increase of 55.1 per cent in Leinster and 67.1 per cent in Dublin (ibid.: 12). At the end of the Celtic Tiger, these entrenched regional inequalities are seen to have persisted. The division of the country into two regions in the early 2000s for the purpose of accessing EU structural funding, allowed for a comparison between the poorer Border, Midland and Western Region (BMW) and the Southern and Eastern Region (S&E) containing the most developed part of Ireland, particularly around Dublin. In 2006, the BMW region contributed just 19.3 per cent of national output despite employing 26 per cent of the country's workforce while Dublin contributed

39.5 per cent to national output. The growth of unemployment in 2008 also had a regional disparity to it as employment fell by 6.5 per cent in the BMW region as against 3.2 per cent in the S&E, with a 91.2 per cent increase in the former compared to a 60.8 per cent increase in the latter. This reflects what O'Donoghue describes as the BMW's reliance on productive activities such as agriculture, construction and primary industries with 34.3 per cent of men in the region being employed in agriculture or construction. He writes that without a structural shift away from primary production to higher value sectors and activities, 'economic growth will continue to concentrate on Ireland's core regions with the highest value-added sectors and this will exacerbate regional inequalities in growth, productivity and incomes' (O'Donoghue, 2009: 15). This points to a failure to address the roots of these disparities with any effectiveness during the course of the Celtic Tiger boom; amid the depth of the recession and with state finances being very scarce, there are far fewer chances of bridging the regional inequality divide.

Gender inequalities

One positive social impact of the Celtic Tiger has been significantly to increase women's participation in the labour force as has been shown in Chapter 2. Though the rate was 35 per cent as recently as the mid-1980s, it had increased to 44 per cent by the late 1990s and to over 58 per cent by 2006, well above the EU average. However, Fahey et al. point out that among women with children under five years of age, Ireland still had the lowest activity rate in Europe; in Ireland, along with Italy and Greece, less than half this group are active in the labour market whereas in Denmark 80 per cent are. Similarly Irish mothers with children up to ten years of age had participation rates among the lowest in Europe. They pointed to the extremely low provision of early childhood and publicly funded childcare services in Ireland compared to Europe as constituting an obstacle to higher levels of participation by women in these groups (Fahey et al., 2000: 258).

Gender differentials in pay, measured in terms of hourly levels, decreased from 20 to 15 per cent over the Celtic Tiger boom. However, since 2000, evidence shows the gap has stabilised with female levels being around 85 per cent of male pay, and with even greater gaps for older women and those with lower education levels. This was found to be relatively wide in Ireland compared to other European countries. Furthermore, women are less likely to have control and autonomy in relation to their day-to-day work which reflects their lower positions in the occupational hierarchy (McGinnity et al., 2007: 202–3). O'Connor and Murphy report that 'the risk of poverty for women in Ireland has remained consistently high throughout the 1990s and into 2000s' with 18.5 per cent of all women at risk but with higher rates for lone parents (most of them women) and older women. They write that: 'In practical terms women experience greater physical and mental stress when living in poverty and managing debt. This has significant consequences for women's overall participation in society' (O'Connor and Murphy, 2008: 42). The consequences of this situation for women's health was emphasised in a report by the Money Advice and Budgeting Services (Mabs) and the Women's Health Council which found that almost 70 per cent of women surveyed identified a link between debt and their health problems while 27 per cent said debt affected the health of their family. Some 12 per cent of the women surveyed did not have a medical card or a GP visit card despite being on low income while 15 per cent of women with a disability felt ill health had contributed to their debt (Carroll, 2007).

Turning to health inequalities, Burke surveys a wide range of evidence and concludes that, despite women's greater longevity than men in Ireland, 'they experience poorer health and endure more chronic diseases during their later years of life then men' (Burke, 2008: 55). Women on low income are more likely to experience poor health and die younger then women on higher incomes; most notable is the experience of Traveller women (members of the nomadic group known in Ireland as Travellers) who live on average 12 years less than settled women. Unemployed women are twice as likely to give birth to low birth-weight babies than those from higher socio-economic groups, putting the children at greatly increased risk of early death, serious illness and lifelong disability. Irish women have the highest rate of death from heart disease in the EU15 and the death rate from cancer was higher in Ireland than in any other EU country except for Denmark. Women are twice as likely to experience depression than men and are more likely to experience two or more mental health difficulties at one time and thereby more likely to attempt suicide. Finally, 42 per cent of Irish women are reported to experience sexual abuse or violence at some time over their lives (Burke, 2008: 54–6). As Barry concludes about the position of women as Ireland emerges from its boom years: 'A gender equality perspective is sometimes applied in the policy-making process but fundamental areas of economic and social policy are *gender blind*. A consequence of this is that many women have failed to benefit from recent economic and social development and remain trapped in situations of poverty and disadvantage' (Barry, 2008: 29; emphasis in original).

Quality of life

At the height of the Celtic Tiger boom, the *Economist* magazine in 2005 produced a global quality of life index for 111 countries which classed Ireland as the country with the highest quality of life in the world. While this received a lot of media attention, less attention was paid to the fact that what really distinguished Ireland from other countries were the high scores it received for family and community life, factors that owed more to the legacies of the past than to the Celtic Tiger, what the *Economist* called 'the interplay of modernity and tradition in determining life satisfaction'.

This is consistent with the fact that measures of life satisfaction in Ireland in the late 1990s were no higher than they were in the 1970s though they dipped for a time in the late 1980s (Fahey, 2007). Meanwhile, other surveys have shown that Irish people report a deteriorating quality of life during the Celtic Tiger. For example, Dr Elizabeth Cullen has examined the high price in health, quality of life and the social environment paid by Irish people for the economic boom (Cullen, 2006). Evidence is assembled here of some disturbing trends in the quality of life in post–Celtic Tiger Ireland, namely the growth in violence, drug abuse and suicides.

Speaking in early 2009, the commissioner of the Garda Síochána, Fachtna Murphy, admitted that Ireland is becoming a more violent society with more people than ever willing to resort to fatal shootings or stabbings to settle drug-related or personal disputes. As he stated, 'young people are prepared to be aggressive [and] ... in recent times it's been taken to a higher level, particularly with a number of stabbings taking place' (Lally, 2009). While provisional figures for 2008 showed a decrease in murders and man-slaughter over the previous year (from 77 cases to 52), overall 2008 showed a five per cent increase in crime driven by higher levels of drug dealing, robbery and public order offences. Significantly, drugs offences, including importation, possession and supply, increased by 23.5 per cent and pos-session of firearms increased by 19 per cent (Lally, 2008). These indicate Ireland's greater integration into global flows of illegal trade in drugs and firearms, one of the darker sides of globalisation. In his review of crime trends over the course of the Celtic Tiger boom, O'Donnell found that crime rose between 1990 and 1994, fell between 1995 and 1999, and then fell, surged and declined again between 2000 and 2004. He added that this see-saw pattern highlights the unreliability of police data in Ireland so that a new method of compiling and presenting data may account for the big falls in the second half of the 1990s. He found that the rate of lethal violence, while not out of line with other European cities, 'has increased dramatically at a time when the international level is downward' (O'Donnell, 2007: 252). He furthermore also reported that in 2003 more than one in twenty people said that they had been victims of at least one of a listed number of crimes over the previous year, a doubling of the rate since 1998.

With Ireland's growing integration into illegal global networks of drugs trafficking, it is not surprising that rates of drug abuse have been increas-ing significantly in Ireland. One report found that five times as many Irish teenagers have used cocaine as their European peers, 41 per cent of the Irish surveyed had used cannabis compared to 21 per cent in Europe while 11 per cent had used cocaine compared to two per cent in Europe (Holland, 2008). Another report found that Ireland has the fourth-highest rate of drug-related deaths in Europe: 54.2 deaths per one million people compared to a European average of 20.9. Only Estonia, Denmark and Luxembourg were found to be ahead of Ireland (Minihan, 2008). Irish teenagers were found to have the second-highest level of drunkenness in comparison with eight other European countries and the US. This found that 29 per cent of the sample claimed to have been drunk at least once in the previous month compared to an average of 21.7 per cent among the comparator countries. Only Austria had a higher rate (Minihan, 2009). The rate of suicides increased by 12 per cent in 2007 over the previous year, with a jump from 409 cases to 460. Ireland has the fifth highest rate of suicide in Europe among young men aged 15 to 24, though its overall rate is low by European standards (McGreevy and Moriarty, 2008). Finally, it is worth noting that while the Celtic Tiger era 'was less transformational for family and sexual life than the decades that preceded it' since economic growth encouraged more marriage and more children, the increase in the average number of sexual partners of those who are sexually active resulted in 'a very substantial increase' in sexually transmitted diseases from 4781 in 1995 to 11,153 in 2003 with the largest increase being among those aged under 25 (Fahey and Layte, 2007: 174, 161–2).

Conclusions

The chapter has assembled evidence that casts severe doubts on the claim that the boom years in Ireland were the 'best of times'. As is clear from the evidence, these were the best of years for an elite of Irish society who were enriched immensely by the years of growth. However, the data also clearly show that, in the case of many other sectors of society, they either benefited far less or were further marginalised. The chapter has also shown the many structured inequalities of Irish society which, if anything, became even more entrenched over these years. Finally, there are many reasons to conclude that the quality of life in Irish society worsened over the course of the boom, though here subjective judgements are necessarily involved. This chapter, then, has raised many critical issues about the way the boom has been interpreted. Why, when the evidence is so mixed as to its impact on society, did the Celtic Tiger evoke such a positive assessment, indeed a euphoric sense of self-congratulation? This touches on the frameworks of understanding through which the phenomenon was understood and interpreted; these acted as filters which emphasised certain features and elided others. To this issue of interpretation we turn in Part II.

Part II Different Readings of the Celtic Tiger

4
Dominant Readings

Irish economists are not alone in tending to distrust their politicians in the sphere of economic policy. In fact, elegant papers have been written to show that the more remote from the voters the policy makers are, the better the economic outcome in the long run.

Peter Clinch, Frank Convery
and Brendan Walsh (2002: 61)

The three chapters in the previous part have described the contours of the Celtic Tiger boom and its aftermath. In this part, we move to a more analytical treatment, showing how there is no one understanding of any social phenomenon like the Celtic Tiger boom, but that different theoretical frameworks offer different interpretations or readings. The origins of disagreements and debates can, therefore, usually be traced back to these theoretical frameworks so that, if we want to gain a deeper understanding, we need to examine the theoretical frameworks used to interpret the social phenomenon in question. The fact that disagreements and debates have their origins in different theoretical approaches is usually missed by media and popular accounts with the result that one reading or interpretation can become dominant and others be disregarded or marginalised without any in-depth examination or assessment of where the real differences lie and of their significance. This was very true of the Celtic Tiger period in Ireland where an interpretation based on neoclassical economics became widely accepted, celebrating the free market and dismissing the role of the state and public policy as illustrated in the quote with which this chapter opens. The sudden collapse of the Irish boom has therefore raised important questions about the adequacy of the dominant reading and how more critical readings were marginalised from mainstream discussion and influence on policymaking. This part examines these questions through surveying the different readings of the Irish boom and identifying the different theoretical approaches that inform them. This chapter examines the dominant or

mainstream reading while the following chapter examines critical readings. The final chapter in this section develops a fuller and more adequate
theoretical framework through which to offer a more rounded and complex
interpretation of the Irish boom and its aftermath. In examining the dominant interpretation, this chapter begins by outlining explanations of the
Celtic Tiger offered by some leading economists, interrogating in particular
the reasons they offer as to why its success should continue and, more
recently, the reasons for its collapse. The chapter then critically elucidates
the understanding of economic growth and of the links between growth and
social well-being which find expression in these mainstream explanations.
Finally, it reveals assumptions which inform mainstream explanations, both
those derived from neoclassical economics and from modernisation theory
in sociology. The latter is illustrated by the role that the economists and
sociologists of the Economic and Social Research Institute (ESRI) played in
providing a very benign interpretation of social change during the Celtic
Tiger period (Box 4.1).

Explanations from mainstream economics

The explanations for the emergence of the Celtic Tiger which have had most
influence on public attitudes and policies are those offered by mainstream
economists, that is economists working within neoclassical economic theory
or variations of it such as new growth theory. For these economists, Ireland's
high economic and employment growth in the 1990s derives from its ability to achieve high levels of productivity and maintain cost competitiveness
with its trading partners. While there are disagreements about the relative
contributions to these outcomes of different elements such as exchange rate
policy, social partnership or industrial policy, the essential features of this
explanatory paradigm were summed up by Krugman in a paper on Ireland's
economic success: 'Given the combination of good productivity growth and
wage restraint, the success of the economy is in a macro sense not hard to
explain' (1997: 42).

　Barry (1999: 26) defines 'the Irish economic problem' as 'the need to
achieve competitiveness in internationally-tradeable sectors other than
agriculture'. He finds that, whether measured in GDP or GNP per worker,
productivity growth in Ireland was substantially higher than the EU average since the late 1960s. This is due both to the fact that Irish productivity within individual sectors has been catching up with average European
levels and also that traditional low-productivity sectors have been replaced
by newer higher-productivity ones. He calculates that manufacturing
productivity grew very impressively to overtake UK levels, though it was
substantially higher in foreign-owned than in indigenous industry (34–7).
However, it was not until the 1990s that employment growth took off which
he attributes to factors such as the increase in foreign investment in the

manufacturing sector and, for the financial services sector, the extension of the low rate of tax on corporate profits to that sector (38–9). Barry was also influential in a debate in the early 2000s on whether the Irish boom was a question of delayed convergence to the economic performance of Ireland's western European neighbours or a regional boom created by active industrial policies and structural fund spending. He highlighted the implications of this debate: 'If the convergence view is correct, it suggests that we can now rest on our laurels: as long as we do not introduce inappropriate policies we are unlikely to fall behind average EU living standards. If the regional view is correct however, it suggests that external shocks to our ability to attract FDI might have serious long-term consequences for the economy' (Barry, 2002: 90). In more recent contributions, he has emphasised the importance of continuing to attract high levels of FDI, particularly foreign firms engaged in the offshoring of research and development activities (R&D) and of the need to develop more effective policies to improve the 'highly uneven performance of Irish schools' (Barry, 2006: 54).

Leddin and Walsh (1997) take issue with those who see the cuts in public spending between 1987 and 1989 as resulting in 'expansionary fiscal con-traction' as the improvement in public finances restored private sector con-fidence and led to a fall in the private sector savings ratio and a resurgence of private consumption and investment spending. This, they argue, neglects the extent to which the fiscal correction was a more gradual process than a 'shock therapy' (9). They emphasise the importance of the 1986 devalu-ation of the Irish pound in stimulating exports to Europe which played an important role in economic expansion while they are more sceptical than some of their colleagues about the role of social partnership in moderat-ing wage growth and inflation, pointing out that countries like the US and Britain 'have combined falling unemployment with low price and wage inflation in a decentralised wage bargaining framework' (13). In explaining the factors which sustained longer-term high growth rates, they refer to institutional factors such as the high degree of consistency and continu-ity across the main political parties on the main parameters of economic management and industrial policy. Interestingly, however, in discussing the role of EU grants and subsidies, they emphasise that 'as a general rule the international evidence does not support the view that foreign assistance is growth promoting' (18). Examining the transformation of the Irish labour market between 1980 and 2003, Walsh attributes its exceptional perform-ance to a combination of favourable shocks on the demand side such as exchange rates and interest rates facilitated by a favourable set of supply-side developments such as the growing stock of human capital as a result of rising levels of educational attainment, wage moderation brought about by the centralised wage bargaining of social partnership, declining union power, a decline in the tax wedge on earnings and a stricter approach to pay-ing unemployment benefits. He comments: 'The juxtaposition of so many favourable demand and supply side developments makes the economic 'miracle' relatively understandable!' (Walsh, 2004: 99).

In an earlier work, Bradley has pioneered the application of new growth theory to the Irish case, arguing that neoclassical economics has problems in explaining the determinants of economic growth (Bradley et al., 1993). Drawing on work by Paul Romer and Robert Lucas, endogenous growth theory has allowed economists to focus on how growth can be generated without appealing to exogenous factors such as technical progress or human capital formation, as does orthodox neoclassical theory. Instead they postulate four mechanisms which may be responsible for generating economic growth: human capital, public capital or infrastructure, industrial policy and technology and trade. Thus new growth theorists emphasise the room for manoeuvre open to countries to stimulate competitiveness and growth internally by investments in knowledge and in people. For example, Bradley's account of Ireland's economic success highlights that 'individual small nations and regions have less power to influence their destinies than in previous periods of industrialisation, other than by refocusing their economic policies on location factors, especially those which are relatively immobile between regions: the quality of labour, infrastructure and economic governance, and the efficient functioning of labour markets' (2000: 13–14). His account therefore concentrates on such factors as the state's success in attracting in 'sufficient firms in the computer, instrument engineering, pharmaceutical and chemical sectors to merit a description of sector "agglomerations" or "clusters"' (ibid.: 13) and the role of EU regional policy and related structural funds in improving physical infrastructure, education and training (14). In identifying the danger that a dominant foreign industrial sector might destabilise competitiveness in the traditional indigenous sector because of wage pressures it generated, he argues that 'wage-setting policy and social partnership is a crucial component' in helping avoid this danger (24). This approach has proved influential in Irish policymaking and, for example, provides much of the framework for the OECD's explanation of the origins of Ireland's economic boom (OECD, 1999: 25–62).

Fitz Gerald (2000: 27) argues that the Irish boom is better seen as a belated catching up with its neighbours rather than an economic miracle. Stating that 'economics alone is not sufficient to explain the successful process of economic development in Ireland in recent years' he writes that cultural and social environment plays a vital role in determining the relative success or failure of economic policy. He identifies three main factors: Ireland's opening up to the outside world both to new ideas but also to the influx of skilled labour with new ideas; government policy in relation to education and to attracting foreign direct investment and enabling factors such as the emergence of a low dependency ratio, the fiscal correction of the 1980s and social partnership. Fitz Gerald places a lot of emphasis on the growth in the supply of skilled labour (consequent on earlier investment in education) to meet increasing demand, which he says contrasts with the situation in many EU countries where the labour force is growing quite slowly and where the major benefits of the post-war investment in human capital have already been reaped. This difference in factors affecting labour supply, taken together with the other social and economic factors he identified, 'explains why the Irish economy is growing more rapidly than those of other EU countries' (2000: 54). Following the economic collapse in 2008, asked to address what needed to be done to help recovery, Fitz Gerald placed the emphasis on the need to improve competitiveness through cutting the costs of production. Among the options he mentions are cutting public sector pay rates which, if they mirrored cuts in private sector rates, would result in a major gain in competitiveness with a consequential big reduction in unemployment after three or four years. He also mentions cutting the number of public sector jobs and reducing the costs of welfare. On the taxation side, he recognises the need to redress the weaknesses of the taxation system – its limited coverage and even more limited yield – but cautions about the negative repercussions on output and employment that can result from raising taxes, recommending a widening of the tax base through a carbon tax and a property tax. Finally, he recognises that these cost-cutting efforts must go hand in hand with continuing investment in education and R&D (Fitz Gerald, 2009: 15).

As collapse hit the Irish economy, economists analysed the reasons for the increase in the cost base of the economy and the consequent loss of competitiveness. Leddin attributed this to the rounds of pay awards under the national agreements of social partnership that were among the factors which left the Irish economy at its most uncompetitive since the early 1970s, raising costs and fuelling inflation. He wrote that 'the country's immune system has been suspended, leaving the economy vulnerable to a whole variety of adverse shocks, giving rise to the possibility of a prolonged economic slowdown' (Leddin, 2008: 4). Interestingly, Leddin acknowledges that as the boom took over between 1988 and 1997, workers in both the public and private sectors 'received a relatively small share of the prosperity associated with the booming Irish economy' as pay awards constrained their increases in earnings; over this period the wage share of national income fell over 25 per cent. For Leddin 'the seeds of Ireland's competitiveness destruction were sown' from 2000 on with pay awards of 24 per cent for the public sector and 18 per cent for private sector workers. He writes that 'between 1997 and 2004, Ireland was transformed into a high-cost, high-price economy' (ibid.).

What, then, based on these mainstream explanations, are seen as the explanations for economic success and failure? Differing emphases can be deduced from the literature, what Walsh (1999: 4) calls the optimistic and the pessimistic scenarios. True to the parameters of the explanatory paradigm being used, these concentrate on factors such as productivity and cost competitiveness, the 'real economic fundamentals' as Sweeney (1999: 226) puts it. Reading the output of these mainstream economists following the economic collapse of 2008 illustrates that their focus on 'economic fundamentals' led them to overlook such structural weaknesses that persisted over the period of growth, most importantly the dual nature of the Irish economy and its dependence on winning high levels of FDI if it was to continue to be successful. Barry and Crafts argued at the height of the boom that there appeared to be something more than just delayed catch-up in Ireland's economic transformation. This was suggested by the evidence that Irish manufacturing sector productivity appeared to have surpassed that of the UK and that, compared to East Asia, Irish total factor productivity growth was far more impressive (1999: 42–3). They concluded: 'If Ireland can maintain its "capture" of high-productivity foreign direct investment into the future, this will bode well for a continuation of the country's strong economic performance' (44). Fitz Gerald's account placed emphasis on Ireland's declining dependency ratio as representing 'a window of opportunity that will last for fifteen or twenty years' allowing a rapid rise in living standards to take place. He forecast that, from the middle of the next decade 'the driving factors behind the rapid growth will begin to slow and the rate of growth in output will gradually decelerate towards the EU average' (2000: 55). Walsh foresaw an earlier slowdown in growth (1999). Among the issues he highlighted was a likely reduction in productivity growth as the shakeout of low-productivity employment and the inflows of FDI declined in importance, and the erosion of competitiveness as lower unemployment generated higher wage inflation. With the slowdown in economic growth following the bursting of the dotcom bubble in the US and the effects of the 9/11 attacks in 2001, Clinch, Convery and Walsh summarised their advice for the future growth of the Irish economy into a number of principles; among them was the importance of productivity, the role of investment in human and physical capital and the need for flexibility in response to ever-changing circumstances and unforeseeable shocks. Interestingly, they also urged rejection of 'the fear and suspicion of market forces (including the profit motive) that is a strong undercurrent in the Irish debate on public policy' (Clinch et al., 2002: 181–2).

In contrast to Irish economists' optimistic emphasis on the 'real economic fundamentals', a number of prominent international economists were highlighting greater risks for the Irish economy, even at the height of the boom. Krugman (1997: 52) pointed to potential labour and skills shortages and Ireland's vulnerability to a shift in technology 'that might vitiate the advantages of a European location'. He also pointed to the threat to Ireland's attractive tax regime for foreign investors: '[A]t some point one can all too easily imagine French politicians noticing that Ireland pays wages well below the EU average, taxes capital far less than other European states, and that partly because of those low wages and taxes it has become a favourite export platform for non-European firms serving the European market. If Brussels ever does start to impose rules aimed at preventing social dumping, they would probably bite even more severely on Ireland than on the UK' (53). Both Krugman (1997) and Sachs (1997) pointed to the risk to Ireland from other countries in search of foreign investment, such as eastern European and Latin American ones. Jarrett (1999: 198–99) pointed to the challenge of alleviating the housing constraint and mentioned Ireland's 'excessively generous' tax treatment of owner occupiers as 'contributing to the current housing boom' while highlighting the fact that Ireland still lags behind the OECD average in educational attainment. Most significantly, however, these foreign observers of the Irish scene highlighted what is perhaps the greatest dilemma facing the Irish growth model, one largely ignored by Irish economists. Jarrett drew attention to the fact that 'Ireland is the only OECD country whose social spending has actually fallen in relation to GDP since 1980' (ibid.: 200). But Sachs (1997: 62) emphasised that government spending as a percentage of GDP is very high in Ireland compared to East Asia and, as a result, Ireland's economic status 'is still far from secure in the long term'. He argued that Ireland needed to cut the burden of expenditure and taxation further. Barry and Crafts (1999: 47) echoed this when they argued that at lower government spending levels relative to GDP, the impact of public expenditure appears generally to be positive for economic growth and is in contrast to the higher levels prevailing in most present-day OECD countries. In strict economic terms, this may be true, but it ignores the conclusion drawn by the editors of the ESRI volume on the Irish experience of growth and inequality that 'the decline in welfare effort relative to national income raises fundamental questions about the quality of social citizenship rights in Ireland into the future' (Nolan et al., 2000: 352). They continued:

> [A] policy which leaves Ireland with a relatively low proportion of national income going on social spending will inevitably lead to a situation where the scope, level and quality of public provision and social protection fail to match higher living standards from the market. Reversing this trend would require a re-negotiation of the terms of social partnership in a manner that would entail a greater share of the fruits of growth being channelled through social rather than market wages.
>
> (ibid.: 352)

The severe collapse of the Irish economy in 2008 offers a revealing vantage point from which to view these mainstream explanations of the Celtic Tiger boom. While economists did point to the unsustainable nature of the growing reliance on the construction industry in the mid-2000s, what is revealing about this dominant reading of Ireland's transformation is its focus on a set of economic principles, all very valid in themselves, but lacking any focus on the structure of the Irish economy and how well it served the needs of society. While there were great advances made over this period, they tended to obscure ongoing structural weaknesses that were not sufficiently addressed; foremost among them in the productive sphere was the weakness of indigenous industry and services and continuing heavy reliance on FDI, while in the social sphere the weak ability of this economy to distribute through higher levels of social spending and infrastructural upgrading the resources it generated was not sufficiently addressed. These explanatory weaknesses point to a more fundamental problem relating to mainstream explanations of Ireland's Celtic Tiger, namely the understanding of economic growth that informs them and how they view the link between economy and society.

Understanding economic growth

While there is no final agreement in economics literature on what constitutes economic growth,[1] the concept and measures of it exercise a major influence on public discourse. Since the middle of the twentieth century and with the active encouragement of international organisations, the production of national accounts based on comparable concepts and methods has become the dominant way of analysing and measuring economic growth. The most widely used concept as the basis for such studies is gross domestic product at constant prices, or real GDP. This can be defined as 'the total output of goods and services for final use produced by residents and non-residents, regardless of the allocation to domestic and foreign claims. It is calculated without making deductions for depreciation of "manmade" assets or depletion and degradation of natural resources' (World Bank, 1994: 232). A related concept, of importance in the Irish case because of the large contribution made by multinationals to Irish economic growth, is gross national product (GNP). This comprises GDP, adds to it the income received by nationals from labour or property ownership outside the country and then deducts the payments made to non-residents who contributed to the domestic economy.

Due to our concern with social impacts, a number of comments on this measure of economic growth are warranted. The first relates to the fact that as a measure it takes no account of how the growth in output is distributed. Thus, for example, an overall increase in GDP may be accompanied by an absolute decline in the incomes of the lowest income group. Secondly, GDP/GNP measures have been criticised for reasons related to the important role they have assumed in public discourse. In his Nobel Memorial Lecture in 1975, Gunnar Myrdal criticised this role as follows:

> Our politicians, of all political parties, stick to the inapt concept of 'growth' which is embodied in the gross national product or one of its derivatives. We economists, by not having scrutinised more intensively

that even statistically rather spurious concept, and by ourselves commonly utilising 'growth' in that sense uncritically as a main value premise in our discussions of practical economic policy, have unfortunately contributed to restricting the mental horizon of politicians and of the common people.

(Myrdal, 1989: 14)

The main criticism of this measure of growth is that it measures aspects of the productive capacity of the economy and is in no way a measure of national well-being, even though it is often used in public discourse as being equivalent to such a measure. For example, certain costs associated with economic growth such as pollution of the environment or traffic congestion are not taken into account when compiling GDP/GNP measures except to the extent that they increase market transactions. Thus, paradoxically, a major oil spill adds to GDP/GNP because of the costs associated with cleaning it up. Similarly, other social ills such as crime or divorce increase GDP/GNP since they involve increased spending in the marketplace (on security, lawyers, purchase of new goods, etc.). Furthermore, it is mostly only goods and services traded in the market which are considered to increase (or decrease) GDP/GNP. Therefore, drawing into the market economy activities previously done at home (cooking meals, minding children) is deemed to increase GDP though it may harm people's welfare since it increases their costs and worsens their quality of life. Related to this is the fact, as feminist critiques point out, that much of the work traditionally done by women goes unmeasured by GDP/GNP growth rates. For this reason, a number of alternative measures of human welfare or development have been elaborated,[2] most notably the annual human development index (HDI) of the United Nations Development Programme (UNDP, 1990 onwards) which measures development using a combination of health, education and income measures. This produces some striking contrasts between countries in terms of their place on the GDP/GNP index (produced annually by the World Bank) and on the HDI index.

The UNDP's promotion of a concept of human development and the attempt to quantify this for each of the countries of the world is a good illustration of the view that economic growth is not equivalent to social well-being. These concerns, however, have been weakly reflected in the mainstream literature or in public discourse on the Celtic Tiger where GDP/GNP growth rates are assumed to equate with measures of social development.[3] In adopting the concept of economic growth from mainstream economics therefore we are mindful of the fact that 'GDP is simply a gross measure of market activity, of money changing hands. It makes no distinction whatsoever between the desirable and the undesirable, or costs and gain. ... As a result the GDP not only masks the breakdown of the social structure and the natural habitat upon which the economy – and life itself – ultimately depend; worse, it actually portrays such breakdown as economic gain' (Cobb et al., 1995: 60).

Growth and well-being: Theorising the link

Following from this restrictive understanding of economic growth, two distinct conceptualisations of the link between growth and well-being can be identified. The first rests on the assumption that economic growth (usually measured in terms of GDP/GNP growth) is a process logically distinct from well-being. Its impact on social well-being happens through distributing the fruits of that growth. Such assumptions are clearly expressed in the following 'summary statement about recent trends in poverty' formulated by one of Ireland's leading poverty researchers, Professor Brian Nolan:

> We have so far failed to use our new-found wealth to make serious inroads into poverty, to ensure that everyone has enough to live with dignity and participate fully in our society.
>
> (Nolan, 1998: 16)

Though he writes that this formulation 'does not capture the full complexity of what has been happening', he adds that 'it does convey what I see as the core issue now' (ibid.). Thus the implication is that economic growth is distributionally neutral and that the task of ensuring it to have an equitable social impact depends on efficient mechanisms of redistribution. This view pervades official policy on poverty reduction. For example, the Irish government's National Anti-Poverty Strategy (NAPS) is based on the view that economic growth provides extra resources that could subsequently be more equitably shared (NAPS, 1997: 3). It is official policy to do this through 'measuring the impact of programmes and improving their design and delivery to achieve the required results' rather than through any departure from 'prudent management of public expenditure'. It is explicitly stated that 'higher levels of public spending are not necessary for a successful anti-poverty strategy' and that significant tax increases could damage the strategy (NAPS, 1997: 7, 8).

Those working within the dominant reading of the economic boom and its aftermath have devoted little attention to issues of well-being. An exception is a report written for the National Competitiveness Council on the links between well-being and competitiveness (NCC, 2008). This surveys the literature on well-being as a way of overcoming the limitations of GDP/GNP as measures of social progress. Drawing on the UNDP HDI and on Eurobarometer surveys, it finds that Ireland has relatively high measures of well-being though it acknowledges the limitations of these measures. However, the report fails entirely to acknowledge the extensive literature that links well-being and equality (see Wilkinson and Pickett (2009) for a recent overview) and, for example, overlooks Ireland's low position on the UNDP's Human Poverty Index for industrialised countries (see Table 3.5). Most problematic about this report is its conceptualisation of the links between well-being and competitiveness as it simply assumes that economic growth produced by the current growth model results in enhanced well-being. As it states, 'having an emphasis on policies that support sustainable economic growth and competitiveness can play an important role in maintaining and enhancing national and individual wellbeing' (NCC, 2008: 21).

This benign view of economic growth and the possibilities it offers for social well-being is countered by a more critical view that identifies a link between economic growth and the generation of poverty and inequality. As Joyce and McCashin (1982: 86) put it: '[T]he social and economic changes which have taken place have had dual effects – impoverishment and enrichment. The changes have not affected all groups equally or similarly – some have benefited and others have lost'. One strong expression of this view is found in different varieties of dependency theory that posit a link between the development of core countries in the world system and the underdevelopment of peripheral countries (Martinussen, 1997: 85–100). O'Hearn has applied such an analysis to the Irish case, arguing that its 'open, foreign-dominated, free-enterprise regime' (1989: 579) has resulted in 'higher inequality of direct incomes' (ibid: 590) (see Chapter 5). One does not have to accept the tenets of dependency theory, however, to posit a link between economic growth and poverty. Writing before the advent of dependency theory, Karl Polanyi identified a link between the emergence of industrial society (the British industrial revolution in the early nineteenth century) and 'the incomprehensible fact that poverty seemed to go with plenty' (Polanyi, 2001: 89). Polanyi regarded this as one of the 'baffling paradoxes' (ibid.: 85) of the new industrial society, which was due to the fact that society was made subservient to the self-regulating market economy and that 'such harmonious self-regulation required that the individual respect economic law even if it happened to destroy him' (ibid.: 85).

Polanyi's view has been returned to by political economists and social theorists as a way of understanding the forces in today's more internationalised or globalised economy that are generating greater poverty and inequality, both within countries and also between the North and the South in the global economy (Latham, 1997; Jordan, 1996: 222–5). This phenomenon has been referred to as 'the growing conflict between economic systems and the fulfilment of our social needs' (Wilkinson, 1996: 211) and it is seen by some theorists as one of the major economic and social challenges of our time. In seeking to understand the nature of this challenge, Hoogvelt writes that 'poverty and wealth-creation are but two sides of the same historical process, even if that historical process itself undergoes fundamental changes in the manner in which it is organised' (Hoogvelt, 1997: xii). This is a less benign view of the social impact of economic growth, understood not just in terms of growth of output but also in terms of the organisational processes through which this takes place. In this view, poverty amid plenty derives from the process of growth itself; they are, in Hoogvelt's view, two sides of the same process.

Most of the literature on the Celtic Tiger accepts the benign view of the link between economic growth and social well-being. Unfortunately, the challenge posed by Joyce and McCashin in 1982 has been largely neglected in treatments of Ireland's boom economy in the 1990s (see Chapter 5 for a summary of the small number of works which take a more critical approach to the issue). They wrote: 'It is important to confront the question of the relationship between economic growth and poverty because in the Irish case the impression is sometimes given that economic growth *per se* is a sufficient answer to the problems of poverty and inequality' (86; emphasis in original). They expressed the hope that 'the necessarily brief treatment of these questions will prompt more substantive research work in the future' (86). This hope has not been realised; despite extensive work by the social science community on issues related to poverty and inequality in Ireland, they are largely treated in isolation from any consideration of how the growth model followed by Ireland may generate greater poverty and inequality. This reflects the theoretical assumptions that underpin the dominant readings of the Celtic Tiger as a period of economic transformation and social development. The next section identifies these key theoretical assumptions.

Dominant assumptions

Neoclassical economics

Neoclassical economics defines itself as a neutral, value-free science (Norton, 1994: 3–16) which studies 'the relationship between human objectives and the scarce means, which normally have alternative uses, by which individuals and groups attempt to attain these objectives' (ibid.: 9). However, the choice of what are worthy human objectives cannot be value-free and neutral. As Robbins put it: 'There are no economic ends. There are only economical and uneconomical ways of achieving given ends .... There is nothing in economics which relieves *us* of the obligation to choose' (Robbins, 1995: 255, 259; emphasis in original). Applying this to the issue of equality, he writes: '[I]f we regard a society which permits inequality of incomes as an evil in itself, and an egalitarian society as presenting an end to be pursued above all other things, then it is illegitimate to regard such a preference as uneconomic' (Robbins, 1995: 261). In theory, therefore, objectives such as poverty reduction and equalising income distribution are as valid subjects for economists to study as is economic growth. In practice, however, efficiency and equity are seen as objectives which are opposed to one another and 'most economists concern themselves only with questions of efficiency,' writes

John in an essay on economic policy objectives (John, 1995: 63). He goes on to argue that 'a complete analysis of economic policy must ... address the efficient allocation of resources both at a point in time and through time, and consider both intragenerational and intergenerational equity' (66) and acknowledges that there are almost certainly trade-offs between growth and equity (83). For example, he writes that economic growth need not imply increased welfare if it leads to increased negative externalities such as environmental pollution (79, 80). Growth may make intragenerational redistribution possible without reductions in anyone's absolute standard of living but the validity of this argument depends on whether one considers the extra income from growth accruing directly to individuals or to society as a whole (81). Finally, he argues that 'the success or failure of economic policies can be assessed in part using measures of employment, equity, and growth' (50) and acknowledges that 'efficiency takes no account of distributional issues ... [a] society where millions are starving while its ruler lives in unimaginable luxury may be using and distributing its resources efficiently' (62).

However, the concerns raised by John find little echo in the mainstream Irish economics literature. Discussions of social well-being in Ireland and its link with economic growth are, therefore, rare in Irish economics literature. The closest one comes to it is the literature on poverty measurement, treated below. O'Shea links this concern with efficiency over equity to the utilitarian version of radical individualism on which the neoclassical paradigm is based. One result of the assumption that individuals seek to maximise their utility, he argues, is that it is the satisfaction of individual preferences that provides the catalyst for growth and development in the economy. Equity and distribution are secondary objectives which, when they arise, are reduced frequently to technical arguments about what the exchequer can bear (O'Shea, 1996: 236–7). Other assumptions have also been identified as reasons for these emphases. Neoclassical economists in the main absorbed the late nineteenth-century faith in progress and the benevolence of its consequences, writes Barber (1991: 164), and directed their attention instead to the functioning of the market system and its role in allocating resources efficiently. As O'Shea (1996: 212) writes: 'Most economists accept the basic insight of Adam Smith that, under certain conditions, an economic system based on free or competitive markets will ensure that questions of allocation are answered in an optimal way. The same economists are likely to concede a role for government when market failure occurs or gross inequality exists, but would continue to argue for the primacy of efficiency in all areas of resource allocation.'

Welfare economics

The dominant and most influential social science literature on poverty in Ireland, that of the ESRI team of poverty researchers, finds its most appropriate disciplinary home in welfare economics (Nolan and Callan, 1994; Nolan and Whelan, 1996; Callan et al., 1999). Here some key theoretical assumptions informing its approach are identified through examining the rationale expressed by two of its leading scholars for the choice of poverty as the focus of their research (over, for example, inequality or social exclusion) and their choice of deprivation indicators to measure it.

They describe their main motivation in focusing on poverty as being a concern for the limitation of the lives that some people are forced to live in. Poverty, they define, is the inability to participate owing to lack of resources and they distinguish it from either multiple deprivation attributable to factors other than lack of resources, or deprivation that is enforced but only in an isolated area of life. Thus it refers to enforced and generalised deprivation and they identify what is distinctive about it: 'Poverty is not inability to participate owing to unemployment, it is not inability to participate owing to racial discrimination, it is not inability to participate owing to ill-health: it is inability to participate owing to lack of resources, which each of these factors may but does not necessarily produce' (Nolan and Whelan, 1996: 187–8). They also distinguish it from the concept of social exclusion, a term they find to be poorly defined. 'Talking of social exclusion rather than poverty highlights the gap between those who are active members of society and those who are forced to the fringes, the increasing risks of social disintegration, and the fact that for the persons concerned and for society, this is a process of change and not a set of fixed and static situations' (189). While acknowledging that social exclusion may help to sensitise researchers and policymakers to dynamics, processes and multiple disadvantage, they say that it would be at the cost of 'the spark that "poverty" ignites because of its everyday usage and evaluative content' (195).

To measure this enforced and generalised deprivation they construct a series of 24 deprivation indicators broken into three sets. These they combine with relative income poverty lines to arrive at a measure of the percentage of the population consistently poor. They state: 'Our poverty measure includes direct measures of the limited lives that people are actually leading, and our findings regarding the extent of poverty and processes generating it do differ from those produced by a focus on income poverty lines alone' (183). Justifying their choice of deprivation indicators against a wider choice that would include, for example, not voting as an indicator for non-participation in society, they say that it is 'an *inability* to participate rather than non-participation that represents what most people would regard as deprivation' and they add that this occurs because people do not have the income and other financial resources to do so (186; emphasis in original).

These arguments betray a set of assumptions consistent with the standard neoclassical approach within welfare economics based upon a utilitarian philosophical framework (O'Shea and Kennelly, 1995: 1). Central to those assumptions is that social welfare consists of the sum of individual utilities (the satisfaction of their needs or wants) and that this is a function of income plus consumption of goods (including such 'goods' as individual hobbies or holidays). Barr (1998: Chapter 6) highlights two deficiencies in this philosophical framework. Firstly, it ignores non-material sources of well-being which may explain why Nolan and Whelan (1996: 183) dismiss the Swedish approach of measuring well-being through a combination of indicators measuring resource deprivation and indicators measuring security of life and property, political participation and family and social integration (Erikson, 1993: 68). Secondly, its individualism excludes consideration of the fact that individual welfares may be interdependent, namely that individual needs and their satisfaction 'are defined, shaped and constrained within social structures' (Welch, 1989: 263). As Barr points out, such individualist assumptions rest uneasily with a relative definition of poverty since acknowledgement of welfare interdependence raises issues of judgement about such issues as income distribution and, more generally, social inequality. Though the ESRI poverty researchers pioneered a relative definition of poverty in Ireland, their preference for focusing on poverty rather than inequality[4] appears to rest on classic individualist, utilitarian assumptions.

The point in this discussion is not that their approach is invalid. It obviously has many strengths, not least of which is its methodological rigour. But, considering in particular its predominant influence in informing government policy towards poverty in Ireland, its limitations need to be acknowledged and attention given to alternative approaches. For example, O'Shea and Kennelly have sketched out some alternatives from within welfare economics (1995). It also needs to be acknowledged that sociology has, from early in its development, abandoned utilitarianism because of its heuristic weakness as the quintessential 'individualist' social theory and developed a more structuralist understanding of poverty and inequality (Welch, 1989: 262–3). Such an understanding also has a vital contribution to make.

Box 4.1 The ESRI reading of the Celtic Tiger: Science or ideology?

In June 2007, the leading sociologists and welfare economists working at the ESRI published *Best of Times?* (Fahey et al., 2007) a book that purported to offer a scientific view of the 'social impact of the Celtic Tiger' (this was the book's subtitle). For a book written entirely by academics, it received a remarkable level of media attention. *The Irish Times* (29 June 2007) alone give the editors space for a lengthy op-ed piece but also made the book the lead front-page story and devoted an editorial to it. Clearly then, this was a book of exceptional importance, making a major contribution to a lively public debate on whether the Celtic Tiger boom had improved Irish society and its quality of life. In surveying in their opening chapter some examples of critical commentary on this issue, the editors clearly situated the book as a response to critics of the social impact of the boom, an assessment of whether 'the combination of stasis and advance' of the Celtic Tiger 'could be judged a success or failure' (ibid.: 5).

Coming from the thorough quantitative social science tradition of the ESRI, the book threw empirical light on many contested areas of Irish life, among them income inequality, the quality of employment, social mobility, poverty and economic vulnerability, health and health care, housing, education, family and sexual practices, the fabric of life in new suburbs, gender work-life balance, immigration and crime. On a number of these subjects, the book updates and confirms an analysis already well known by those familiar with the work of the ESRI over recent years. In addition, the editors draw on work being done outside the ESRI to shed light on some contested features of Irish society, such as the quality of life in fast-growing suburbs, and trends in crime. The book therefore offers a snapshot of Irish society today at the end of the boom. Much of the evidence is aggregate statistical or survey evidence. However, such generalised statistical evidence tends of its nature to aggregate into broad categories thus eliding much of the nuance and detail that lies behind the statistics while the positive views reflected in opinion surveys taken in the midst of an economic boom are inevitably coloured by the feel-good factor that predominates at such a time. None of this invalidates the evidence but it highlights its limitations, adding up to a somewhat more partial picture than is claimed by the editors who, in their opening chapter, conclude that the Celtic Tiger 'on the basis of its social as well as its economic impact, certainly deserves two cheers and perhaps even three' (ibid.: 10). Unfortunately, the editors offer no criteria to weigh the list of positives over the list of negatives that they then go on to outline.

This highlights a major problem with the book, namely the gap between the inevitably partial evidence presented and the claims made for this evidence, that this was the best of times for Irish society. This gap relates to serious methodological and theoretical weaknesses yet these were very unlikely to have been evident to the general public to whom it was presented as a definitive scientific account. Indeed, the book limits itself by and large to considering a very limited range of evidence, mostly that produced by the ESRI, while failing to acknowledge scientific evidence that points to conclusions different to those it draws. Furthermore, the book fails to make explicit the theoretical approach being used to structure and interpret the 'facts' it presents about Irish society so that the facts chosen and the weight of conclusions derived from them lack foundation, rest as it were on thin air. It is not that the evidence presented lacks validity but rather that the choice of this evidence over other evidence rests on assumptions that are not made explicit. Finally, the book presumes a causal connection between its evidence and the Celtic Tiger whereas much of it shows rather a remarkable continuity with processes of modernisation pre-dating the boom raising the question as to whether it is about the social impact of the Celtic Tiger at all. Overall, then, the book seems more motivated by a desire to refute critics of the boom which has the effect of eliding the many ambiguities and limitations of the evidence and preventing a more balanced and nuanced conclusion about the nature of social change in contemporary Ireland, its causes and its consequences (see Kirby, 2008a).

Modernisation theory

Identifying modernisation theory as an influence on treatments of the Celtic Tiger moves us from economics into sociology. As an academic discipline, sociology is relatively new to Ireland and has its origins in two distinct traditions – the largely empirical tradition of nineteenth-century political economy informed by an optimistic belief in progress (Daly, 1997), and the dominance of Catholic social teaching in the twentieth century. This latter was strong on principles but weak on empirical research (Clancy et al., 1995: 14–16). While the discipline has established itself since the 1970s, it still displays some of the legacy of its divided origins. Thus, much contemporary Irish sociology devotes itself to empirical research into aspects of Irish society; however, less sustained attention is devoted to the theoretical frameworks which inform such work or to the theoretical implications of its findings. Neither has the tradition of Catholic social thought stimulated a concern for theory-building in Irish sociology. While this tradition remains vigorous as a source of social critique (particularly in the work of the justice and education commissions of the Conference of Religious of Ireland, CORI) and has stimulated attention among some academics to the values informing economic theory (see, for example, O'Shea and Kennelly, 1993 and Healy and Clark, 1998), its influence on the practice of sociology has been minimal. As a result, Irish sociology is most developed in the methodological sophistication with which it can explore a wide range of diverse research themes – poverty and inequality, education and health, gender and sexuality, religion and the family, voluntary groups and community action, entertainment industries and the media. However, the discipline's strengths on these subjects have resulted in a certain theoretical and empirical fragmentation; it has been less successful at offering a more holistic interpretation of what has been called 'the lack of fit between economy, state and society on the island' (Clancy et al., 1995: 18) or of the impact of global forces on the national and the local.

The lack of sustained attention to the larger theoretical picture which this reflects has resulted in a certain dualism in social theory. While the optimistic tenets of an evolutionary modernisation have been widely challenged within the various specialist areas into which the discipline is divided,[5] the assumptions of modernisation theory still exercise extensive influence, even if this is rarely acknowledged explicitly. This influence is most clearly seen in the underlying assumptions through which Irish social development is often interpreted. Here key assumptions of modernisation theory can be identified such as the view that development is a movement from the traditional to the modern, that this is progressive and beneficial to all, that it takes place through elites imbibing modern values such as individualism, entrepreneurship and achievement-orientation, and that accepting technology and advice from outside Ireland, particularly through the influences of foreign direct investment and membership of the EU, serves as the principal means to spur modernisation. These assumptions are central to what Maguire calls the elitist, assimilationist project through which Irish society since the early 1960s has been integrated into the world capitalist system in a dependent way (Maguire, 1988: 64, 69). As O'Dowd has written, both in the Republic and in Northern Ireland 'development strategy remains identified with modernisation theories, i.e. with the view that the diffusion of entrepreneurial skills, technology and capital investment are the keys to economic growth' (O'Dowd, 1986: 200). And, as he put it elsewhere, 'the strength of the modernisation theory may be gauged from the extent to which its assumptions are taken for granted as common sense by its adherents who frequently fail to realise or acknowledge that they are subscribing to a particular theory of social change' (O'Dowd, 1995: 168).

Evidence of the influence of modernisation theory is thus to be sought in some deep-rooted assumptions and values which find expression in the literature on the Celtic Tiger, rather than in explicit treatments. The work of O'Donnell, a leading political economy theorist of the Celtic Tiger (see Chapter 5 for a treatment of his approach) offers a good example. For his view of what he calls Ireland's re-invention and transformation rests on juxtaposing a modern, liberated, creative Ireland to a traditional, inward-looking and stagnant Ireland, what he calls 'the road from nationalism to liberation' (1999: 3). He writes: 'The social and cultural change of recent decades has transformed the individuals in Irish society in a way that has unleashed enterprise and demands new patterns of organisation. It is for this reason that the changes in the public sphere – European integration and social partnership – can be seen as the beginning of the reinvention of Ireland, much as the cultural movement of the late nineteenth and early twentieth century were shown, by Kiberd, to have invented Ireland' (2000: 211).[6] It is not surprising that O'Donnell refers a lot to the work of the journalist Fintan O'Toole,[7] since modernisationist assumptions have also been identified in the latter's influential writings (Cronin, 1998: 4,5). In a revealing essay on the worldview of O'Toole, Ó Séaghdha identifies the role that the dualities of rural/urban, Catholic/secular, traditional/modernising, nationalist/internationalist play in his work. As he puts it, 'the effect has been to confirm rather than to question stereotypes and to encourage political and historical complacency' (Ó Séaghdha, 2002: 158). Just as the neoclassical explanations of the Celtic Tiger tend, as we saw above, to neglect its social impact, so too modernisationist assumptions have tended to inform much social analysis of contemporary Ireland, and to underpin the dominant social reading of the Celtic Tiger.

Conclusions

This chapter has mapped out the contours of the dominant readings of the Celtic Tiger, both economic and sociological. It has interrogated the assumptions that inform such readings, thereby drawing attention to their limitations and biases. In particular, it has highlighted the gap that exists between economic and social concerns in the dominant readings, informed as they are by utilitarian, individualist and anti-social assumptions. The next chapter turns to more critical readings of the Celtic Tiger that seek to overcome the weaknesses evident in the dominant readings.

5
Critical Readings

> Even a cursory understanding of financial markets and a
> brief look at the history of economics show that profes-
> sional economists can rarely forecast economic booms and
> busts, and even when they do, they are usually so few in
> number or so at odds with consensus opinion that their
> advice is not acted upon.
>
> Michael O'Sullivan (2006: 60)

The unexpected collapse of the Celtic Tiger raises serious questions about
the ability of the dominant readings surveyed in the previous chapter to
offer real analytical and explanatory insight into Ireland's model of development. For example, Ireland's most authoritative source of independent
economic analysis, the ESRI, had been forecasting as late as May 2008 that
Ireland's GNP would grow by 1.6 per cent in 2008 and by 2.9 per cent in
2009 (Tansey, 2008a). By October 2008, it had decreased its forecasts to a
growth of 1.3 per cent in 2008 and 0.7 per cent in 2009 (Slattery, 2008). Yet,
in early 2009, this had been further slashed to an estimate of –3.1 per cent
decline in 2008 and a forecast of –9.2 per cent in 2009 (Barrett et al., 2009:
32). With a widespread consensus among economists that the international
recession was responsible for only around one-third of the Irish recession
and that domestic causes were responsible for most of it, the ESRI cannot
blame the international recession for its inability to identify the major weaknesses that have plunged Ireland so swiftly into what may be its greatest economic crisis since independence. By contrast, throughout the Celtic Tiger
boom, critical readings of the Irish development model had been pointing
to the severe structural weaknesses which by late 2008 were beginning to be
taken more seriously by political and economic leaders and by the general
public. Yet, up to then, those writing these critical readings tended to be
dismissed as the 'begrudgers' (Foster, 2007: 11–12).

The purpose of this chapter is to survey these critical readings of the Celtic
Tiger and, more generally, of Ireland's development. These adopt a wider

and more critical theoretical approach than do the dominant readings examined in the previous chapter. They usually straddle the distinction between economic and social life which was seen to divide the disciplines of economics and sociology, taking a more holistic analytical approach. Furthermore, they tend to adopt a more global perspective, probing more critically the influence of global forces on the domestic economy and society. They can, to a greater or lesser extent, be described as critical theory which 'stands back from the apparent fixity of the present to ask how the existing structures came into being and how they may be changing, or how they may be induced to change' (Cox, 1995: 32). Such an approach is all the more important at a time of fundamental change like the present. Two distinct critical approaches can be distinguished in the literature on Irish development and both have made important contributions to our understanding of the Celtic Tiger. The first constitutes approaches drawing on variants of Marxism and the second is constituted by a number of theorists who can loosely be grouped under the label political economy. Within this, a particular group of scholars working in the field of cultural political economy is also surveyed. Conclusions are drawn about the poverty of theory in the Irish social sciences.

Dependency theory, Marxism

Neo-Marxist approaches and, more specifically, variants of dependency theory which expect growth to result in growing inequality (in the case of dependency theory, for those countries following a dependent model of development) have informed a corpus of literature on Irish development (O'Hearn, 1998, 1995, 1993, 1989, 2001; Munck, 1993; Mac Laughlin, 1994a, 1994b; Crotty, 1986, 1979; Wickham, 1983, 1980). Dependency theorists situate Ireland within a global capitalist economy divided into core and periphery regions (with, for world-systems theorists, semi-periphery regions displaying features of both core and periphery[1]), and identify mechanisms whereby external forms of dependence create internal forms of uneven development. Munck (1993) has identified this uneven nature of development as the main internal aspect of dependency which causes widespread poverty, unemployment and, often, mass migration (2–3).[2] Dependency theory therefore seems to offer a more promising theoretical framework through which to explore aspects of the Celtic Tiger such as the correlation of high levels of economic growth with increasing social inequality.

O'Hearn (1989) has most systematically applied a dependency analysis to the case of Ireland and, specifically, to the Celtic Tiger (1998, 2000, 2001). He identifies three characteristics that he says distinguish the nature of Irish dependency – radical free trade, radical free enterprise and foreign industrial domination. These mean the Irish market is penetrated by imports and the state restricts its role to marketing Ireland as a profitable location for foreign business. The result was the decimation of indigenous industry much of which could not withstand the competitive pressures of free trade. He argues that Ireland's high rates of growth and of total factor productivity may be in part illusory, an artefact of corporate accounting. This 'dependent, export-oriented development', as he calls it, has gone through periods of boom and bust since the 1960s and, in the 1990s, entered into an extended period of boom as it succeeded in capturing a crucial segment of foreign investments, particularly in the computer industry, which clustered their production facilities close to one another so that they could respond more flexibly and more rapidly to changing market conditions. He places particular importance on the IDA's success in attracting Intel which, in 1991, located its European site for the production of computer chips near Dublin. In this way, Ireland 'bought economic tigerhood' (2000: 74) as nearly every major player in information technology followed Intel to Ireland. He sums up:

> The association between FDI, exports, and economic growth is clear-cut. Foreign chemicals, computers, and electrical engineering directly accounted for more than 40 per cent of Irish economic growth in the 1990s, exceeding 50 per cent in some years. And these sectors are dominated by a few large TNCs. Ten US TNCs in computers and chemicals accounted for a third of value added in southern Irish manufacturing in 1994. In 1998, the economy grew by nearly 10 per cent, and much of this resulted from a 60 per cent rise in organic chemical exports, mainly due to phenomenal sales of one new drug produced in County Cork: Viagra. In the main, the Irish tiger economy boils down to a few US corporations in IT and pharmaceuticals.
>
> (2000: 75)

One of the principal contributions O'Hearn makes is in comparing the Irish tiger to the East Asian ones. Here he shows that, unlike Ireland, Taiwan and South Korea developed through creating strong indigenous sectors and avoiding dependence on foreign investment though he identifies a typically East Asian pattern of industrial upgrading as Japanese firms subcontracted to local firms in these countries, in the process providing them with access to technology and training. He sees Ireland as being closer to Singapore which also attracted a lot of US multinational companies through offering incentives similar to those offered by Ireland. However, as a city state, Singapore has been more successful in spreading the benefits more widely and, like the other East Asian tigers, the Singaporean state intervenes more actively in its economy than does the Irish state, through its control of labour, its direct involvement in industry and its system of forced private savings (1998: 1–32). He also highlights the contrast between the high investment rates in East Asia where the four tigers increased their investment ratios from around 20 per cent in 1965 to more than 35 per cent in 1990 with

Singapore maintaining an investment ratio of 41.3 per cent during 1980–92. By contrast 'perhaps the greatest anomaly of the Celtic Tiger has been rapid growth without investment', he writes (2000: 77) with Irish investment rates of less than 15 per cent being the lowest in Europe in the mid-1990s. He concludes that Irish growth was 'disarticulated' as 'it was not based, like that in small European economies which earlier developed to core status, on the development of a local market for products that could be the centre of innovation and expansion' but instead was driven by 'rapid external growth' (2001: 192).

O'Hearn links rising social inequality to the nature of the Irish growth model, identifying three factors that are causing it: firstly, the fact that profits and high professional income are the basis of Irish economic growth; secondly, the concentration of employment creation in low-paying service jobs and, thirdly, the commitment of the state to fiscal policies which heavily favour the rich (1998). The shift from consumption and investment to profits results from the fact that the state must provide low tax rates to attract foreign investment and wage moderation to ensure competitiveness. Through the neo-corporatist wage agreements it holds down wages growth while profits increase. Thus O'Hearn points to growing income inequality as a direct result of this model (2000: 78). He argues that the proportion of part-time and contract work among new jobs is high and that the flexibilisation of labour has taken on a characteristic pattern in Ireland as many TNCs adopt a dual-employee structure with core workers having relatively good conditions and performance-related pay work side by side with what he calls a 'buffer' of part-time, temporary and contract workers (2000: 80). As he writes: 'A relatively small number of jobs were created in the high-tech sectors that led the Irish surge of growth, and only some of them were relatively well paid. The vast majority of new jobs were in services, predominantly low paid and insecure' (2001: 192). He also accuses the Irish state of avoiding 'any serious attempts to end poverty, instead giving small increases to social welfare recipients and introducing fairly innocuous temporary job schemes for the unemployed' (1998: 142).

A distinctive aspect of dependency theory is its global approach, drawing links between a country's position within international capitalism and its domestic levels of poverty and social inequality. O'Hearn argues that a global approach is required if a realistic picture is to be gained of the barriers to industrialisation and the limitations of locally defined solutions. Most of the studies of Irish development fail to take such a global approach, he argues, and therefore fail to recognise the extent of external control over local events. He also argues that the Irish model is unsustainable due to its extreme dependence of US FDI and that for this reason Ireland is not a model as 'other countries will find it hard if not impossible to follow the Irish path simply because there is not enough foreign investment available to sustain growth in more than one or two peripheral European zones'(2001: 194).

While O'Hearn has made the most extensive contribution to analysing the Irish case from the perspective of dependency theory, other theorists have also contributed. Wickham draws some different conclusions than does O'Hearn arguing that Irish industrialisation has been a success story in terms of living standards. He points out that growth in the service sector in Ireland, which superficially seems similar to what has happened in many Third World countries, is in fact different since much of the service growth is in 'modern'-type employment. However, he adds that dependent industrialisation has shifted the balance of class power away from the working class, despite the increase in that class' relative size (Wickham, 1980). Mac Laughlin (1994b) has used a world systems analysis to interpret the persistence of emigration from Ireland, rejecting dominant explanations based on the mobility or aspirations of young Irish adults in favour of an explanation rooted in Ireland's peripheralisation within the international economy.

The only unique Irish contribution to development theory has been the work of Raymond Crotty. Though it has been described as being 'similar to Frank's[3] early dependency analysis' (O'Hearn, 1995: 92), Crotty's work is in fact highly idiosyncratic since it seeks the cause of what he calls 'undevelopment' in the imposition of European 'individualist capitalism' on other societies throughout the world, starting with Ireland (Crotty, 2001: 81). Furthermore, for Crotty, capitalism emerged around 2000 BC in the forests of central western Europe with the early accumulation of capital in the form of crops, shelter, winter fodder and cattle. He outlines at length how Ireland, despite appearances, is a good example of capitalist undevelopment as the cost of land and that of capital have been kept cheap while labour has been made expensive so that profit is made from owning the former rather than from employing the latter; this results in about half the labour force having to emigrate in order to earn a living. However, due to this export of people, Ireland has, unlike any other capitalist colonial undeveloper, been able to increase the living standards of those who remained in the country and it now provides the conditions for showing how undevelopment can be undone through distributing the nation's economic resources in equal measure to citizens through a national dividend and instituting taxes on land and on financial deposits (ibid.: 253–70). For Crotty also, growing poverty and inequality is what defines 'undevelopment': those countries 'with more people worse off than formerly, or fewer better off than before' (ibid.: 255).

The main contribution of dependency theory is that it focuses attention on the structural inequalities that are a central part of the world economic system. But a major problem is that it emphasises the external structural constraints on a country's development to such an extent that it appears to leave little room for internal actors to influence the course of development. As Ó Riain put it in reviewing O'Hearn, the dependency/world systems theory approach, while being a powerful tool in revealing the power of global forces over local and national workers, states and societies, is a 'blunt instrument for analysing the variety of ways in which these actors can strategise in order to pursue different development options within an overall context of globalisation' (Ó Riain, 1998: 133). O'Donnell takes issue with Crotty and O'Hearn arguing that their studies, which saw Ireland's engagement in European integration and the international economy as the source of ongoing failure, never offered a guide to practical action (O'Donnell, 2000: 179). Furthermore, a certain theoretical imprecision attaches to the category of dependency as applied in these writings to the Irish situation. While adequate as a descriptive term, dependency theorists elevate it into a cause of underdevelopment while failing to reveal adequately the mechanisms that make it so. For O'Hearn, one of these mechanisms is decapitalisation as multinationals drain capital from the national economy. This, however, is hotly contested by many economists who point out that the net outcome of inward and outward capital flows results in substantial economic and financial gains to the domestic economy.[4]

Allen (2007, 2000, 1999) offers a more conventional Marxist analysis of the Celtic Tiger which also emphasises how it has enriched a small elite while leaving the majority relatively less well off. In his study of the corporate takeover of Ireland, he states that the focus of much social scientific scholarship on the poor and marginalised has left 'a great gap in the study of Irish society', namely that 'links between the political and economic elites, the activities of business people and the networks they form' are under-studied and he sets himself the task of trying 'to reveal a structure of corporate privilege which is immensely damaging for society' (Allen, 2007: xi). Rejecting a Weberian model of social stratification because it takes little cognisance of class conflict, he contends that the Marxist concepts of late capitalism and class polarisation present a useful framework within which to analyse growing inequality amid economic growth. Defining social class above all by its relationship to the means of production allows him to conclude that the working class includes many sectors of white-collar workers whose employment is characterised by the absence of control and autonomy over conditions of work, and he identifies a process of class polarisation as resources are redistributed away from the working population to the owners of capital. He illustrates the power of the owners of capital by examining the pressures of corporate interests on education and children, the emergence of 'the corporate university' (142) and the 'corruption of science' (149) through reliance on corporate funding, corporate influence in the health care system, environmental damage and the weakness of regulatory agencies, and privatisation. He argues that the Celtic Tiger has produced a 'discontented majority' leading to a 'sharpening of conflicts' which 'make the emergence of new political forces virtually inevitable' (2000: 6). Arguing that what is needed is 'the collective strength that workers have when they mobilise together', Allen concludes that 'the Celtic Tiger has laid a new basis for this politics to emerge. He identifies that such campaigns in the mid 2000s as the Save our Seafront campaign in Dún Laoghaire, the campaign against water charges, the protests against Irish Ferries moves to outsource staff, and the big march in Dublin in February 2003 against the war in Iraq constitute networks with 'the energy and enthusiasm to offer an alternative vision of Ireland.' Yet the trade union movement 'has been in a Rip Van Winkle style sleep for two decades' and the official left offers little real support to the 'broad movement that relies on protest, direct action and people power' (2007: 247). For all the strengths of his work, Allen fails to situate inequality within a particular political economy of growth; this allows him to overlook gains to workers such as increased employment and real increases in living standards as a result of economic growth. Furthermore, he views the state as simply a vehicle for the wealthy to impose their sectional interests on the rest of society while his view of a discontented majority lending support to the left is overstated.

These analyses of the Celtic Tiger raise serious critical issues about the social impact of high levels of economic growth and the sustainability of a model of development which results in growing inequality. Their main weakness, however, is a methodological one in that they display a tendency to use evidence to substantiate an already established theoretical case rather than engaging in a careful empirical examination, guided by theory, to develop a more adequate theoretical exposition of the Irish case which might yield more useful insights for action. For this, we turn to political economy approaches.

Box 5.1 Garvin on the causes of Ireland's underdevelopment

For long, the literature on Ireland's underdevelopment was dominated by economists and sociologists with virtually no contribution from political scientists. Even some of the key works on the Irish state are by sociologists (Ó Riain, 2004; Breen et al., 1990). For this reason, the publication of Tom Garvin's *Preventing the Future: Why Ireland was so poor for so long?* (2005) and the popular reception it received, seemed to herald an important contribution by a leading political scientist; the influence of its central thesis was mirrored in the end-of-year editorial in *The Irish Times* (31 December 2005) which stated: 'Much of the economic growth over the past decade has been simply a catching-up process after decades of economic failures caused by the stranglehold of vested interests on public policy and by bad political decisions.' For Garvin, politics determines economics and he turns to the US political scientist Mancur Olson's influential work for an explanation of how organised elite vested interests such as business, trade unions, farmers' organisations, government, professional associations and ecclesiastical organisations all reinforced one another to discourage innovation and slow up change in the period between 1945 and 1960. Essentially, he focuses almost exclusively on actors and pays cursory attention to either ideas or institutions.

If Garvin limits his argument to one variable, namely veto groups, the methodology he uses to determine how far these groups help explain Ireland's developmental failures is most unsatisfactory since the author nowhere addresses how he proposes to test his hypothesis, nowhere defines with any precision what groups he is talking about and nowhere identifies the precise ways in which such groups prevent development. The closest the book gets to any clear statement of the author's basic thesis is as follows: 'The delayed character of Irish economic develop-ment can be traced directly to the limited, inegalitarian, non-technical and ideologised educational system that was enforced on the polity by the lobbies of the period' (125), essentially the Catholic Church and Irish language revivalists. Assertion, therefore, replaces any careful examina-tion of evidence in this book and is based on a set of presuppositions that are taken for granted. It is highly individualistic and believes strongly in the virtues of the free market while decrying public enterprise and state involvement in the economy. It is viscerally anti-Catholic and sees a secular and scientific education as the key to development. In these ways it mirrors modernisation theory in its first crusading phase in the 1950s and early 1960s.

While the book fails to throw any light on the issues it purports to address, namely why Ireland stayed so poor for so long, its highly posi-tive reception makes it of interest. For it reveals more about the domi-nant concerns that interested the reading public at the height of the Celtic Tiger boom and the theoretical presuppositions they shared so unquestioningly. It may be a very unreliable guide to understanding the causes of Ireland's underdevelopment and to offering any insight into the nature of the Celtic Tiger boom, but it illustrates very well why many of the public had such a myopic and self-serving view of social change in Ireland, and lacked any sense of the dangers that lay ahead.

Political economy

A variety of studies on Irish development can be grouped under the heading of political economy. While the term 'political economy' is a contested con-cept, in this context it is used in a general sense to denote an approach which seeks to examine the interaction of political power and economic outcomes and which devotes central attention to the links between state and market (Hettne, 1995: 1–6; Jones, 1988: 1–26). A number of scholars of Irish develop-ment can be identified whose work is characterised by the centrality of this theoretical approach, among them Ó Riain (2008, 2004, 2000) and Ó Riain and O'Connell (2000), Smith (2005), O'Sullivan (2006), O'Donnell (2008, 2000, 1999), Fink (2004, 2007, 2008), O'Malley (1998, 1992, 1989), O'Malley and McCarthy (2006), Girvin (1989), Mjøset (1992), Kennedy (1998, 1993, 1992a, 1992b) and Kennedy et al. (1988).

The diverse works included under this section have in common that they eschew grand theoretical frameworks in favour of a broad-ranging empirical examination of Ireland's economic and social development. In these works, theory plays a very different role to the one it plays both in the neoclassical and modernisation approaches outlined in the previous chapter and in the dependency-type and Marxist approaches outlined in the section above. Thus neoclassical economics and modernisation theory both assume outcomes about rising living standards and growing social mobility and equality; the failure to achieve these outcomes over Ireland's longer-term development trajectory has not resulted in an interrogation of the theoretical frameworks, rather it has meant that the disjuncture between expectations and outcomes has been given far less sustained theoretical attention than it merits. In a similar way, dependency and Marxist approaches presume that capitalist development results in growing poverty and inequality, benefiting elites rather than the majority, and they assemble evidence to show how this is the case. In doing so, however, they neglect a more detailed empirical examination which might uncover the specific ways in which economic and social processes interact in a particular case, from which both policy and theory could be usefully informed. Instead of working from within a set of assumptions and the expectations to which these give rise, the scholars using political economy approaches achieve a finer dialectical interplay between theory and empirical examination which has resulted in gaining useful insight into the genesis, nature and weaknesses of the Celtic Tiger and, more generally, into the nature of Ireland's development trajectory.

Ó Riain's work (2004) proposes that the state can make a real difference to how countries position themselves in the international economic order and that Ireland offers an example of a new kind of developmental state, the Developmental Network State (DNS), 'mediating between the global and the local, connecting them and shaping the nature of their relationship' (28). He distinguishes between the Developmental Bureaucratic State (DBS) (South Korea and Singapore) and an emerging DNS of which Taiwan and Israel are examples as well as Ireland, and devotes detailed empirical attention to how this Irish DNS emerged. Central to this, he argues, is the emergence of the software sector in Ireland as the Irish state shaped its growth through the networking of state agencies, industry associations and university research centres. But Ó Riain also analyses the class politics underpinning the emergence of this network state, particularly the alliance between a rising technical–professional class, but also the 'seething politics' that lies beneath the seemingly seamless shift towards a 'postindustrial, professionalized labour force' with its 'noisy clash of two middle classes' (the emerging technical professional private sector and the social-service professionals of the public sector) with the growing marginalisation of low-paid service workers (140). He draws attention to the contradictions that characterise Ireland's development, the deepening inequality it is fostering and the inability of decentralised state institutions to deal with these. As he puts it, the DNS 'will face an increasingly contentious politics of national inequality because unequal integration into the globalization project undermines solidaristic national social contracts' (38). This account of the Celtic Tiger period, Ó Riain places in a longer historical reading of the emergence of different developmental regimes in Ireland out of a combination of crisis, political responses to it and the fashioning of new institutions as a result – firstly, the emergence of the foreign investment regime in the late 1950s and, more recently, the emergence of 'network developmentalism' out of the crisis of the 1980s. His more recent work (2008) takes this further in tracing the competing state projects of the Celtic Tiger: neo-corporatist stabilisation from 1987 to 1994, learning and developmentalism from 1994 to 2000 and 'disciplining development and democracy' in the post-2000 period when a tax cutting agenda took over from the attempt to build economic capacity. 'The institutions that were built in the 1990s to support innovation and to promote social solidarity were always threatened by the official story of the Celtic Tiger as a market-driven economy', he writes. These tensions were obscured during the boom period but 'the choice between free markets and innovation and equality' is posed more starkly as recession hits (2008: 183).

Fink (2004) explicitly distinguishes his approach from that of dependency theory, instead using a neo-institutionalist framework with its concepts of state autonomy and capacity. Drawing on the work of Ó Riain, Fink's analysis leads him to conclusions that are the very opposite of Ó Riain's. Instead of ascribing a key role to the Irish state in transforming the economy, Fink sees the multiple dualities that characterise Ireland's development model and the growing polarisation of society that is resulting, as deriving from 'the incapacity of the Irish State to effectively tackle the problems born of its growth model' which he describes as 'the self-restricted role of the Irish State in the development process' (Fink, 2004: 139); indeed, for Fink the Irish state's 'inefficient redistributive measures and low level of expenditures on social protection have exacerbated' problems (139). In linking the economic and the social, Fink gives central attention to the concept of dualism as he writes that 'the existence of a dual industrial structure has led to a dual employment structure, which has fed through to induce a social dualism characterised by polarisations between skilled and unskilled labour' (121). This helps draw attention to the essential continuities masked by the boom of the late 1990s and early 2000s and that ascribes the growth in inequality and relative poverty to the dualistic nature of the Irish economy, with a high productivity and high-tech foreign-owned sector side by side with an indigenous sector characterised by lower productivity, profits and innovation. Fink argues that the Irish state 'has experienced a traditionally high degree of autonomy owing to a specific socio-economic set-up, which has guaranteed a low level of internal influence on the setting of developmental goals' but that 'its capacities to implement these goals have been weak' (27). This autonomy derives from the populist nature of Irish politics and the lack of a strong social democratic movement which might have challenged the essentially liberal, free-market orientation of state development policy. As a result, the state restricted its role to offering incentives to the private sector, 'nurturing and not coercing capital to invest productively' (53), thereby weakening its capacity to achieve the developmental goals it set itself.

Smith's examination of the 'political economy of the Irish Republic' (the subtitle of her book) focuses on Ireland as 'perhaps *the* test case for globalisation' (Smith, 2005: 2; emphasis in original). She examines the exogenous and endogenous factors that account for Ireland's boom and concludes that 'it is possible to understand Ireland's developmental trajectory without any reference to globalisation in analytical terms' (143) since the economy was an open liberal economy long before globalisation began to be employed. She contends that far from being globalised, what is happening in the Irish case is a deeper integration into the US and particularly the EU economy. She treats the distinctive nature of the Irish economic and social adaptation to the pressures of the global economy as being not pure neoliberalism but rather 'the ebb and flow of tendencies and counter-tendencies', so that the Irish case does not present a neat dichotomy of either an activist or an auxiliary state but rather a bit of both (113). Among Smith's major contributions is her analysis of the role of discourse in the shaping of policy. Acknowledging that many senior policymakers believe Ireland is becoming more globalised, she documents in a very revealing way the use of the category in political discourse, arguing that it provides the rationale for the emphasis on competitiveness in such discourse. However, she concludes that, given the lack of evidence that the Irish economy is indeed subject to the competitive pressures of globalisation, the discourse about globalisation as a source of external compulsion 'is in significant part a (discursive) construction' (177). But the book does not adequately explain why this is so, largely because the author fails to situate discourse within the institutional framework in which it takes place (consensus-oriented political institutions and culture, internal struggles between different departments within the public service) and which is essential to explaining the outcomes achieved.

While O'Sullivan's work (2006) comes from a more economic perspective, his wide-ranging treatment of political and social issues, his critical focus on globalisation, his appreciation of the key role the state plays, and his scepticism about the claims made for the Celtic Tiger boom make it appropriate to include in this section. While acknowledging the economic successes of Ireland's adaptation to globalisation through making itself attractive to foreign capital to establish subsidiaries, O'Sullivan emphasises that, as a result, 'someone else either owns or controls the levers of the Irish economy' (75). He is unimpressed by the Irish business class which he describes as 'fast, aggressive and shiny, not unlike the newly monied classes of other emerging economies' and he adds that 'Irish companies have only got poor corporate governance as a distinguishing characteristic' (83). Indeed, O'Sullivan quite refreshingly dismisses the complacency of so many of his fellow economists, by stating that 'Ireland has become too fond of and familiar with the steady flow of investment capital from abroad, principally from the US' (95) and that it can leave as easily as it came. He finds little evidence of an exceptional Irish economic model such as exists among the Asian Tigers or in the Nordic region and fears that external factors will not be as kind to Ireland in the future. But if the Irish economy has been fast globalised, this masks the fact that a great part of Irish society is untouched by globalisation and he assembles a range of evidence on the growth in poverty and inequality, on human underdevelopment, the lack of social mobility and the rise in racism that have accompanied economic success, concluding that 'not enough is being done by the state to mediate the effects of globalisation on Irish society' (119).

For this reason, he describes 'the lop-sided nature of globalisation in Ireland' (128) as it has not been harnessed to spread wealth to the parts of society that need it most. O'Sullivan describes major challenges facing Irish policymakers: the first is to derive growth from new sources and minimise the risks to the drivers of economic performance during the Celtic Tiger period; the second is 'to spread the benefits of growth in a more far-sighted manner' (98). These will require a greater role for the state, an increase in taxes to yield more resources for the state and a reform of state institutions to make them more effective. He focuses on the challenge for policymakers who 'operate with a limited policy arsenal' but who have the opportunity to distinguish themselves through innovations in policy to develop 'a discernible Irish model of economic management' (99). Though published before the collapse of the Celtic Tiger, O'Sullivan's critique was remarkably prescient and stands in stark contrast to the dominant readings produced by most of his fellow economists.

O'Donnell has made a major contribution to the literature on the Celtic Tiger in tracing the multiple interactions and outcomes that have given rise to it. Central to these is the role of the European Union and Ireland's innovative social partnership. In tracing what he calls the 're-invention of Ireland' (1999: 32), he writes that 'European integration and governance have been centrally important in the economic transformation of the past decade' particularly through 'the alignment of state strategy with the action of economic and social interests' (2000: 162). Thus, the state of the European Union and a correct understanding of its nature are of critical importance to Ireland, he asserts. For him, it was 'the period of closure' from the 1930s to the 1960s and the values it incubated (165), that can now be seen as exceptional and he traces two distinct periods in Ireland's internationalisation: from EC membership on 1 January 1973 to the economic and social crisis of the 1980s (1973–87) and the period since 1987 in which Europe was relaunched and Ireland transformed. As a result, 'Ireland's approach to market regulation, and the relationship between market, state and society, has been significantly reshaped by membership of the EU' and he instances the list of regulatory agencies established. This reconfiguration of market regulation is 'a major change in Irish public administration and policy' (184). He identifies social partnership as 'the major innovation' which led to more than a decade of 'negotiated economic and social governance' (177) and in more recent work describes the Irish state as a 'partnership state' (2008). He argues that the institutions of partnership have played a key role in helping the economy adjust successfully to the international environment, in structuring a more collaborative relationship between the state and civil society and, somewhat less so, in changing administrative practices, pushing the government to seek consistency between different policy areas.

The emphasis of these scholars on the Irish state's key role in achieving the country's 'tiger' status marks a departure from earlier political economy analyses of Ireland's development in which the emphasis was on the state's failure to foster successful development. O'Malley's work straddles both phases. His 1989 study draws on the literature on East Asian development to argue that countries like Ireland with a weak industrial base face daunting challenges to industrialise in today's world economy. Such latecomers, as he calls them, need to develop industries that can compete in the international marketplace but they are at a severe disadvantage in doing so due to the head start gained by a wide range of industries, most of them based in the advanced industrial countries. Elements such as advanced technology, large capital requirements, highly skilled labour and economies of scale all constitute 'barriers to entry' for the latecomer. In this context, the success of Japan, South Korea and Taiwan with their selective and active state guidance to nurture indigenous industries so that they overcome the barriers to entry facing the latecomers is looked to as the source of lessons for Ireland. In later work (1992, 1998), O'Malley examines the ways in which a more active state policy since the mid-1980s to develop indigenous industry has resulted in 'a substantial improvement in the growth performance of Irish indigenous industry … without historical precedent in twentieth century Ireland' (1998: 57) and argues that at least some of these developments in Irish industrial policy look like an appropriate response to the barriers to entry for the industrial latecomer analysed in his earlier work (ibid.: 57).

In his study of the Irish economy in a comparative institutional perspective, Mjøset (1992) broke substantial new ground in the literature on Irish development by drawing explicitly on development theory and by comparing Ireland to a number of small European states which, unlike Ireland, have been developmental success cases – Sweden, Finland, Denmark, Austria and Switzerland. He draws distinctions which are very useful for understanding the Irish experience, particularly that between autocentric development (growth with development under national direction) and peripheral or dependent development (growth without development where the benefits flow out of the national economy). He situates Ireland between these two categories to understand the deep-rooted causes of Ireland's malaise. Mjøset refuses to identify one primary cause of Irish underdevelopment, writing instead of clusters of causal factors (the nature of agrarian modernisation, the sluggish growth of the home market, a paternalist family structure) all re-enforcing each other and leading to a vicious circle which, at the time he was writing, Ireland had yet to break out of. The key to successful development he regards as being a system of national innovation which he defines as 'the institutions and economic structures which affect the rate and direction of innovative activities in the economy' (45). Instead of developing a system of national innovation, Ireland has tried to import a system of innovation, he argued.

Though alluding to dimensions of development theory, Girvin's study (1989) is a largely empirical examination of economic policymaking from the foundation of the state until 1961. He argues that the crisis of the 1950s was not a crisis of the model of native industrialisation but a crisis of agriculture, 'the result of the failure of a traditional society to move beyond the limits imposed by this' (Girvin, 1989: 202). Again he argues that decisions taken during the 1960s constrained policymakers thereafter but adds that there were alternatives open to the Irish state during the second half of the 1960s, such as the possibility of deepening the planning process and of further state intervention to direct the economy. Instead, the state opted for a seemingly painless strategy that 'could be introduced with few changes to the traditional political structure, to society or its culture' (207). The result was that 'Ireland became dependent on others to provide for its welfare without developing a society that could provide for itself' (207). Girvin concludes that Ireland remains a developing rather than a developed society and that it requires 'a strong state to direct the economy and to provide for the welfare of the society' (211).

The work of economist Kieran A. Kennedy has persistently interrogated the record of Irish economic development and found it wanting. The economic history of Ireland in the twentieth century which he co-authored (1988) reviews specific aspects of Irish economic performance such as capital resources and investment, foreign trade, agriculture and manufacturing, and finds that 'it has to be conceded that this performance often fell well short of potential – even making due allowance for the constraints' (257). The authors identify three weaknesses operative in all major areas of policy throughout the period – failure to grasp the implications of the small size of the country, absence of long-term perspective and neglect of human resource dimensions.

In other works, Kennedy acknowledges that these weaknesses 'are clearly symptoms of something deeper, the more fundamental explanation of which may lie in the culture, political framework, distribution of power and resources' (1992a: 21) or other forces. The unemployment crisis of the 1980s, he saw as 'not so much a new problem, as a new manifestation of a deeper problem that has been endemic in Irish history', in large part 'a long-standing problem of underdevelopment' (1993: 4, 43).

The great strength of the political economy literature is its empirical examination of the distinctive nature of the Irish case and, in particular, its dissection of the relationship between state, market and society. However, its weakness can often be that its empirical investigation is insufficiently grounded in theory with the result that conclusions can rest on assumptions derived from partial evidence. As argued above, there has been a tendency in the recent political economy literature on the Celtic Tiger both to prioritise the relationship between state and market and to neglect their relationship to society, and to assert benign conclusions rather than deriving them from a more thorough empirical investigation. Most noteworthy is the very different assessments of the role of the state, between the very positive readings of Ó Riain and O'Donnell and much more critical accounts of O'Sullivan and Fink. This discussion points to the need for a more thorough political economy approach to the Celtic Tiger, investigating rather than asserting the changing relationship of market, state and society and grounding this relationship within an explicit theoretical framework. This is the task undertaken in the three chapters of Part III.

Cultural political economy

A lively critical literature has emerged analysing cultural dimensions of the Celtic Tiger boom. While scholars from the humanities as well as the social sciences have contributed, it can usefully be called a cultural political economy. Acknowledging that the constitution of a dominant meaning embodies power, a cultural political economy approach 'focuses analytical attention on the meaning attributed to ... change and allows an examination of how a certain meaning achieves dominance despite the fact that other far more critical meanings of the same phenomena also exist' (Kirby, 2002b: 22). This, therefore, moves beyond a cultural critique to examine how the constitution of meaning affects power relations between state, market and society. The discourse analysis of Smith (2005), outlined above, in which she examined how the perceptions of globalisation held by senior policymakers influenced the Irish state's policy prescriptions is one example of a cultural political economy.

Scholars using this approach have adopted a variety of foci. For Kuhling and Keohane (2007), the concern is to examine the globalisation, and commodification, of Irish identity. They show how such cultural artefacts as

Riverdance or advertisements for drinks such as Guinness stout, Jameson whiskey and Ballygowan mineral water 'tap into collective representations or shared cultural values with regards to identity, community and authenticity' to create a new sense of Irishness (Kuhling and Keohane, 2007: 77). These draw on traditional motifs and practices to constitute a new and attractive Irish identity that appears liberated from the limitations of the past, a cosmopolitan and globalised identity but one still rooted in a sense of tradition. However, Kuhling and Keohane ask whether this is functional to neoliberalism and a public realm that 'is impoverished, dominated by predominantly commercial interests' (192), thereby hiding the real power relations constituting Irish society. In probing another key constitutive feature of contemporary Irish identity, Ging examines how the rise of consumerism 'is affecting the ways in which we mediate and talk about gender behaviours, identities and relationships in contemporary Ireland' (Ging, 2009: 52). While this is not unique to Ireland, its reception in a society with its own history of gender relations is of obvious concern, she writes. For example, she suggests that 'the blatant sexualisation of girlhood in child-directed advertising and marketing imagery raises further questions about consumerism's impact on children's self-identity' (63). Looking at a range of consumer practices, media texts and debates, and TV programmes, Ging concludes that 'the Celtic Tiger years have led us into new discursive arenas, in which ideological consensus is increasingly achieved at the level of the symbolic, the rhetorical and the discursive' with 'attitudes to gender ... being (re)constituted through subtle processes of consumption and economic rationalisation, which are channelled through an increasingly profit-driven media' (67).

If cultural political economy examines how dominant meanings are constituted and achieve their power, it is also concerned with the constitution of critical meanings that challenge power, seeking to understand how these meanings are marginalised and so disempowered. Taking one example of a vigorous contestation of dominant meanings during the Celtic Tiger, namely the determined protests by local people in north Mayo against a proposed Shell gas pipeline through their area, Garavan illustrates very concretely the ways in which critical meanings about development and progress are shaped and disempowered by the institutional settings through which they are mediated (Garavan, 2009). This happens to an extent through the need to make the critique understandable to the various interlocutors involved such as the local government, the planning authorities, the Environmental Protection Agency, the Health and Safety Authority, the state authorities, the media, the local public and even academics. For each audience, the critique is named and framed in a particular way, such as a land-use issue, an environmental issue, an industrial safety issue or a natural resources issue. Yet, argues Garavan, beyond these ways of presenting the critique 'there is also in practice an argument about what is really meant by key concepts of modernisation such as progress and development' but this is often implicit rather than overt (86). He concludes that both sides in this dispute struggled to make sense of one another but, even though they may be talking past one another, this does not lead to a paralysis of decision-making 'because the decision-making process largely favours the corporate/"rational" view of the world' (90). The constitution of meaning, however, may serve to make such moments of contestation rare as was all too evident in the lack of critical challenge over the years of the Celtic Tiger. Through examining the seemingly benign state discourse on 'active citizenship', Cronin illustrates how this was achieved. He argues that the discourse on active citizenship, actively propagated through a state-established Taskforce on Active Citizenship which engaged in a public consultation process and issued a major report, became reduced to 'a language of pious abstraction and studied evasiveness' due to its inability to acknowledge power relationships and socio-economic inequality (Cronin, 2009: 75). He concludes that 'by refusing to provide a critical context for the understanding of the operations of the market economy, the Taskforce deals with problems it can neither understand nor resolve. The result is that the active citizen is left to believe in a familiar credo of Faith (in the current politico-economic setup) and Good Works (volunteering)' (68).

A very different example of using a cultural political economy approach is given by Bradley and Kennelly (2008). They draw on the lively cultural renaissance of the end of the nineteenth century and the beginning of the twentieth century in Ireland to argue that the distinctive sense of Irish identity cultivated at that time through such activities as the Gaelic League (founded to revive the Gaelic language as the vernacular), the Abbey Theatre and the Gaelic Athletic Association (GAA) (founded to revive Irish games) is now badly needed to give Ireland a global competitive advantage in today's globalised and highly competitive marketplace. As they write:

> The evidence is clear: sustainable competitive advantage in the twenty-first century will be determined by *creating value* from resources that are rare, inimitable and non-substitutable. ... This facilitates innovation and continuous transformation by the application of knowledge in creative ways.... Yet Ireland still suffers the consequences of ruptured roots from the loss of its language, primarily during the nineteenth century. To summarise, the best way for Ireland to generate a sustainable competitive advantage is through understanding and appreciating its inimitable resources, particularly intangibles, and implementing practical approaches to create value from these.
>
> Bradley and Kennelly (2008: 4–5; emphasis in original)

Cultural political economy therefore offers a range of critical readings of the Celtic Tiger; what unites them is their focus on how meaning underpins a particular relationship between state and market with major implications for society. The literature surveyed here illustrates the added value that such an approach brings to analysing and explaining the nature and weaknesses of the Celtic Tiger model of development, as well as to probing possibilities for change.

Conclusions

These studies show the potential that exists for overcoming the poverty of theory that was recognised to characterise the Irish social sciences in the early Celtic Tiger period (Kane, 1996).

Mac Laughlin had written of 'the neglect of theoretical explanation' in Irish economics, political science and sociology (1994a: 45) and for Kane the fault lay in the dominance of a particular theoretical paradigm and the outdated nature of that paradigm (a positivist belief in an objective social reality based on laws and mechanisms, which could be observed by the detached observer and knowledge generated through empirical testing) (Kane, 1996: 138). Yet, as the previous chapter illustrated, even if theoretical and methodological innovation is taking place, it is still kept at the margins of the generation and dissemination of social knowledge. This has meant that an ultra-positive, self-congratulatory and myopic reading of Irish 'transformation' dominated public perception and debate of Irish society over the Celtic Tiger years and the critical readings being disseminated failed to generate a more critical engagement with the great weaknesses of the Irish development model. Its swift and dramatic collapse is one consequence. The poverty of the social sciences' contribution to knowledge derives from a widespread failure to recognise that empirical research and the methodologies it employs are based on theoretical assumptions and that its results have theoretical implications; a failure to devote sustained and creative attention to these theoretical issues impoverishes research and limits its potential contribution to understanding society. Taking these considerations into account, Chapter 6 is devoted to elaborating a more adequate theoretical framework for the subject of this study.

6
Elaborating Theory

> Theory is always *for* someone and *for* some purpose.
>
> Robert W. Cox
> (1996a: 87; emphasis in original)

Discussion of the dominant and the critical readings of the Celtic Tiger period in the previous two chapters highlighted the limitations of the theoretical lens through which the Celtic Tiger has been viewed. It identified some central deficiencies: the tendency in some of the literature to see economic growth as an end in itself, the failure to specify what constitutes development and what the social objectives of economic growth are, and giving priority to the needs of the economy and of the state over those of society. The purpose of this chapter is to elaborate a theoretical approach designed to address these weaknesses and therefore to offer a better guide to uncovering and identifying in a more comprehensive way the nature and developmental impact of the Celtic Tiger period. Furthermore, a test of such a theoretical approach is that it should have the analytical ability to uncover the central weaknesses of the Irish growth model, making it a more sure guide than other theoretical approaches to what lies ahead. For, as Cox states in the quote with which this chapter opens, theory needs to be assessed in terms of which sectors it favours and what purpose it serves. Therefore, the chapter begins by situating its theoretical approach within the emerging self-understanding of the social sciences. It then identifies the elements required for a more adequate theoretical framework through which to understand the Celtic Tiger and the inbuilt weaknesses of the development model on which it was based. Following this, it discusses a number of contributions to the theoretical framework being elaborated. The chapter closes by specifying the theoretical framework as an international political economy of development and outlines how it can be applied to a study of the Celtic Tiger in Parts III and IV that follow.

The changing self-understanding of the social sciences

As illustrated by the accounts of theoretical approaches to analysing the Celtic Tiger outlined in the previous two chapters, social theory is constituted by a range of theoretical frameworks, some of them hermetically sealed from one another and yielding widely differing (even contradictory) interpretations of the same social phenomena. Having argued that none of these frameworks is adequate to explain the nature and social impact of the Celtic Tiger and to identify its core weaknesses, it could be concluded that the intention here is to formulate yet another theoretical framework, to add as it were to the menu of theoretical choices available. This, however, would be to neglect the changing self-understanding of the nature and role of theory in the social sciences; it is this changing self-understanding which offers a way of superseding the problems identified in the previous two chapters rather than simply adding to them.

Giddens identified three main characteristics of mainstream social science in the post-war period, what he described as the 'orthodox consensus'. These are naturalism, the notion that the social sciences could be modelled on the natural sciences (he says he prefers the word 'naturalism' to 'positivism' though they mean much the same thing); social causation, whereby social science purports to uncover deeper causes of the actions of human agents of which they are unaware; and functionalism, the view that the social sciences deal in systems which resemble biological wholes. This orthodox consensus about social theory is today no more, says Giddens (though he acknowledges that it may continue to hold sway in empirical social research). Having given way to a diverse range of perspectives,[1] he now finds signs of a renewed synthesis emerging concerning the role of the social sciences and their theoretical components (Giddens, 1996: 65–7).

A number of the elements of this renewed synthesis are pertinent to elaborating a theoretical framework for this study. For example, he foresees that the pre-existing disciplinary divisions within the social sciences will become progressively less sharply defined and that a theoretical synthesis will emerge giving a renewed coherence to debates. While he makes clear that he is not suggesting that a unified theoretical framework is either desirable or possible in a discipline like sociology, he does foresee a new phase of theoretical development: 'The time when it seemed that the advocates of the competing theoretical schools simply inhabited different universes, hermetically sealed off from one another, is now surely past. The new synthesis which is likely to emerge will differ from the old not only in its content, but in respect of its recognition that key aspects of the interpretation of social life are likely to remain contested. However a certain degree of "closure" of the diversity of standpoints will no doubt generally be accepted as desirable and possible' (1987: 31).

These changes in the understanding and role of theory go hand in hand with a changing understanding of the concerns of the social sciences and of how theory responds to these concerns, according to Giddens. He foresees that the recent emphasis on empirical research will be balanced by a renewed interest in large-scale, long-term processes of social transformation. Furthermore, in addressing the role of theory within such concerns, he expresses reservations about the notion of 'theory building', namely the construction of generalisations about the social world, and instead argues that 'conceptual innovation (coupled to empirical research) is at least as important in social science as is the formulating of novel generalizations' (ibid.: 43). For Giddens, a double hermeneutic distinguishes the social sciences from the natural sciences since the former consist not of a body of theory and research insulated from its subject matter (as do the natural sciences) but interact in a two-way manner with their subject matter, both appropriating concepts from the social world and finding their theories and concepts in turn appropriated by the social world. Based on this view, he concludes: 'The most far-reaching practical consequences of social science do not involve the creation of sets of generalizations that can be used to generate instrumental control over the social world. They concern instead the constant absorption of concepts and theories into that "subject-matter" they seek to analyse, constituting and reconstituting what that "subject-matter" is' (ibid.: 48).

The theoretical framework for this study can be seen as reflecting these trends in the social sciences. Its concern is not narrowly empirical but is rather with the larger-scale and longer-term process of Irish economic and social transformation. Furthermore, it does not aspire to build a new theory or set of generalisations but rather to offer explanation and insight into the ambiguous nature of the Celtic Tiger and its weaknesses as a sustainable and egalitarian development model.

Towards an adequate theoretical framework

By adequate theory in the context of this study is meant the ability of a theoretical framework to guide an examination of the subject so that insight might be offered into its nature and causes, thus maximising its explanatory power. In doing this, it clarifies whose interests it serves and for what purpose. It can be contrasted with inadequate theory which declares limits to its ability to offer understanding. An example of such theoretical inadequacy is given at the end of Paul Krugman's discussion of rising inequality in the US. Having discounted the increased integration of the US into the world economy as the cause and having made a few inconclusive comments on what he calls 'the all-purpose explanation known as "technology"', Krugman concludes: 'The bottom line of all of this is that while we can make some interesting speculations, we really don't know very well why inequality has increased' (Krugman, 1994: 145–50). The implication of this statement is that Krugman is awaiting some incontrovertible form of explanation; until such is found, all that is left is speculation. This betrays a narrow and positivist view of what constitutes causal explanation and greatly restricts the possibilities of explanation, insight and conceptual innovation offered by the social sciences.

Elaborating a theoretical framework therefore requires devoting careful attention to the elements and dimensions that constitute it. The nature of the subject being studied suggests the following. The first is that the dominant disciplinary boundaries in the social sciences weaken the potential of any one discipline to provide adequate explanatory tools for a subject that, by definition, straddles such disciplines as economics, political science, sociology, development theory and political economy. Therefore a multidisciplinary theoretical framework is needed, one which can combine some of the rigorous problem-solving and quantifying approaches of these disciplines with broader explanatory power. The theoretical framework needs to be able not just to examine the nature and extent of economic change in Ireland but to link this in a robust way with social outcomes, identifying in a detailed and rigorous way how the former is shaping the latter.

Related to multidisciplinarity is a second element derived from the distinction between problem-solving theory and critical theory. As explained by Robert Cox, problem-solving theory takes the world as given and is concerned with specific reforms aimed at the maintenance of existing structures; critical theory, on the other hand, is concerned with how the existing order came into being and how to change it. Political science and economics are examples of the application of problem-solving theory since they take as their starting point some fixed assumptions about the framework or parameters within which action takes place (the political system or the market). Political economy, by distinction, is not simply another problem-solving theory concerned with the interrelatedness between politics and economics but is rather 'concerned with the historically constituted frameworks or structures within which political and economic activity takes place. It stands back from the apparent fixity of the present to ask how the existing structures came into being and how they may be changing, or how they may be induced to change. In this sense, political economy is critical theory' (Cox, 1995: 32). Cox acknowledges the strengths of problem-solving theories as being their ability to set limits to a particular problem area with the result that the problem can be reduced to a limited number of variables amenable to relatively close and precise examination. Thus statements of laws or regularities can be arrived at which appear to have a general validity. However, he points out that the assumption of fixity on which these strengths depend is merely a convenience of method and rests on a false premise since social reality is in constant multidimensional flux. Furthermore, its claim to be value-free, though correct in a methodological sense since it treats the variables it considers as objects, is belied by a conservative bias inherent in its positing of a fixed order as a fundamental point of reference. For, as Cox puts it, since its aim is to solve the problems arising in various parts of a complex whole in order to smooth the functioning of the whole, it 'can be represented, within the broader perspective of critical theory, as serving particular national, sectional, or class interests, which are comfortable within the given order' (Cox, 1996: 87–91).

By contrast, critical theory is directed towards an appraisal of the very framework which problem-solving theory accepts as given. It is directed to the social and political complex as a whole rather than to its constituent parts. Like problem-solving theory, it is interested in the practical problems of the real world and takes as its starting point some particular aspect of human activity. Unlike problem-solving theory, it does not then further limit and sub-divide the problem to be dealt with; rather critical theory 'leads toward the construction of a larger picture of the whole of which the initially contemplated part is just one component, and seeks to understand the processes of change in which both parts and whole are involved'. It therefore approaches the resolution of practical problems from a perspective which transcends the prevailing order that problem-solving theory accepts as given and it allows for a normative choice in favour of an alternative social order. However, its range of choice of alternative orders is limited to those that are feasible and one of its concerns is to clarify the range of possible alternatives. 'In this way critical theory can be a guide to strategic action for bringing about an alternative order, whereas problem-solving theory is a guide to tactical actions which, intended or unintended, sustain the existing order' (Cox, 1996a: 87–91).

The reference to critical theory requires a third dimension to the theoretical framework, namely that it be normative. This is a dimension with which the social sciences have tended to feel uneasy since it appears to introduce subjective elements into a science that seeks to be impartial and objective. This unease derives from the attempt to make the social sciences replicate the natural sciences as much as possible in their search for objective and generalisable laws and theories. Since the Kuhnian revolution, however, with its argument that the natural sciences themselves are based on paradigms that rest on complex sets of assumptions, the role of values in scientific theorising has had to be addressed. This is particularly true in social science theorising where values intimately inform differences in theoretical perspectives. The theoretical framework for this study therefore seeks to acknowledge this and to adopt approaches that incorporate in an explicit way normative dimensions. As has already been argued, most studies of the Celtic Tiger (with the exception of those based on dependency and Marxist theoretical approaches) neglect explicit consideration of the social objectives of economic growth or of what constitutes development and lack the structural focus to probe and uncover fundamental weaknesses of the model being followed.

Theoretical contributions

Having specified three elements or dimensions that are essential to the theoretical framework for this study, we can now turn to the task of elaborating this framework through specifying contributions from different disciplinary areas, literatures and theorists.

Contributions from development theory

Development theory is chosen as a starting point since both in its self-understanding and in its subject matter it comes closest to offering a theoretical approach which addresses the concerns of this study. Thus, it sees itself as taking a multidisciplinary approach, is concerned not just with problem solving but with wider social transformation and takes an explicitly normative view based on its understanding of what constitutes development. Its concern with broad processes of social change means that it has devoted extensive attention to the links between economic growth and social equality.

Development theory was first elaborated in the years after World War II to explain the problems of what were beginning to be defined as 'underdeveloped countries'. Though heavily influenced by the context in which it arose and developed (both by the geographical regions which were regarded as the areas of its analysis and application, and by the ideological climate of the times), development theory is now seeking a new lease of life and is being applied to the development problems of areas like Europe. For example, Hettne argues that some of the insights arrived at by development theory as it studied the problems of the so-called 'Third World' have relevance to the development problems now facing Europe, both east and west (1995: 206–48).

The first contribution development theory can make is its multidisciplinarity. Amid the mono-disciplinary approaches that dominate Irish social scientific analyses, development theory provides an approach that is holistic, combining economic, social, political and cultural dimensions in the search for a more adequate explanatory framework. Its second strength is its concern for development which offers a locus from which to criticise dominant theoretical approaches to economic and social progress. As Leys puts it, there is 'an urgent need to revive development theory, not as a branch of policy-oriented social science within the parameters of an unquestioned capitalist world order, but as a field of critical enquiry about the contemporary dynamics of that order itself, with imperative policy implications for the survival of civilised and decent life, and not just in the ex-colonial countries' (Leys, 1996: 56). Development theory can therefore be described as a form of critical theory.

Development theory, however, is also marked by weaknesses that limit its usefulness for this study. Firstly, it remains constrained by its focus on the nation state which limits its ability to theorise both extra-state processes, particularly those associated with globalisation, and intra-state processes through which changing correlations of market, state and society can influence developmental outcomes. A second weakness derives from the 'impasse' in development theory as the twin grand paradigms that had dominated its formative years – modernisation theory and dependency theory – have lost both their explanatory and their prescriptive power. This has resulted in a concentration on empirical studies of development, but the fear is that the field is losing its distinctive theoretical core (Booth 1994: 12; Hoogvelt, 1997: x–xi). Related to this is its failure to generate an adequate theory of social change, particularly its difficulty in dealing in a nuanced and multifaceted way with the actor–structure relationship. One result of this is that development theory proved poor at predicting development in the Third World, both the successes and the many failures.

The weaknesses in development theory prompt a turn to political economy, following the example of development theorists such as Hoogvelt and Hettne. However the contribution to this study of one particular literature associated with development studies is briefly outlined before turning to political economy.

Contributions from 'Growth with Equity' literature

Since, as has been argued in Chapter 3, the concept of equality emerged as a means through which to identify the social impact of economic growth and, in the Irish case, as a fundamental weakness of the development model being followed, the development literature on 'Growth with Equity'[2] provides a wider theoretical framework through which to understand the links. Three phases in this literature can be identified:

The Kuznets curve hypothesis

An early hypothesis about the link between economic growth and social equality was that proposed by US economist, Simon Kuznets, in 1955 and was subsequently known as the Kuznets curve. Kuznets was very tentative in advancing this hypothesis writing that his paper was 'perhaps 5 per cent empirical information and 95 per cent speculation' (Kuznets, 1955: 26), yet his hypothesis dominated development literature on the subject for at least two decades, and up to the mid-1990s empirical studies were still finding evidence to corroborate it. Examining the experience of the UK, the US and Germany in the early phases of their industrialisation, Kuznets likened to a inverted U the pattern of inequality as it widened in the early phases of economic growth when the transition from pre-industrial to industrial society was most rapid, then stabilised for a while before narrowing in the later phases (Kuznets, 1955: 18).

Subsequent empirical studies of a large number of developing countries found evidence to substantiate Kuznets' hypothesis (for a survey, see Lecaillon et al., 1984: 7–22). Within the relationship between growth and inequality specified by the Kuznets curve, policy measures were identified which might help offset the tendency for the benefits of growth to be concentrated in the early stages. This approach came to be known as 'Redistribution with

Growth' after a celebrated study of the same name (Chenery et al., 1974). Some went further than Kuznets: in a widely referenced study, Adelman and Morris (1973) admitted to be shocked by their results which found that 'the process of economic modernization shifts the income distribution in favour of the middle class and upper income groups and against lower income groups. Since levels of industrial development and agricultural productivity show a similar U-shaped relationship to the income shares of the poorest groups, the dynamics of economic development appear to work against the poor' (Adelman and Morris, 1973: 188). As Birdsall put it, the conventional wisdom in this first phase of the literature saw a trade-off between augmenting growth and reducing inequality (Birdsall et al., 1995: 477).

Identifying how growth can be egalitarian

From the early 1980s, the validity of the Kuznets curve hypothesis began to be questioned. Fields, surveying a range of studies, stated that the evidence shows no tendency for inequality to increase or decrease systematically with economic growth nor is there a tendency for inequality to increase more in the early stages of economic development than in the later stages (Fields, 1989: 170–6). He concluded: 'This suggests that the decisive factor in determining whether inequality increases or decreases is not the rate of economic growth but rather the kind of growth' (1989: 177). A more recent survey of the literature which also examined new cross-country data similarly concluded: 'Effects of growth on inequality can go either way and are contingent on a number of other factors' (Bruno et al., 1996: 21). Studies of the East Asian miracle helped identify what some of these factors might be. Birdsall et al. summed it up as follows: 'Our argument is straightforward: policies that reduced poverty and income inequality, such as emphasizing basic education and augmenting labour demand, also stimulated growth. Moreover, low levels of income inequality may have stimulated growth' (Birdsall et al., 1995: 478). A virtuous circle was identified through which growth and equality become mutually reinforcing.

Growth and human development

The literature on economic growth and human development is associated with the work of the United Nations Development Programme (UNDP) and, in particular, that agency's annual Human Development Report. Human development has been defined by the UNDP as 'a process of enlarging people's choices' in a way that enables them 'to enjoy long, healthy and creative lives'. It has two sides: the formation of human capabilities and the use people make of their acquired capabilities (UNDP, 1990: 9, 10). Working with this concept, various studies have sought to specify the elements which link economic growth to human development. Ramirez et al. (1997) describe what they call 'the two chains' linking them (1). Thus, economic growth will lead to human development by fostering equality in income distribution, more female education, higher levels of priority social expenditure, and a more effective contribution of social capital, including community organisations and NGOs (7). Human development will aid economic growth through attuning education to the needs of the economy, higher levels of investment, more appropriate technology and better economic policy setting (14). The strength or weakness of these chains can result in virtuous, vicious or lop-sided development, according to Ramirez, Ranis and Stewart, and they categorise the development experience of up to 67 developing countries between 1960 and 1992 according to these categories (30–1).

Pieterse is critical of the human development approach, arguing that it 'does not challenge neo-liberalism and the principle of competitiveness but endorses and feeds it'; thus it 'may enable development business-as-usual to carry on more competitively under a general "humane" aura' (Nederveen Pieterse, 1997: 138). He contends that human development 'follows the *human capital* argument which is part of the paradigm of neoclassical economics' and that 'in assuming the *individual* as the unit of human development', it 'shows its intellectual roots are in liberalism' (Nederveen Pieterse, 1997: 137; emphasis in original). His central concern seems to be that, in merging market and social concerns, human development does not specify on whose terms these are to be merged. Since it does not challenge but rather goes along with market logic, it does not address the problem of the unregulated market in a principled way (137). These concerns raise again the issue of the relationship between state and market, already raised in Chapter 5 and are best addressed through a theoretical framework derived from political economy.

Contributions from political economy

Political economy has been defined as dealing with 'the interaction between economics and politics' (Lane and Ersson, 1997: 1). However, different schools of political economy conceptualise these interactions in very different ways which makes the term a very broad one. Following R. J. Barry Jones (1988), we can say that the realist or mercantilist school of political economy sees the political as having dominance over the economic whereas in both liberal and Marxist schools, the economic is viewed as predominant with the political subordinate to or determined by the economic (9–10). Despite these divergent beliefs, the essence of political economy lies in exploring their interconnections (Crane and Amawi, 1997: 4). It is, therefore, more than an amalgam of two traditional and well-established disciplinary approaches. Rather, as Crane and Amawi make clear, 'the endeavour of political economy is a critique of the scope and methods of both economics and political science' (4); what it attempts is a new synthesis of these two approaches. Cox's definition of political economy as critical theory, as outlined earlier, is an example of this.

A central contribution which political economy has to make to this study, then, is what Strange calls its 'close attention to the role of power in economic life', something found lacking in many studies of the Celtic Tiger, a lack that meant they failed to see the weaknesses of the reliance on private market forces that proved the principal cause of its downfall in 2008. She describes it as follows: 'It is power that determines the relationship between authority and market. Markets cannot play a dominant role in the way in which a political economy functions unless allowed to do so by whoever wields power and possesses authority. The difference between a private-enterprise, market-based economy and a state-run, command-based economy lies not only in the amount of freedom given by authority to the market operators, but also in the context within which the market functions. And the context, too, reflects a certain distribution of power. Whether it is a secure or an insecure context, whether it is stable or unstable, booming or depressed, reflects a series of decisions taken by those with authority. Thus it is not only the direct power of authority over markets that matters; it is also the indirect effect of authority on the context or surrounding conditions within which the market functions' (Strange, 1994: 23). In this way, therefore, political economy provides theoretical tools better able to address the relationship of actor and structure, particularly in the context of the relationship of state and market, as illustrated in Chapter 8 of this book.

Another contribution of political economy derives from its concern for the social impact of economic growth and transformation, a central focus of this study. Insights from the work of Karl Polanyi are especially pertinent since they provide a more critical understanding of the relationship of the market to society than the benign understanding that pervades the literature on the Celtic Tiger.

Contributions from Karl Polanyi

The subject of Polanyi's classic work (1944) deals with the stresses and strains generated by 'the conflict between the market and the elementary requirements of an organized social life' (2001: 257). While his analysis deals with nineteenth century Britain, it does, as Cox recognises, bear great similarities to today's world where 'the market appears to be bursting free from the bonds of national societies, to subject global society to its laws' resulting in 'greater polarization of rich and poor, disintegration of pre-existing social bonds, and alienation' (Cox, 1995: 39). Furthermore, as Hoogvelt has noted, even those political forces which for most of the last century have provided the principal critiques of the market economy, have now come to accept it: '[S]ocialist and social-democratic arguments for emancipation and universalist provision *perforce* do so on the basis of an a priori determining position of the economy. They take the formal market economy as a given, and they attempt to squeeze the excluded back into it' (1997: 243, emphasis in original). In this context, Polanyi's critique of the self-regulating market, a system invested by its supporters 'with almost mythical faculties' he writes (2001: 31), is full of contemporary relevance.

For Polanyi, the conflict between market and social life provided the dynamic of nineteenth-century society and produced the stresses and strains that ultimately destroyed it (2001: 257). His research into the economic systems of earlier societies convinced him of the falsity of the belief which informed classical economics, namely that a self-regulating market economy based on self-interest was a natural institution which 'would spontaneously arise if only men were let alone' (257–8). He goes on: 'The tendency to barter, on which Adam Smith so confidently relied for his picture of primitive man, is not a common tendency of the human being in his economic activities, but a most infrequent one. ... Economic history reveals that the emergence of national markets was in no way the result of the gradual and spontaneous emancipation of the economic sphere from governmental control. On the contrary, the market has been the outcome of a conscious and often violent intervention on the part of government which imposed the market organization on society for noneconomic ends' (258). Polanyi concludes that, in all previous societies, 'markets were hedged around by a number of safeguards designed to protect the prevailing organisation of society from interference on the part of market practices' (65).

Central to the functioning of the self-regulating market economy was the elevation of gain into a key principle. 'All types of societies are limited by economic factors,' writes Polanyi. 'Nineteenth century civilization alone was economic in a different and distinctive sense, for it chose to base itself on a motive only rarely acknowledged as valid in the history of human societies, and certainly never before raised to the level of a justification of action and behaviour in everyday life, namely, gain. The self-regulating market system was uniquely derived from this principle' (31). This led to a presumption that economic interests were the dominant motivating factors for individuals. Based on his research, however, Polanyi argued that other factors were uppermost in motivating people's behaviour: '[E]ven where money values were involved, they were secondary to other interests. Almost invariably professional status, safety and security, the form of a man's life, the breadth of his existence, the stability of his environment were in question' (161). Too narrow a conception of human interest must lead to 'a warped vision of social and political history', Polanyi wrote. An example of this warped vision can be identified in the work of those who argued that statistics showed people's standard of living had actually increased in the Industrial Revolution. Polanyi vehemently disagreed that this implied an improvement in these people's welfare; for him 'a social calamity is primarily a cultural not an economic phenomenon that can be measured by income figures or population statistics' (164). He went on: 'Not economic exploitation, as often assumed, but the disintegration of the cultural environment of the victim is then the cause of the degradation. The economic process may, naturally, supply the vehicle of the destruction, and almost invariably economic inferiority will make the weaker yield, but the immediate cause of his undoing is not for that reason economic; it lies in the lethal injury to the institutions in which his social existence is embodied. The result is loss of self-respect and standards, whether the unit is a people or a class, whether the process springs from so-called "culture conflict" or from a change in the position of a class within the confines of a society' (164). These considerations raise important questions about the impact of market processes on social well-being which have obvious relevance to theorising the Celtic Tiger and its sustainability.

Polanyi identified a 'countermovement' (136) or 'double movement' (157) in society in reaction against the destructive inroads of market forces. He wrote that this was more than the usual defensive behaviour of a society faced with change but rather 'a reaction against a dislocation which attacked the fabric of society, and which would have destroyed the very organization of production that the market had called into being' (136). It manifested itself in an array of social legislations in regard to public health, factory conditions, social insurance, public utilities and so on. He invested great significance in this countermovement, though he recognised that it happened in a spontaneous, undirected way and was motivated by a pragmatic spirit (147). Defending the measures of social protection against the attacks by economic liberals who saw them as thwarting the benefits of the free market, Polanyi saw them as a naturally occurring self-regulating mechanism for the protection of society. This idea of a double movement by which society seeks to defend itself against the disintegrating impact of market forces is actively invoked by today's theorists of globalisation (Inayatullah and Blaney, 1999; Birchfield, 1999).

Box 6.1 Begg on Polanyi and the collapse of the Celtic Tiger

Amid the collapse of the Celtic Tiger in late 2008, the general secretary of the Irish Congress of Trade Unions and Ireland's leading trade unionist, David Begg, wrote an article in *The Irish Times* drawing attention to the relevance of the work of Karl Polanyi for the crisis that was breaking. He wrote that 'Polanyi's great attraction lies in his concern to advance both freedom and social justice. He believes that allowing the market to control the economic system was a fundamental error because it meant no less than the running of society as an adjunct to the market. Instead of economy being embedded in social relations, social relations are then embedded in the economic system.'

Begg sees the most obvious manifestation of this Polanyian insight as being the treatment of labour as a commodity. 'Polanyi points out that human beings are not a product made for sale. Nevertheless, upon the fiction that labour is a commodity is the whole market system organised. It is therefore based on a lie.' Turning to the present crisis, he writes that 'under the pressure of globalisation, Europe has been moving in the direction of the US model and, in truth, Ireland and Britain are part of that Anglo-Saxon construct. But the events of recent times require us all to reconsider. The problem we have to transcend is that many intelligent people have put their faith in the idea of self-regulating markets as piously as others put their trust in God. Now that this god has failed, perhaps people will have the freedom to see things more clearly again, reclaim responsibility and organise the future in more promising terms.'

David Begg, general secretary,
Irish Congress of Trade Unions (2008)

Contributions from international political economy

Political economy also offers the prospect of redressing the other major weakness identified in development theory, namely the lack of a more adequate theoretical framework for considering the links between the global, the national and the local. In this context the contribution of International Political Economy (IPE) is especially relevant.

The internationalisation of the world economy over the last 30 years has seen the emergence of IPE as a discipline in its own right with a number of well-recognised contending perspectives – the liberal, the Marxist and the statist (Frieden and Lake, 1995: 1,5, 10–13). Though it has focused primarily on activities between international actors such as states, multinational corporations, international organisations and social movements, it is 'currently undergoing something of a renaissance' as, in the context of globalisation, it is being seen as 'pivotal to any contemporary analysis of processes of social, political and economic change (whether global, regional, international, national or local in scope and scale)' (Hay and Marsh, 1999: 5, 14).

This study situates itself within what has been called 'the new International Political Economy' (Murphy and Tooze, 1991) rather than within any of the schools into which the discipline has traditionally been divided. Murphy and Tooze identify three ways in which the new IPE deviates from the orthodox perspective on theory and methodology: firstly, through its willingness to recognise and confront the necessary subjectivity of the social sciences; secondly, through its openness to a wide variety of forms of historical and social explanation and their combination rather than resorting to explaining everything in terms of the rational egotistical action of some axiomatic individuals; and, thirdly, through examining the explanatory frameworks in their own terms rather than forcing them into the tripartite divisions of the discipline (6). For these authors, 'the positivist epistemological basis of

IPE' (22) resulted in the privileging of certain issues (free trade, the interests of the US in the global economy) and the exclusion of others (poverty, inequality and social exclusion). They point to the irony that a discipline which has, in its mainstream liberal school, purported to derive its priorities from the concerns of Adam Smith (for example, a free trading system) has given far less priority to 'Smith's ultimate concern – fostering human dignity and the ethical life' (27). As a result, they conclude that 'orthodox IPE can say very little more than common sense can about the primary questions about the global political economy raised by most people – questions of dependency, fundamental insecurity, powerlessness, and, above all, the question of how to identify opportunities for fundamental change' (27).

The theoretical work of Robert Cox is seen by some as making a major contribution to this 'new IPE'. Hoogvelt writes that Cox has 'managed to synthesise and transcend the neo-realist and neo-Marxist approaches, re-integrate the separate subfields of international economic relations and strategic studies, and overcome the structure/agency dichotomy. Indeed, for a growing number of scholars in the field Robert Cox has become the founding father of a new international political economy' (Hoogvelt, 1997: 10). His work contributes in a number of ways to the theoretical framework for this study.

Contributions from Robert Cox

One contribution of Cox derives from his understanding of the nature of the global economy and its impact on the local. This helps identify mechanisms generating social inequality at local level. For Cox, central to the changes in the global economy is the internationalisation of production. This has resulted in a cleavage in the populations of nation states throughout the world between those most directly linked to the global networks of production who are in well-paid and relatively secure employment and those more linked to the local economy who are mostly poorly paid and in insecure employment. By and large the salaried middle classes have fared relatively poorly as have the peasantry, while increasing numbers of people, often migrants from the countryside, are eking out a living in the informal economy. This global social reality resulting from the restructuring of production has changed the core/periphery cleavages in the world economy from ones which primarily related to geographical location ('First/Third World') to ones now also describing social relations within national economies. 'The new production organizations have a relatively small core of permanent employees, and a larger number of peripheral employees whose relationship to the production network is more precarious. Moreover, this peripheral body of employees is fragmented (segmented is the word more commonly used by labour economists) into distinct groups separated by location, by ethnicity, and by gender. One obvious result has been the weakening of the cohesion and power of the labour movement' (Cox, 1995: 40).

Other consequences of the internationalisation of production are pertinent for this study. One is its effects on the nation state as the new capitalism has revived in a more rigorous form the distinction between the economic and the political and seeks to protect the economic sphere from political intervention. 'By and large, the state is conceived as subordinate to the economy. Competitiveness in the global economy is the ultimate criterion of public policy' (Cox, 1996b: 529). From this subordination of the state to the demands of the market comes a growing disenchantment with politics, particularly among the most marginalised. 'By removing the economic sphere from political control – whether this is achieved by law or by ideology – what determines the condition of people in their everyday lives is removed from their control. Politics becomes irrelevant. The sense of civic efficacy is removed, and many people, the most disadvantaged, are left in the futility of alienation. Their rage is unchanneled, ineffective, self-consuming. It marks an impasse. It does not herald the construction of a future' (533).

Cox's work also deepens our understanding of how social change happens and does this in two ways. The first is his concept of historical structure. Derived from Gramsci's notion of hegemony, namely the fit between ideas, power and institutions that provides stability to a particular class-dominated capitalist social order, Cox develops this concept to explain stability in international relations at any particular historical juncture (1996a: 91–116). He argues that the dominance of a powerful state is not sufficient to explain the particular form this international stability took (for example, the dominance of US power in the post-war period was not strong enough to ensure a stable world order). Instead three categories of forces interact – material capabilities such as forms of production, ideas which reinforce the prevailing structure of power or open possibilities for challenging it, and institutions such as states which stabilise and perpetuate a particular order. Each of these three interact in such a way as to impose pressures and constraints on the action of individuals and groups without however determining them; thus individuals and groups may move with these pressures or resist them but they cannot fail to take them into account. While the particular form of hegemony that may result from the interaction of these forces may never be clearly predicted, this conceptualisation offers a way of identifying how change happens. New forms of production (such as the internationalisation of production) lead to changes in social forces and in the institutions through which the prevailing power relations are expressed and organised. On the basis of this, one can speculate about the likely form of world order that might result from these changes.

Cox's second contribution to understanding social change derives from his distinction between a synchronic view of reality and a diachronic view. The first, concentrating on the entities and relationships that are the key to understanding what happens in a particular sector of human activity at a particular historical juncture, have been fairly well captured by social science, he writes (1995: 34–5). However, the problem of structural change, what he calls the diachronic dimension, has been less well dealt with. Cox outlines three approaches to social change: the first is to take the dominant tendencies in the present and project them into the future, the second is to deny that change can be understood so that one is left with a disconnected sequence of events, the third is historical dialectic. For Cox, each historical structure contains both coherence and elements of contradiction or conflict. Structural transformation comes from these points of conflict.

The different theoretical contributions outlined in this chapter can be drawn together under the rubric of an International Political Economy of Development.

Towards an International Political Economy of Development

This chapter has elaborated theoretical approaches to understanding development and social change that address the major weaknesses identified in the social science literature on the Celtic Tiger. It has argued that this requires a normative, multidisciplinary and critical theoretical approach which pays special attention to the role of power in economic life and how this serves to establish a particular relationship between market, state and society. It draws widely on literature from a range of social science disciplines such as sociology, economics, political science, cultural studies, anthropology, political economy, development studies and geography to offer as full an insight as possible into the nature and developmental impact of the Celtic Tiger. For, as Ragin puts it: 'By looking for similarities in unexpected places, social researchers develop new insights that advance theoretical thinking' (Ragin, 1994: 85). The concern with development ensures that this market–state–society relationship is interrogated in terms of its impact on social well-being. Situating this study within international political economy helps to overcome the parochialism that characterises much of the Celtic Tiger literature and seeks to offer a more critical and well-grounded understanding of how the Irish case is a particular response to the challenges of globalisation. Finally, drawing on theories of social change from Polanyi and Cox permits a wider historical approach to be taken towards the longer-term trajectory of Irish development, avoiding the static, self-congratulatory, end-of-history quality of a lot of the Celtic Tiger literature. By combining the inductive empirical approach of positivist social science with the deductive theorising of the grand theorists, the International Political Economy of Development can be seen as contributing 'to a revival of the classical tradition of a unified historical social science' (Hettne, 1995: xiii).[3]

Part III Ireland's Political Economy

7
State: Developmental or Competition?

> Contemporary Ireland is an exemplar of the competition state, where social policy is subordinated to the needs of the economy.
>
> Nigel Boyle (2005: 16)

The purpose of this book is to explain the weaknesses of the Irish model. Chapters 4 and 5 have surveyed the principal theoretical approaches to analysing that model and identified their limitations. For the dominant readings, these limitations relate to the narrow and fragmented focus of much of the economic and sociological analyses and the utilitarian and individualist assumptions that inform them, particularly in terms of the relationship of the economy to society. As was argued in Chapter 5, the critical readings offer a broader and more satisfactory examination that overcomes many of these limitations; yet weaknesses remain in terms of the theorisation of the nature and role of the state, of the understanding of the productive economy that informs some, though not all, of the works covered, and the causal connections between state and market on the one hand and social outcomes on the other. Chapter 6 has outlined a theoretical approach that seeks to overcome these limitations, with a particular focus on making explicit the bases for theorising the relationship between political economy configurations (namely how state and market interrelate) and processes of egalitarian social development, in the context of today's more globalised world in which the national and the international interpenetrate one another.

This Part contains three chapters that develop an analysis of the distinctive nature of the Irish model. As was stated in Chapter 6 quoting Susan Strange, close attention has to be paid to the role of power in economic life and how political authority both configures markets (through the nature of regulation and taxation, for example) but also creates the context or surrounding conditions in which the market functions. Because of this, Part III begins with a chapter on the nature of the Irish state as it has both moulded the market and, in turn, been itself reconfigured by its relationship with the market over the course of the Celtic Tiger. Chapter 8 then turns to the kind of market economy that has developed out of this interrelationship of political and economic power. The final chapter in this Part examines how this distinctive Irish political economy configuration shapes social outcomes and the nature of civil society. This chapter on the Irish state takes as its central focus the lively debate between those who argue that the Irish state is an example of a new kind of developmental state, overcoming key limitations of the East Asian developmental state, and those who argue that it is a competition state. Before it gets to this debate, the chapter opens by examining briefly the historical neglect of the state in the Irish social sciences and the lack of debates on characterising what kind of state it is. It then examines the one characterisation of the state that was developed, namely Ireland as a welfare state, identifying the distinctive features that distinguish it from other welfare states. The following section examines the characterisation of Ireland as a developmental state before going on in the subsequent section to report the argument that Ireland is, instead, a competition state. The final section identifies the key differences at issue between both characterisations and offers a way of understanding the Irish state that largely overcomes them. Conclusions then are drawn about the role of the state in Ireland's development.

Characterising the Irish state

Few Irish social scientists would disagree with the assertion that, in the Irish case, 'the state has been deeply implicated in the entire process of managing both economic development and the welfare state' (Ó Riain and O'Connell, 2000: 310). Based on this, as was stated in the Introduction, claims have been made that 'the Irish growth experience and its distributional consequences is not a simple story of globalisation, forced withdrawal of the state and the promotion of neo-liberalism' (Nolan et al., 2000: 1). Indeed, 'it has been widely argued that a central ingredient of this success was the role of the state in various guises' (Adshead et al., 2008: 1). Yet, as O'Donnell states, 'there has been, in fact, a remarkable scarcity of detailed empirical research on particular parts of the Irish state and public policy, compared with, say, work on elections and political culture' (O'Donnell, 2008: 79). As recently as 1990, a groundbreaking study of the Irish state concluded that 'the state's capacity – so formidable on paper – on closer inspection proves to be illusory' (Breen et al., 1990: 213). How this state suddenly in the course of a few short years came to have such formidable capacity to develop a model that made Ireland a leading example of developmental success only came to be addressed towards the end of the Celtic Tiger period (see Ó Riain, 2004).

Therefore, it is only very recently that sustained attention has been devoted to analysing the nature of the Irish state. Not all analysts are convinced that this is a useful exercise. For example, O'Donnell is sceptical of efforts to characterise states, seeing in it echoes of Marxist theory and politics in the inter-war period when much hung on whether a particular state was characterised as socialist, imperialist or fascist. 'Nothing equivalent hangs on our current characterisations and we might indulge ourselves (and mislead ourselves) if we use descriptions in such a categorical way' (O'Donnell, 2008: 74). In her examination of the Irish political economy, Smith finds it impossible to characterise the Irish state as she finds both 'strong tendencies towards prioritising economic competitiveness' but also some distributive and developmental tendencies (Smith, 2005: 120). She therefore concludes that Irish state policy has entailed elements of both the developmental and the competitive. O'Donnell agrees with Smith that what are being examined are dimensions of the Irish state in which one can identify tendencies and counter-tendencies.

In keeping with his preference for examining dimensions of the state, O'Donnell focuses on Ireland as a 'partnership state' since, in his view, social partnership has played a key role in helping Ireland adjust successfully to the challenges of policymaking in the context of today's globalisation. Taking into account the growing complexity of governance, he sees the partnership state as developing a shared understanding among a wide range of social partners through analysis and dialogue, as facilitating new forms of relationship between the national state and those affected by policy such as policy entrepreneurship, promoting joint action between social interests and supporting interest-group formation, and as placing a new relationship between policymaking, implementation and monitoring at the centre of policy development. He sees the partnership state as being 'characterised by a problem-solving approach designed to promote consensus' (O'Donnell, 2008: 78). Central to the challenge of the partnership state is developing a consistency between three broad types of policy – macro-economic, distributional and structural or supply-side. For O'Donnell, therefore, the 'partnership state' is not so much a type of state as a set of relationships between various actors, both state actors among themselves and state actors with actors outside the state. As he writes, it 'should be viewed as a practical project, with all the complexity and ambiguity that characterises collective experimentation, rather than as a theoretical entity' (ibid.: 98).

Something closer to a characterisation of the state is O'Connor's 'Irish patriarchal state' (O'Connor, 2008). She argues that state theory has privileged the relationship between state and class while ignoring 'the gender of those involved in the state structures or the gendered implications of state policies' (O'Connor, 2008: 143). She goes on to examine three dimensions of the Irish patriarchal state – the gender composition of its administrative, executive and corporatist structures, its policies and discourses related to gender (such as gender policies, social welfare and childcare and economic growth), and its 'crisis tendencies and contradictions' (ibid.) such as the decline of religion and the rise in women's educational levels that allow new political possibilities to emerge. She concludes: 'Despite rapid and fundamental social change, continuity rather than change is the dominant motif of the Irish patriarchal state to date' and she notes 'the effective weakness of the Irish state in challenging those in hegemonic positions' (ibid.: 162–4). While a major contribution to our understanding of the Irish state, and undoubtedly a characterisation of that state, O'Connor's Irish patriarchal state refers to the gendered nature of power and does not touch centrally on the political economic nature of the power of the Irish state, namely the power configurations that structure the relations of state, market and society in the Irish case.

The importance of characterising the Irish state derives from the need to understand the central logic of the Irish model of development. The problem with O'Donnell and Smith's accounts is that they fail to recognise that a central logic characterises the core actions of the state, even if that central logic is not consistently or effectively applied in all the actions of the state (either through ideological contests within the bureaucracy or through inefficiency in the state's capacity). In other words, what are the overriding logics that guide state policy and that help determine options when choices have to be made between different objectives? The importance of seeking to characterise a state derives from the need to search out and identify this central logic as it manifests itself in the actions of the state. Furthermore, this central logic also manifests what political actors and the political system perceive as the constraints and opportunities of the wider international context in which the state operates, in this case deriving from perceptions of globalisation. In other words, what is important to identify is how the domestic political system and bureaucracy understands, filters and responds to the constraints and opportunities of globalisation. While O'Donnell is sceptical of the task of characterisation, it should be remembered that the characterisation of 'welfare state' became broadly accepted during the era of national capitalism. Though there were many varieties of welfare state, they could all be seen as responses by particular national political systems and cultures to the opportunities and constraints of the dominant international political economy context of the time. Our search for a characterisation of today's Irish state begins therefore by going back to the only characterisation of the Irish state that did become widely accepted before the Celtic Tiger era, namely the Irish state as a welfare state.

A welfare state?

In contrast to the universality of coverage which characterised the British welfare state in the post-war period, the Irish system has, in Cousins' words, 'remained essentially fragmented and showed little commitment to interclass solidarity' (Cousins, 1995: 20). One can conclude from the account of Breen et al. (1990) that the Irish welfare state was never intended to be redistributive and was inspired not by equality but by charity. In a characterisation of the Irish welfare state that has been widely quoted, O'Connell and Rottman describe it as 'a pay-related welfare state':

> Inequalities were neither eliminated nor even greatly abated. While all citizens may have come to have virtually equal entitlements to a comprehensive range of social rights, services and benefits, the interaction of those rights with market-generated inequalities generally results in the reproduction of inequality. What has evolved is a pay-related welfare state in which minimal levels of universal entitlement to income and services are supplemented by market-based resources. Thus, we argue that the expansion of the welfare state, and of social citizenship, was accomplished in such a manner as to leave privilege essentially undisturbed.
>
> (1992: 206)

Thus middle-class citizens can benefit from state spending on pensions, education or health care while supplementing this through their own private spending (224–5). The Irish welfare state has, therefore, proved ineffective in modifying in any significant way the inequalities generated by market forces and, indeed, may even have exacerbated them.

Unlike the British system where there were periods of fundamental reshaping of the system (the Beveridge and Fowler reforms), the Irish welfare system developed in an incremental and ad hoc nature, with new benefits being added as new needs became apparent. As O'Donoghue describes the Irish welfare system as a whole: '[The] process of temporary responses to particular problems in the system has resulted in one of the most complicated benefit systems in Europe. This level of complexity, besides the in-built poverty traps, causes itself negative behavioural disincentives' (O'Donoghue, 2003: 54). Murphy argues that there exists a 'path dependency of highly targeted ungenerous and inadequate payments' which 'may be an important explanatory factor in explaining recent Irish reform' since payments were already so low and targeted that there was no room or reason to reduce them even further as happened in other liberal welfare states as welfare was reformed into workfare (Murphy, 2006: 53). In terms of expenditure, around 60 per cent of the Irish state's social expenditure is funded out of general taxation while around 40 per cent is through social insurance. Around 25 per cent of social insurance contributions are paid by employers and 15 per cent by employees. Overall employer and employee contributions in Ireland in 1997 amounted to just 13.7 per cent of total taxation compared to an EU15 average of 26.7 per cent; by 2003 this had remained static in Ireland at 13.9 per cent but the EU15 figure had declined to 24 per cent. Timonen (2003: 46) concludes: 'In short, contributions play a considerably smaller part in financing the welfare state in Ireland than they do in other European countries.' Most of Ireland's social spending is funded from central taxes, and one can trace a growth in Ireland's total taxes from about 15 per cent of GNP in the mid-1950s to 39 per cent in 1987 before falling back throughout the 1990s to 35.5 per cent in 2003. However, as Table 7.1 shows, from having a tax take that was exactly the EU average in 1987, by 2003 Ireland was significantly below the EU15 average (Ireland's figure for GDP and for GNP is given as the latter is more comparable).

Table 7.1 Total tax as a percentage of GDP/GNP, 1987–2003

	1987	1991	1995	1999	2003
Ireland GDP	36	34.1	32.8	31.9	29.7
EU15	39.6	39.4	40.1	41.5	40.5
Ireland GNP	39.6	38.8	37	37.5	35.5

Source: O'Toole and Cahill (2006: 208).

In Ireland, expenditure on services has been among the lowest in the EU15 so that income transfers constitute a greater part of the Irish state's welfare effort (Timonen, 2003: 19). Overall, means-testing forms an important part of the Irish welfare state: throughout the 1990s the percentage of social benefits that were means-tested and paid out of general taxation fluctuated between 31 and 35 per cent whereas the EU average was around ten per cent. Social insurance has expanded substantially with coverage increasing from around 60 per cent of the workforce in 1955, to nearly 85 per cent in 1985 and it has continued to increase since then. However, in 1998 only 75 per cent of those covered were insured for all benefits while, generally, they consist of a flat rate benefit unrelated to previous earnings. The Irish welfare system therefore relies substantially on non-contributory benefits, many of them means-tested. Covering various contingencies, some not covered by social insurance (such as lone parenthood and low income if in work), the benefit system can be classified into four types of cash payments – out of work payments, in work benefits, universal child benefits and housing benefits with additional in-kind benefits such as butter vouchers, fuel allowances and free transport (O'Donoghue, 2003: 42–8).

How effective has this two-tier welfare state been in reducing poverty? One way of answering this question is through examining the adequacy of welfare payments for those in poverty. Tracing Irish replacement rates from 1955 to 2002, which is the ratio of the value of welfare payments to average earnings, O'Donoghue found that for single people it was 'quite low by European standards' fluctuating between 25 and 30 per cent for most of this period. For a married couple with two children, the rate moved from 57.3 per cent in 1987 to 53.4 per cent in 2002 (O'Donoghue, 2003: 49 and Table 4). Over a shorter time period, Walsh traced minimum welfare rates and the level of the state pension as a percentage of 60 per cent of median income (a widely used poverty line) from 1994 to 2005, as shown in Table 7.2. He correlates the rise in relative poverty, particularly the dramatic rise in poverty among the elderly at the height of the Celtic Tiger period, with the relative decline in these welfare payments.

Table 7.2 Welfare rates 1994–2005 (as percentage of 60% of median income)

	1994	1997	2001	2003	2005
Minimum welfare rate	70	62	56	68	77
State pension	72	64	63	78	86

Source: Walsh (2007: 31).

Another way of examining the effectiveness of Ireland's welfare state in reducing poverty is to place it in a comparative context. Table 7.3 shows the extent to which pensions and social transfers reduced the risk of poverty in Ireland and in the EU in 2000 and in 2006. This shows that Ireland lags well behind the EU average in its ability to reduce poverty.

Table 7.3 Effect of state transfers on reducing the risk of poverty, Ireland and EU, 2000 and 2006

	Ireland 2000	EU15 2000	Ireland 2006	EU25 2006
Initial risk of poverty rate	37	40	40	43
After pensions	31	23	33	26
After pensions and social transfers	20	15	18	16
Risk reduction	17	25	22	27

Source: CSO (2003: Table 5.6) and CSO (2008b: Table 4.4).

Data given by Smeeding and Nolan (2004) tell a similar story based on the Luxembourg Income Study (LIS). They compare market income (pre-tax and transfer) poverty with disposable income poverty, namely the poverty rate after taxes and transfers are factored into income. Seven western European countries plus the US and Canada are compared at dates from 1997 to 2000 (the Irish data are for 2000, the height of the boom). This finds that market income poverty in Ireland at 24.9 per cent is below the average of 26 per cent (reflecting a tight labour market) whereas post-transfer poverty is second highest in Ireland at 16.6 per cent, well below the average of 10.5 per cent and only just behind the US at 17 per cent. The authors comment: '[D]etailed analysis shows that higher levels of government spending (as in Scandinavia and Northern Europe) and more careful targeting of government transfers on the poor (as in Canada, Sweden and Finland) produce lower poverty rates' (Smeeding and Nolan, 2004: 16–17).

Box 7.1 Boyle on 'Europe's most anorexic welfare state'

When US political scientist, Nigel Boyle, came to Ireland to study its welfare policy, he was puzzled by the fact that Ireland's declining welfare effort at the height of the Celtic Tiger went hand in hand with spending around two per cent of GDP on active labour market measures, double the OECD average, putting it firmly in the league of the high-spending Nordic countries and the Netherlands (Boyle, 2005: 11). To find an answer to this paradox, he studied the state's labour market agency, FÁS (An Foras Áiseanna Saothair), which is unusual among such European agencies for the breadth of its responsibilities. Established in 1987 by the then Minister for Labour, Bertie Ahern (who was Taoiseach from 1997 to 2008), FÁS quickly established itself as an effective and influential agency of the Irish state. Through establishing its own channels of communication to the EU in Brussels and through convincing Irish officials that it could spend EU funds effectively, it succeeded in winning one-third of the total funds the state received in the first EU Delors funding round (1989–93) and a quarter in the second round (1994–9). As Boyle summed up its appeal: '[T]he Irish state quickly learned that it could address myriad problems cheaply and effectively by using FÁS. Other government departments and agencies became increasingly bypassed and FÁS became an all-purpose solution to various problems – the 'Swiss army-knife' of the Irish state' (71). ('The Swiss army-knife performs myriad functions, none of the well,' he writes (113).)

FÁS achieved its position not through any ideological programme (social democracy versus neo-liberalism) but, rather, through accommodating itself to the inherent clientelism of Irish politics. The support for its activities at local level in towns, cities and rural areas by constituents who benefited from its programmes, was immediately picked up on the antennae of Irish members of parliament (TDs) who provided a strong backing when it was criticised in academic and consultancy reports. For Irish politicians, the criticisms mattered not a bit when their supporters voiced active support. According to Boyle, 'FÁS is too useful to the Irish state as a source of relatively cheap and relatively effective solutions to problems, including the management of the social problems of the Tiger economy and the political consequence of high relative inequality' (110–11). He adds that an understanding of the nature and role of FÁS 'helps to resolve the riddle of why Europe's most anorexic welfare state coexists with a stable form of social partnership and a frozen policy discourse on social and educational policy' (115).

These data would indicate that even though welfare rates increased in Ireland from the mid-2000s, they are insufficient to improve the state's ability to reduce the country's risk of poverty. Significantly, in a study of what it would take to emulate in Ireland the success of the Danish and Dutch welfare system in reducing poverty, Callan et al. found that the differences in poverty outcomes between Ireland and those two continental countries could not be explained by differences in age profile, pattern of labour force participation and household composition but rather by levels of welfare effort. They estimated that the standard and top rates of Irish income tax would have to be raised by 11 percentage points (to 35 and 57 per cent, respectively, based on the then Irish rates) for Ireland to afford Danish and Dutch levels (Callan et al., 2004).

In the Irish case, much discussion has taken place of where Ireland stands in the typology of welfare states developed by Esping-Andersen (1990). While he places Ireland as part of the Anglo-Saxon 'new nations' together with Australia, the US, New Zealand, Canada and the UK, Cousins points out that subsequent references to Ireland in later chapters of the book place it in different clusters and he comments: 'The Irish welfare state is obviously a very moveable feast but not one which Esping-Andersen attempted to digest' (Cousins, 2005: 10). Cousins finds Esping-Andersen's typology problematic for a case like Ireland as it pays no attention to post-colonial peripheral countries that have been highly dependent in the global political economy. Cousins' discussion places Ireland in a group of Atlantic countries as it bears similarities to the British welfare state but also to southern European countries like Italy, Spain and Portugal sharing with the latter Catholicism and relatively late development (ibid.: 136–58). O'Shea and Kennelly similarly find problems with Esping-Andersen's typology and suggest that a classification developed by Alber based on two crucial sets of relationships in social care provision, one between church and state and the other between centre and periphery, is potentially a much more interesting framework for peripheral, post-colonial countries like Ireland (O'Shea and Kennelly, 2002: 57–63). Despite these valid criticisms of Esping-Andersen's typology, however, there is a widespread recognition in the Irish literature that Ireland is closest to the liberal model. For example, Murphy and Millar take issue with the NESC document on the developmental welfare state (see Box 7.2) since it argues that Ireland is a hybrid welfare state. They see this as 'confusing and unhelpful' since it 'obscures the reality of a failed welfare state, hides the role tax and social welfare policy plays in growing inequality and treats high levels of relative income poverty as less problematic than they really are' (Murphy and Millar, 2007: 83). While Ireland has been characterised as a welfare state, therefore, it has been a weak and fragmented one that has served to re-inforce privilege rather than overturn it.

A developmental state?

In the context of the widespread neglect of the Irish state by scholars, Ó Riain's argument that the Irish state constitutes a new form of developmental state

opened a significant new debate on the role of the state in Ireland's development (Ó Riain, 2000, 2004). This takes as its starting point the literature that
developed in the 1980s out of analyses of the role of the East Asian state in
that region's developmental success and which elaborated the concept of
the 'developmental state' (see Johnson, 1982; Amsden, 1989; Wade, 1990).
In applying the concept of 'embedded autonomy' taken from Evans (1995)
to the Irish state, Ó Riain initially characterised the Irish state as a 'flexible
developmental state' in contrast to the bureaucratic developmental states
of East Asia, arguing that this constitutes a new model of state-led development that is more responsive to the demands and pressures of globalisation
(Ó Riain, 2000). His later work slightly amended the concept to that of a
Developmental Network State (DNS) as 'network centrality is critical to
this new state – isolation from the local or the global renders it ineffective'
(Ó Riain, 2004: 4).

Ó Riain's starting point is that 'states and other institutions of governance do not simply "regulate" a system with its own logic but rather constantly structure and restructure capitalist social relations, even as they are
constrained by them'. Furthermore, 'forms of state developmentalism vary
enormously across time and space in their developmental strategies and
tactics, institutional and geopolitical foundations, social consequences, and
the ensuing political possibilities' (Ó Riain, 2004: 15). Since, as he writes,
'the developmental state is likely to emerge in different guises under varying *sociopolitical conditions* at different times and places', he identifies such
examples as the Northern European social democracies, the temporary
success of dependent development in Brazil, the East Asian miracle and
'the emergence of fast-growing economies such as Israel, Ireland and even
Taiwan in the 1990s' as examples of 'different types of developmental states'
(ibid.: 19; emphasis in original). In essence, he defines the developmental state as a state that fulfills the following: 'forging a collective strategy
for development despite inequalities and hierarchy in the international
economy, building institutions to pursue that strategy, and fostering self-
reproducing autocentric development through shaping the relationship
between the developmentalist coalition and the national and world-system
structures within which it is embedded' (20). For Ó Riain, this can take the
form of bureaucratic or network-state developmentalism. If, in the past,
developmental states relied heavily on state intervention in their attempts
to industrialise and for this reason he labels them bureaucratic, in the
contemporary era they can achieve their goals 'not by taking on the tasks
of development but rather by shaping the capabilities of society and the
market to do so' (23), and so the need to be much more flexible and devoted
to networking.

Ó Riain's definition of the developmental state is therefore multifaceted
and complex. It goes beyond Skocpol's definition of state capacity as the ability of the state to pursue and/or implement official goals (Skocpol, 1985: 9).

Such an understanding of capacity, namely the creation of institutions to make social transformation possible, forms only one part of Ó Riain's definition. Prior to the creation of institutions, the state must reshape the private self-interests of actors with resources so that they become part of a wider collective interest in national development. Furthermore, the institutions fashioned to promote this wider collective interest must be safeguarded against becoming beholden to private interests in society – it is in this context that Ó Riain adopts Evans' notion of embedded autonomy. Once achieved, these institutions serving a national developmental project are just the first step to ensuring a dynamic of autocentric development; this latter requires the reproduction of a sociopolitical coalition supporting development, a self-reinforcing dynamic or 'feedback loop' between the development of productive forces and such factors as the broad development of skills and learning capacity and wider processes of autonomous political, social and cultural development. Finally, the agility of the state in the face of constant change in the international system so that it can maintain its successful insertion is a final dimension of the developmental state. This conceptualisation of the state therefore embodies three different dimensions – the state's institutional capacity, the state's relationship to society and the various organised interest groups within it, and the state's relationship to the wider international context outside its national arena. All these need to be dynamically managed and developed if developmental transformation is to result.

Applying this to Ireland, Ó Riain bases his claim that the Irish state is developmental on the state's role in the transformation of the Irish economy in the 1990s. As he writes: 'A system of innovation emerged that supported relatively broad industrial upgrading and a particularly dynamic high-technology sector – among both foreign and indigenous firms' (45). This upgrading was supported by three types of state action. The first was a national system of innovation underpinned by state–society alliances based upon the activities of state agencies that defined policy priorities, provided finance and institutional supports, and legitimated this development agenda. The second was the broader set of socioeconomic changes that generated local demand for technology goods and a variety of services, particularly centred on the growth of an Irish software industry which Ó Riain calls 'the leading edge of indigenous industrial upgrading in the Celtic Tiger' (56). The final type of state action relates to the wider socio-economic conditions that helped keep inflation low to improve industrial competitiveness. This was achieved through the neo-corporatist arrangements of social partnership which managed a trade-off between moderate wage increases agreed at national-level negotiations and tax reductions. However, in a reference that links to other treatments of the Irish state being surveyed in this chapter, Ó Riain recognises the eroding of the revenue base of the state's finances that was hidden during the boom but which has become ever more evident as the boom years recede. As he writes: 'The social-partnership agreements ensured that integration into the global economy has not decimated social rights. However, the agreements have also presided over a period of rising inequality and weakening welfare effort' (65). Ó Riain is critical of the competition state concept as it extends 'important observations about the specific features of many contemporary capitalist states into too general an argument regarding a new mode of capitalist regulation' which thereby serves to 'obscure the existence of a political space for struggles within and through existing institutions over how development could and should be structured' (18). Instead, he asks: 'If the institutions of the Celtic Tiger could generate the results they did in the face of domestic neoliberal populism and an international order hostile to state and social shaping of economic life, what might they achieve given a more supportive political order?' (11). Realising the potential for expanding the developmentalist and social rights projects within the Celtic Tiger requires therefore, he argues, an alternative set of concepts and perspectives such as the developmental state.

The concept of the developmental state was taken up more in policy discourse than in the academic literature on the Irish state. This is most marked in the concept of the developmental welfare state adopted by the National Economic and Social Council (NESC) in its 2003 tri-annual statement of the state's economic and social strategy and used as the basis for elaborating a Developmental Welfare State (DWS) for Ireland (NESC, 2003: 29-33) (see Box 7.2). This uses the concept of the developmental state as a label for a new kind of welfare system – 'tax and welfare transfers, the provision of services and activist initiatives' (NESC, 2005: ix). Though not elaborated upon in the documents proposing it, this contains echoes of Ó Riain's concept in that it refers to the state's institutional capacity, its relationship to civil society, and the ways in which the welfare system is seen to reinforce the wider economy's competitive success.

Box 7.2 NESC on the 'developmental welfare state'

In 2005, the NESC issued a major report on Ireland's welfare state, proposing that the country's economic success as it was seen at the time required that it 're-visit the basic architecture and core objectives of Ireland's social policies and welfare state, and in several key respects to reform them' (NESC, 2005: 2). Describing Ireland's welfare state as 'a hybrid system' (34), the report acknowledges the many social deficits and inequalities that characterise Irish society and tentatively states that 'it can be argued that several forms of social spending require higher priority if Ireland is to advance its economy and society in the directions it wishes to' (136). To achieve greater synergies between economic and social policy, it proposes a developmental welfare state based on a core structure of three elements – core services, income supports and what it calls 'activist measures' (156). The state would have the responsibility to provide a set of core services such as childcare, education, health, eldercare, housing, transport, employment services and training, available to all members of society and at high standards in ways that are equitable but tailored to people's circumstances. Income supports, such as child income support, working age income *for* participation (italics in original) and minimum pension guarantees should be 'adequate not just to cover basic subsistence needs but also to buttress satisfactory social participation' (157). The third element would involve innovative responses by a range of bodies such as the community and voluntary, public or private sectors to unmet social needs 'the implications of which for mainstream service provision are not yet apparent' (157). The Council is concerned that adequate support be provided over the life-cycle with particular emphasis on childhood and the elderly and with supports for the working-age population being tailored to helping them back into the labour force. It ends by saying that 'a successful economy requires a successful society, in a double sense' – it is both a moral and a functional requirement. NESC offers the conceptualisation of the developmental welfare state as the necessary framework 'for providing greater impetus, strategic direction and effectiveness in developing the social policies that will reflect and build a successful society in Ireland' (228).

The NESC proposal is an ambitious one but it is not without its problems. The first and most serious problem is that it fails entirely to address the issue of funding. As inadequate funding has been a feature of Ireland's welfare state, a feature that worsened during the economic boom of the 1990s, any expansion and development of the welfare state will require a commitment on the part of the state significantly to increase welfare funding. This report fails both to address how much extra funding might be needed and also where it might come from. Secondly, as Murphy and Millar point out, the report 'is strategically but constructively ambivalent ... it leaves open the way for a positive social democratic interpretation or a more negative neo-liberal variation of welfare reform' (Murphy and Millar, 2007: 79). They illustrate this point by examining the report's recommendation for a more conditional participation income for people of working age, noting the ambiguity of NESC's term for describing this, 'sensitive activation'. The crucial issue as to whether such income is punitive, thus forcing people back into the labour force, or supportive, and therefore easing their way back, relates to the generosity of replacement ratios. Noting that the Dutch and Danish ratios of up to 89–96 per cent of previous earnings are very generous compared to the Irish ratios of 24 per cent, the authors fear that the single 'participation income' that the report recommends should replace the several contingency-based, social assistance payments that currently exist 'would not offer a decent level of social protection and would lock Ireland into a more liberal-type model' (ibid.: 89). Finally, it is disappointing to note that the report 'has not inspired lively debate or reshaped the momentum around welfare reform' (ibid.: 78). Debate on it has been limited to professional and activist specialists and no mention has been made of it either in wider political circles or in political debate; for example, both a general election (2007) and local elections (2009) have taken place since its publication and the objective of a developmental welfare state formed no part of any party's proposals in these elections.

A competition state?

The concept of the competition state was introduced to the Irish debate in the first edition of this book (Kirby, 2002a: 142–4). Following Kirby, Dukelow also adopted the concept for the Irish case as 'the state has taken a selective interventionist role in the manner of a competition state to re-orient social security policy to enhance economic competitiveness by tackling unemployment, yet leaving levels of income inequality and poverty remain relatively high' (2004: 27). Boyle, though seemingly unaware that the concept had already been introduced into debates on the Irish state, baldly stated, as quoted at the beginning of this chapter, that 'contemporary Ireland is an exemplar of the competition state' (2005: 16). In analysing the deficiencies of local government in Ireland, Tierney draws on the concept of the competition state 'with its emphasis on the market and the increasing alienation of many people from government in the process' and argues that these deficiencies can be effectively addressed through local government (Tierney, 2006: 71). Kirby and Murphy further developed and tested the concept through analysing the development of Irish social security policy (Kirby and Murphy, 2008).

The competition state concept emerged from analysing the ways in which developed industrial states were restructuring themselves in response to the constraints and opportunities opened up by neo-liberal globalisation in the 1990s. While initially under pressure from internal causes such as recession and the fiscal pressures on welfare spending, by the 1980s and 1990s, welfare states were also under pressure from outside factors such as international competitiveness, the mobility of capital worldwide and intensified international trade (Pierson, 2004: 100–2). As Ruggie recognised, the globalisation of financial markets and production chains challenged the premises on which the grand bargain between capital and labour rested since that bargain presupposed a world in which the state could effectively mediate external impacts through such tools as tariffs and exchange rates (Ruggie, 2003: 94). In this situation, welfare states are under pressure to reduce costs and erode the level and extent of protection they previously provided (Mishra, 1999: Scharpf, 2000). It is out of analysing the ways in which states are responding to these pressures that the concept of the competition state emerged. Various attempts have been made to characterise the new regime that is emerging as a successor to the Keynesian welfare state. Jessop sees this 'new state form' as a Schumpeterian workfare state (SWS) while Cerny describes the emergence of a 'competition state' out of the tensions between the demands of economic globalisation and the embedded state/society practices that characterised the national welfare state as the priorities of policy move away from the general maximisation of public welfare (full employment, redistributive transfer payments and social service provision) to the promotion of enterprise, innovation and profitability in both private and public sectors. These reactions, however, follow no set pattern or master plan: 'The emerging embedded neoliberal consensus is therefore not simply a developing "from outside" or "from above"; it is also a political construction promoted by political entrepreneurs who must design projects, convince others, build coalitions and ultimately win some sort of political legitimacy "from inside" and "from below"' (Cerny et al., 2005: 19).

In applying the concept to the Irish state, Kirby argues that the competition state accurately described the nature and operation of the Irish state in the era of the Celtic Tiger since it prioritises goals of economic competitiveness over those of social cohesion and welfare (Kirby, 2005). He writes that the concept of the competition state analytically captures in a fuller way than does that of the developmental state the logic of the Irish state's actions. This it does since it links the economic developmental dimension of state actions with the social distributional, unlike the developmental state concept which treats them separately. He concludes that the developmental state concept therefore fails to understand *why* the state has been so unsuccessful in translating economic success into social development. Dukelow rests most of her argument that Ireland is a competition state on a forensic examination of Irish welfare and labour market policy arguing that the combination of policies promoted over the 1990s amounts to a strongly productivist state policy consistent with a competition state. She provides evidence of legislative and administrative reforms focused on implementing a more active form of conditionality and suggests 'the balance has shifted towards greater compulsion, targeting and spending restraint' (22). Boyle argues that the decline in Irish social spending as a percentage of GDP over the course of the Celtic Tiger boom while spending two per cent of GDP on active labour market measures is consistent with the competition state hypothesis that public investment shifts over time to focus on projects that enhance capital or create flexible labour markets that promote enterprise, innovation, learning and training. This pragmatic, low-cost approach to social provision indicates the limits of the state's action and is far from the transformative dynamic one would expect from a developmental state (Boyle, 2005). Murphy (2006) makes an empirical argument that Irish social policy is consistent with a competition state. She argues that showing Ireland as a competition state does not mean proving that welfare spending has been curtailed, but rather it requires demonstrating how social security policy has been structurally reshaped to serve economic over welfare objectives. The most fundamental shift to a competition state arises from a redistributive welfare system that de-commodifies citizens (protecting them from having to depend on the market for an income) moving towards a productivist workfare state that commodifies citizens by encouraging and/or requiring them to depend for resources on labour-market participation. She identifies five types of commodifying social security reform emerging in the Irish competition state: regulation, retrenchment, residualisation, recommodification and defamilarisation. Reviewing how Irish social security policy has changed from 1986 to 2006, she concludes that Irish social security reform has its own distinctive style, pace and discourse and that Ireland is still in the process of becoming a full-fledged competition or 'workfare state' characterised by a distinctive Irish mix of 'supportive conditionality' and 'sensitive activation' consistent with a move towards a competition state (Murphy, 2006).

Ireland as a regulatory state

A competitive logic is especially evident in the new regulatory framework put in place by the Irish state over the 1990s. Apart from the Competition Authority, established in 1991, regulatory authorities were established, at arms length from the state, for sectors such as telecommunications (1996), energy (1999), aviation (2001), financial services (2003) and taxis (2004). Collins identifies two common characteristics of such regulatory agencies: the reduction of regulations to give market forces freer reign in some areas but also the construction of stricter regulatory structures in others where competition is likely to be compromised. He sees a paradox here between reducing regulations in some areas and constructing them in others (Collins, 2007: 120). However, the overriding consideration is the promotion of competition. For example, the Competition Act of 2002 gives the Competition Authority the function of reviewing proposed company mergers and acquisitions to ensure as far as possible that conditions exist for competitive forces to operate. As such, Collins writes that the regulatory process 'is rather more informed by economic theory than democratic principles or electoral considerations' (Collins, 2007: 131).

Following the collapse of the Celtic Tiger in late 2008, the regulatory regime of the Irish state, particularly in relation to financial services, came in for sharp criticism. This was essentially a principles-based regulatory system under which banks and financial firms would abide by agreed codes of behaviour rather than having these imposed on them and supervised by regulatory authorities. However, as Carswell has written, 'the emphasis of the regulator's focus was primarily on issues affecting consumers rather than on prudential matters such as liquidity and funding affecting the banks and their lending practices' (Carswell, 2009a: 5). Indeed, the financial regulator's prudential director who has the responsibility for ensuring that banks lend prudently and set aside sufficient capital to cover risks did not sit on the regulator's board whereas the consumer director did. A report from the Financial Services Consultative Consumer Panel found that the collapse of the Irish financial sector was magnified by the financial regulator's failure to control the property bubble. The report was quoted as stating: 'We are unclear as to why the regulator did not move to dampen the bubble at an earlier stage, for instance by requiring banks to set aside more capital for riskier products' (Madden, 2009b: 1). Similarly, other financial experts asked why the regulator, with access to inside information on the banks' situation, did not act earlier to impose discipline on the banks (McErlean, 2009). For McManus, the problem lies in the suitability of a principles-based regulatory system for the Irish banks. Echoing the nature of the Irish welfare system as analysed by Boyle (see Box 7.1), McManus writes: 'Light-touch regulation is low cost, because the regulator is lean and, ideally, nimble. It is also responsive to industry needs.' He adds that this form of regulation is 'unfortunately completely unsuited to the culture of Irish banking' which, at least in the case of Anglo-Irish bank, was willing to circumvent the agreed rules (see Brennan, 2008: 19). By mid-2009, the Irish government bowed to the wave of criticism of the regulatory authorities and announced a re-organisation of financial regulation, uniting the two regulators into one entity under the chairmanship of the Central Bank governor and with a promise of a significant expansion of regulatory capacity and substantial additional staff (Carswell, 2009a). Light-touch regulation and its role in the systemic collapse of the Irish banking system reflects the priorities and practices of a competition state.

Mediating the differences

The concepts of developmental and competition state are, therefore, quite distinct. However, they do have some common features. Most significantly, both agree that the state can make a difference though, perhaps echoing their different origins, the competition state concept recognises more fully the constraints placed on state actions by the competitive pressures of today's globalisation. Both acknowledge the uneven nature of state actions, though both also claim that a central overarching logic can be identified behind this unevenness. It is the nature of this overarching logic that constitutes the key difference as developmental state theorists claim that such states possess the capacity to achieve outcomes that fundamentally transform the economy and society towards higher levels of development. Competition state theorists, on the other hand, identify a logic that moves state actions away from the maximisation of welfare towards the promotion of enterprise and profitability as national elites respond to the pressures of globalisation. Theorists of both concepts recognise that both developmental and competition states do not confirm to uniform models but reflect the internal political configurations and culture through which the overarching logic of developmentalism or competition is mediated, though it must be said that both literatures have paid insufficient attention to the politics through which these logics emerge and come to dominance.

In terms of their application to the Irish case, the following conclusions can be drawn. Firstly, proponents of the developmental state and of the competition state can both agree that the state played a central role in transforming the industrial base of the economy through the attraction of high levels of high-tech FDI; however, the major disagreement concerns the extent and depth of this productive transformation and the link between it and social development. Secondly, proponents of the developmental state have concentrated on outcomes achieved and claimed state capacity on the basis of this; those who argue for the competition state have drawn this conclusion from a more fine-grained analysis of policymaking and policy outcomes and the ways they are mediated through the institutions and culture of the state and through the political system. These have served to draw attention to the contingent nature of the successes achieved and to the constantly evolving logic of state actions as its elites calculate how best to respond to what they perceive as the opportunities and constraints of the international order. At a time of major economic recession such as the Irish state has faced from mid-2008, this situation grows all the more uncertain and contingent. Ó Riain's 2008 analysis of the competing state projects in the contemporary Irish political economy illustrates well these dimensions of the fast-changing Irish political economy and what a fine-grained analysis can contribute to our understanding. This highlights both the developmental potential of sectors of the Irish state (though they remain relatively weak and marginalised) and also how these were smothered by a neo-liberal fixation with tax cuts from the late 1990s (Ó Riain, 2008). In the light of our knowledge so far, it seems most accurate to characterise the Irish state as a competition state but to acknowledge that despite its overriding logic of global competitiveness, pockets of developmentalism do exist within it. This echoes Kurtz's analysis of the Chilean case as one of 'state developmentalism [but] by no means ... a developmental state', namely that state intervention played a crucial role in Chile's successful integration into export markets but failed to overcome long-term problems of entrenched economic and social inequality (Kurtz, 2001: 16).

Conclusions

One of the major contributions of the Celtic Tiger period to political studies in Ireland is to have focused much more detailed attention on the role of the state than it had been accorded up to recently. Since the Irish state has played such a central role in the country's development, the lack of any active debates on the nature and role of the state allowed unsubstantiated claims about the state to be accepted in scholarly and public debate – for dominant economic analysts the state was easily portrayed as the cause of delayed development as it interfered with market dynamisms; for those of a more statist persuasion, conclusions could be too easily reached about the potential and capacity of the Irish state. Recent debates have begun to offer a more fine-grained analysis that shows the reality to be much more complex. Indeed, the state has been a central actor in the development of the market, without which the levels of development reached by Ireland would not have been possible. Yet the state has also been profoundly implicated in the lop-sided outcomes achieved, particularly dramatically as a result of the Celtic Tiger boom – both in terms of the dualistic nature of the productive economy and also in terms of the deep social polarisation that has been entrenched. Understanding the nature of the Irish state, with all the limitations of our current understanding, has therefore allowed a greater appreciation of what is perhaps the backbone of the Irish model since the model has depended so centrally on the actions of the state (and does so now again as sectors of the market economy are in collapse). The second central feature of the Irish model is how this state has configured a market economy in particular and distinctive ways. This is the subject of the next chapter.

8
Market: Neo-liberalism Irish-style

A unique feature of the Irish system [is] officials' awareness
of just how important foreign investment is for the country's prosperity. The imperative of attracting and keeping
foreign firms has soaked deep into every nook and cranny
of the apparatus of the state in a way not to be observed
elsewhere.

Dan O'Brien (quoted in Collins, 2007: 118)

The Irish economy is essentially a free-market economy with a shrinking
state-owned sector. However, since independence the state has played a key
role in creating the conditions in which the private sector operates and,
even though the Celtic Tiger period saw the emergence of a dynamic private
sector in some areas of the economy, the role of the state remains crucial
(in terms of spending on research and development for example). Chapter 6
quoted Susan Strange when she wrote that 'it is not only the direct power of
authority over markets that matters; it is also the indirect effect of authority
on the context or surrounding conditions within which the market functions' (Strange, 1994: 23). This draws attention to the central insight of the
political economy approach adopted in this book to analyses of the economy, namely that it is the interrelationship of state and market, of public
and private authority, that requires examination in order to understand the
particular and distinctive configuration of any economy. This is particularly
true in a case like that of Ireland in which the indigenous private sector
has shown weak capacity to develop dynamic economic sectors so that the
state has been the key agent in fostering the upgrading of the productive
economy, from agriculture, to industry and, very recently, to an economy
dominated by the service sector and, as the opening quote above states, has
relied heavily on foreign investment to do this.

In analysing the ways in which the state has configured a distinctive Irish
economy, this chapter frames its discussion in the context of neoliberalism.
This book's first edition argued against the then dominant view that Ireland

146

was not a case of neoliberalism because of the active role that the state played in the economy (Kirby, 2002a: 160–3). Seeing neoliberalism as a loose and ill-defined label to describe an economy based on extensive liberalisation from state regulation in which public institutions are restructured to facilitate the efficient and competitive operation of market forces, it was argued that neoliberalism finds different expressions in different countries according to local political traditions and cultures, and to the correlation of political and economic forces that exist at any particular time. It concluded that the Ireland of the Celtic Tiger, with its highly market-friendly state with its subordinate relationship to global market forces, and the inegalitarian social impact of this state–market relationship, constituted an Irish form of neoliberalism. The subsequent development of the Irish economy, and in particular its spectacular collapse in late 2008, has confirmed the Irish model as being strongly neoliberal.

This chapter draws on the evidence of the intervening period to further develop the analysis of 'neoliberalism Irish-style'. Starting from the brief portrait of the Irish economy given in Chapter 2, the treatment here examines key features of that economy in more depth. It begins by analysing the weak culture of innovation that has emerged as a major feature, linking this to the institutional configuration of how the Irish state acted to upgrade the industrial economy in the decades before the Celtic Tiger boom. The second section looks critically at the state's policy for recreating what it now labels a 'smart economy', asking whether the lessons of the collapse have been learnt at all. The third section examines the emerging service sector which, in the 2000s became the motor force of the Irish economy but which was the sector that pulled down the whole economy when construction and banking collapsed in late 2008. A brief section on the nature of the public sector in Ireland follows, as this helps illustrate well some of the key features of 'neoliberalism Irish-style'. The penultimate section takes as its theme the impact of the economy on society through an examination of one of the most successful sectors of the economy, the pharmaceuticals sector, but widening the focus to include the implications of this success for health regulation and promotion in Irish society. Conclusions are then drawn about what more we have now learnt of 'neoliberalism Irish-style'.

Innovation

If one word dominates the Irish state's ambition for the economy, it is innovation. Whether labelled as the 'knowledge economy' or more recently as the 'smart economy', the objective is 'to make Ireland an innovation and commercialisation hub in Europe – a country that combines the features of an attractive home for innovative R&D-intensive multinationals while also being a highly-attractive incubation environment for the best entrepreneurs in Europe and beyond' (Government of Ireland, 2008: 8). Yet while some successes are evident in terms of attracting more R&D by multinationals to Ireland, there is far less evidence of any breakthrough by indigenous firms. As Grimes and Collins summarise the prospects for the state's R&D policies: 'While [policymakers] are acutely aware that this objective [of transitioning Ireland's economic profile towards higher skilled and knowledge-based activities] can only be achieved by building up endogenous capacity within the economy, the reality is that the economy will continue to heavily rely on inward investment for many years to come' (Grimes and Collins, 2009: 64). This failure of the indigenous sector is widely acknowledged (see Box 2.1) but little analysed. What are the deeper reasons for the remarkable innovative weaknesses of the Irish-owned industrial sector, half a century after the state began a highly successful policy of attracting in foreign multinationals?

In a rare examination of this issue by a leading economist, Bradley identifies three stages that Ireland's strategy of 'industrialisation by invitation' has followed. The first, corresponding to the period from the late 1950s to the mid-1980s, 'was "factor" driven, based on low rates of corporation tax, low wages, and subsidised capital formation'. Acknowledging that policymakers in Ireland are now seeking to shift to a strategy based more on indigenous innovation, he writes that 'this has exposed some of the limitations of an industrial strategy that came to be based largely on foreign direct investment' (Bradley, 2002: 44). For example, in analysing technological innovation, he draws attention to the fact that 'the forces that drive innovation in products and manufacturing processes tend to originate in the USA rather than in Ireland' and he concludes that it is 'this feature that presents the most serious threat to the survival and progress of the sector' (ibid.: 34–5). The central anomaly of the Irish growth model, he expresses as follows:

> The crucial role of management is to formulate a corporate strategy that aligns with the nation's wealth-building strategy. So, this issue is usually examined largely from the point of view of domestic corporations adjusting to national strategy. In Ireland however, causality more often as not runs in the opposite direction. In other words, the Irish Industrial Development Agency – the IDA – was constantly scanning the world for inward investment in high technology sectors. Quite often the domestic environment initially was not sufficiently attractive to persuade cutting edge firms to locate in Ireland. But information on firms' needs was fed back to the Irish government authorities by the IDA, and major policy changes could be executed rapidly. The national wealth creating strategy in Ireland often needs to adapt to the requirements of firms in the global corporate environment, and not the other way around.
>
> (ibid.: 38–9)

US academic Fred Gottheil makes a similar point rather more bluntly. He asks: 'What was really Irish about Ireland's economic performance? That is to say, was it really a Celtic Tiger at work in Ireland or a U.S. Tiger caged in a Celtic zoo?' He answers his own question by noting that the profit rates as a percentage of sales of US multinationals operating in Ireland 'were scarcely short of awesome'; for example, US pharmaceutical companies operating in Ireland had profit rates approaching 50 per cent which compares to five per cent profit rates for Irish companies operating in Ireland and for US companies in the US. While there has been some transformation of the domestic economy, the Irish economy still continues to be very much 'a "platform economy" for foreign multinationals – particularly US', he concludes (Gottheil, 2003: 731–3).

Bradley draws the conclusion that, based on international industrial policy frameworks, such as Vernon's product life-cycle framework or Porter's diamond of competitiveness, if Ireland displays behaviour like a less developed region 'it will always remain an underdeveloped country that competes in low cost production of maturing products' (ibid.: 45). His hope is that, based on Best's capability triad, Irish policy can have more influence over creating the conditions for more entrepreneurial Irish firms to emerge in the future.

Recent empirical evidence, however, gives grounds for concern about the possibilities of such an emergence. Examining Ireland's innovation performance over the period of the Celtic Tiger boom, Hewitt-Dundas and Roper find that the proportion of manufacturing plants making product changes has increased by only five per cent over the period while the proportion of plants undertaking process innovation declined by almost seven per cent. They find that manufacturing innovation 'is driven by a relatively narrow range of external knowledge sources aside from knowledge created within the plant through R&D'. This they put down to the low level of business R&D spending in Ireland and 'the lack of any positive link between the extent of innovation activity and links to public knowledge sources' such as universities. Unsurprisingly, they find that externally owned plants and those with access to group R&D are more likely to be undertaking product innovation (Hewitt-Dundas and Roper, 2008: 59).

In pointing to the relationship between the IDA and the state, Bradley is drawing attention to the longer-term influence of state policy on laying the foundations for the weaknesses in domestic innovation about which concern is now being expressed. However, pinpointing these weaknesses requires a finer-grained analysis than what he provides. Ó Riain analyses more fully the power that the IDA achieved within the Irish state and the longer-term consequences of this power. As he writes:

> The IDA, the state agency charged with attracting foreign investment, took on the role of 'hunter and gatherer' of foreign direct investment and became unusually powerful within the national state system. When most national economies were still attempting to negotiate with and

control foreign capital, the Irish state turned to a relatively unconditional pursuit of such investors – creating the first free-trade zone in the world (at Shannon) and providing generous tax incentives and grants, a transnational-friendly environment, a young and cooperative labour force, and, in the 1980s, a world-class telecommunications system.

(Ó Riain, 2004: 40)

While this policy succeeded in laying the foundations of a modern industrial economy in the 1960s, it was in the mid-1990s that it took off as Ireland became recognised as one of the stellar global performers for its success in winning high levels of FDI in key sectors such as electronics, pharmaceuticals and financial services, moving up the UNCTAD index on inward FDI performance from seventy-first position in 1988–90 to fourth position a decade later (Paus, 2005: 50).

While this is a familiar story, what is less examined is the institutional and political underpinning of this success. The IDA was able to attract highly educated people to work there as employment opportunities in the private sector were limited, successive governments were committed to the strategy being pursued and the IDA 'always had a soft budget constraint, which gave it leeway in its aggressive pursuit of foreign investors' (Paus, 2005: 71–2). In 1969, it became an agency outside the civil service structure and 'gradually became the centre of policymaking as the Department of Industry and Commerce became more marginalized' (Ó Riain, 2004: 179). This independence allowed it to keep itself at arm's length from interference from other state agencies and bureaucrats leading to what Ó Riain describes as 'its embeddedness in an international community of potentially mobile firms' (ibid.: 154). However, as a consequence it has come close to being captured by such firms; as Ó Riain puts it, 'it is usually the IDA that speaks most clearly for the interests of the TNCs' within the Irish state (ibid.: 155). Furthermore, given the populist nature of Irish politics and the weak policymaking capacity of political parties, the IDA was left to dominate industrial policymaking and implementation from the 1960s to the 1990s. Paradoxically, the IDA maintained its central role in policymaking following the criticisms of the 1982 Telesis review of industrial policy which was severely critical of the state's over-reliance on FDI, which illustrates the IDA's entrenched and dominant role (Jacobsen, 1994). This situation therefore led to an effective depoliticisation of industrial policy as the IDA was left to dominate policy on attracting FDI. As Ó Riain puts it: 'The FDI regime dominated the traded sector of the economy, whereas nontraded sectors contained primarily domestic firms and were dominated by clientelism' (Ó Riain, 2004: 177).

The principal cost of this dominant focus on FDI was the weak development of indigenous industry. It was only with the spaces afforded by the EU structural funds from the late 1980s onwards that a new alliance of state bureaucrats, young entrepreneurs and university research centres led to the emergence of an indigenous software sector. A new focus on indigenous industry in state policy also led to the break-up of the IDA in 1993 with the establishment of two new agencies: Forbairt (later to become Enterprise Ireland) to concentrate on indigenous industry and Forfás as an advisory and co-ordination board, while the IDA became IDA Ireland with an exclusive brief for foreign industry. However, as Ó Riain reminds us 'the leading executives of ... Forfás, came from the IDA, not from the indigenous development agencies' (ibid.: 179). Despite the reorganisation of the state's industrial policy complex, the IDA has remained a very powerful body. Its continuing influence on policy towards building innovative capacity is identified by Barry who has argued that this policy is too narrow in focus, appearing to be designed primarily 'to ensure that the country is adequately supplied with the kinds of skills and expertise required by MNCs engaged in the offshoring of R&D'. Significantly, he adds: 'In this it would appear to conform more closely to the agenda of the IDA than of Enterprise Ireland' (Barry, 2006: 46). The weakness of policy to develop indigenous innovative capacity therefore derives from the institutional matrix of the state's industrial policy, and in particular the powerful role of the IDA within this which acts as a mouthpiece for the needs of multinationals within the state.

Much has been made in recent years of the fact that Irish companies are now investing ever greater amounts abroad. This grew from €5bn in 2000 to €15bn in 2004, declined substantially in 2005 and 2006 but grew again to €16bn in 2007. In 2006, almost €4.5bn of this went to the UK and €4bn to the US, the two largest destinations (Forfás, 2008a). Yet the profile of the companies investing abroad is very different from those that invest in Ireland, again revealing the distinctive nature of the Irish economy. King calculates that Irish outward FDI is concentrated in four sectors – financial services, construction and property, food, drink and agribusiness, and print, paper and publishing. The large companies with a substantial presence overseas are the non-metallic mineral products company, CRH operating in 26 countries, and the paper and packaging group Jefferson Smurfit, operating in 31. The food company Kerry Group operates in 22 countries and the metal products company, Kingspan, in 17. Among other large Irish multinationals are Fyffes and Waterford Wedgewood (King, 2006). Yet, as Barry points out, 'these Irish multinationals are disproportionately located in non-traded sectors such as construction and paper and packaging and do not exhibit the type of "created asset" intensity (derived from R&D and strong product differentiation) that has been found for Korean and Taiwanese multinationals' (Barry, 2006: 42). This, then, alerts one to the fact that the sectors in which domestic companies have risen to dominance are by and large not high-tech sectors. How the state is seeking to change this is the subject of the next section.

Box 8.1 Fink on Ireland's and Hungary's 'uneven FDI-led development'

A German scholar, Philipp Fink, was struck by the similarities between the economic strategies of Ireland and Hungary – as both countries were very reliant on attracting FDI – and by the outcomes of these strategies in both cases, namely, 'large differences in productivity and profits between the leading foreign-dominated export sector and the underperforming indigenous sector' (Fink, 2007: 2). As a result he wrote a study comparing Ireland and Hungary as similar models of FDI-led development on the European periphery (Fink, 2007, 2009).

Examining the reasons for each country choosing such dependent paths to development, he identified 'development blockages' in both cases resulting from underdevelopment and 'the evolution of defective capitalism' (3). This was due to the historical place of both countries as weak partners in colonial economic unions resulting in a lack of sufficient internal demand and markets for industrial products and therefore the dominance of agricultural exports. Subsequent modernisation attempts therefore needed to overcome these development blockages requiring a very active role by the state in both countries. He writes that 'the inability of the development regimes of socialism in Hungary and import-substitution in Ireland to induce the envisaged developmental results eventually led to their replacement by the current FDI-led development regime' (5). However, due to weak state capacity and the restriction of policy to creating the conditions for TNCs (transnational companies) to invest, he writes that 'the state in both cases displays a high capacity to attract FDI, but a low capacity to ensure the sufficient integration of investing TNCs into the host economy' (6).

Though this development model has resulted in a transformation of the productive structure, economic growth and a substantial increase in per capita incomes in both cases, Fink argues that it has not helped either country to 'overcome their economic peripherality' (242). He identifies a number of features that both countries have in common. In identifying the relative weakness of the indigenous sector in both he questions the suitability of TNCs to act as transfer agents for the diffusion of modern technology into the productive structures of the host economies and the poor absorptive capabilities of indigenous firms to utilise TNC technologies and know-how. He also identifies the growth of social polarisation in both cases, mirroring the dualism in their industrial structures (growth in poverty and inequality) due to 'the low level of state capacity to steer the development process' (17). Noting the unsustainable housing boom in the Irish case and, in Hungary, trade and balance of payments deficits (both driven by increased consumption), he predicted that both countries were in danger of losing their 'tiger' status.

Building a 'smart economy'

In the early phase of the Celtic Tiger collapse in late 2008, the government issued a 'framework for sustainable economic renewal' entitled 'Building Ireland's Smart Economy' (Government of Ireland, 2008). Regular reference to this document in subsequent statements of Ministers and other officials indicates its status as *the* authoritative statement of the state's objectives for economic development. Since economic development policy has been effectively depoliticised over recent decades with all the principal political parties adopting a fundamentally similar approach, it is very unlikely that any change in government would alter this policy in any significant way. As the latest iteration of the goal of creating a high-tech and high-value economy which has dominated state policy since the early years of the Celtic Tiger, the 'smart economy' document warrants critical scrutiny.

This policy document has two clear sources of ideas. One is the dominant international discourse on building a knowledge economy, labelled here as the 'innovation island'. This is simply a repackaging of long-term policy to locate more R&D activity by multinational companies in Ireland and to build the innovative capacity of the indigenous industrial and service sector. The document does not offer any new policy ideas, with the partial exception of the proposal to invest €500 million in creating a new venture fund to support early stage R&D activity by small and medium-sized enterprises. Apart from that, the document contains the usual taxation incentives, the pledge of continuing state investment in R&D in Irish universities, and the existing activities of Science Foundation Ireland (SFI) to help commercialise the outputs of such research. What is new in this document is the second major source of ideas, namely 'Green Enterprise' (ibid.: 17). Reflecting the presence of Green Party Ministers in government, the document pledges investment in renewable energy (wind and wave power and the upgrading of transmission systems), in better insulation in homes, and in sustainable transport (including a target of ten per cent of Ireland's road fleet being electrically powered by 2020). Taxation measures to secure these objectives include a carbon levy, further modifications to the motor tax system and a lower rate of value-added tax for eco-friendly products. Other objectives include investment in critical infrastructure and creating efficient and effective public services (though here the emphasis is more on shrinking the numbers in the public service, securing savings through the pooling of services and better performance management systems than on outlining a reform agenda for creating a more efficient and capable state).

As a plan for putting Ireland on a new growth path, the 'smart economy' is largely a repackaging of long-held objectives and policy mechanisms with the addition of a mild version of the 'Green New Deal' (see Green New Deal Group, 2008). Nothing betrays as forcefully that this marks no departure from the FDI-led development of the past half century than the statement that 'our low corporate tax regime has been a central pillar of Ireland's industrial policy and we will maintain competitive, low corporation tax rates (including the 12.5% rate)' (10). And, as Lucy put it, the over 100 pages of the document are full of aspiration but lack an internal consistency and a clear focus. The challenge of developing a tax base more adequate to the requirements of a state seeking to invest in building the skills and capabilities for a high-tech economy is not addressed while, in relation to the proposal for a venture capital fund, Lucy points out that there is already 'a thriving venture capital sector in Ireland' which is concentrated on buyouts and reorganisation (Lucy, 2008: 15).

If there is nothing new in the much-vaunted 'smart economy' iteration of long-standing state objectives, it requires an examination of the one area of public policy which has seen dramatic changes over the period of the Celtic Tiger to assess the prospects for creating 'an exemplary research, innovation and commercialisation ecosystem' (Government of Ireland, 2008: 13). This is the state's investment in building an infrastructure to develop the research capacities of Irish higher education to become internationally recognised centres of research excellence. It is revealing that Irish state investment began as a result of the economic boom of the Celtic Tiger and was not a cause of that boom. Only in the 1990s was attention devoted to developing policy on science and technology and from 1998 onwards significant funding began to be channelled to the universities for research purposes. The foundation of the Programme for Research in Third Level Institutions (PRTLI) in 1998, of two research councils in 2000 – the Irish Research Council for Science, Engineering and Technology (IRCSET) and the Irish Research Council for the Humanities and Social Sciences (IRCHSS) – and in the same year of SFI put in place the institutional infrastructure to build internationally recognised research capacity in Ireland. Following the identification of biotechnology and information and communications technology (ICT) as the engines of future growth in the global economy, the government created the Technology Foresight Fund with a budget of €646 million to be administered by SFI. Energy-efficient technologies have since been added to the list of strategic areas of research. Meanwhile, the PRTLI programme helped transform the research landscape in Ireland's third-level sector, through its periodic rounds of research funding. In the decade 1998–2008, the Programme disbursed €865 million to these institutions 'to adopt a strategic approach to research, identifying and building on existing strengths ... and [has] fostered a culture of co-operation and collaboration among researchers within and between institutions' (HEA, 2008b: vi) helping create nearly 80,000 additional square metres of research space, funding in excess of 1000 researchers and 2000 postgraduate students.

Paradoxically, it was a private philanthropic organisation that goaded the Irish state into funding research. The state's Higher Education Authority (HEA) has acknowledged the role of Atlantic Philanthropies as being 'central to effecting a real paradigm shift in Irish research' (HEA, 2008b: vi). Atlantic Philanthropies is a US foundation established by a wealthy Irish American, Chuck Feeney, to make charitable grants. First established in Dublin in 1990, it quickly became the higher education sector's largest private donor and spent €69 million in its first seven years across a wide range of areas in higher education including infrastructure, libraries and access programmes. However, Atlantic recognised the very low level of government investment in research at this time (estimated at about 11 per cent of the EU norm in the early 1990s) and the lack of any commitment by government to address this. It decided therefore to focus its attention on upgrading the research infrastructure in Ireland and to do so in partnership with the Irish government (Rhodes and Healy, 2006: 66). Out of this initiative, the PRTLI programme was founded; of the €605 million given in research funding through the first three rounds of PRTLI, €178 million of it was a donation from Atlantic following which it withdrew from funding. Two subsequent funding rounds have been entirely funded by the state. Atlantic evaluates its achievement as follows: 'The PRTLI initiative has resulted in a substantial enhancement in the capacity for world class research in Ireland, the enablement of Irish researchers to participate in the international research community as scientific leaders and peers and the considerable strengthening of the "fourth level" in Irish education' (Rhodes and Healy, 2006: 71).

Yet, despite these evident successes, questions continue to be asked about this policy and about state policy towards higher education. Paradoxically, researchers have found that the greater the frequency of direct interaction with academics, the lower the probability of both product and process innovation in businesses, and they speculate that these findings may reflect differences in work practices and objectives between businesses and academics. They conclude that 'the substantial public investment on research in Irish higher education institutes may have a disappointing, and perhaps even a negative, effect on the innovation performance of Irish business' (Jordan and O'Leary, 2008: 10). This conclusion seems to be supported by the research of Hewitt-Dundas and Roper referred to above. Furthermore, the annual Innovation Index of the German Institute for Economic Research places Ireland third last on its index of 17 countries, just ahead of Spain and Italy. Ireland scored particularly poorly in education, research and development and networking opportunities, perhaps again drawing attention to the weak links between academic research and industrial innovation (Scally, 2008: 14–15). Concerns have also been raised about the state's seemingly inconsistent policy as it fails to increase funding to run Ireland's universities even as it increases funding for research centres within them. As the heads of two leading universities, John Hegarty of Trinity College Dublin and Hugh Brady of University College Dublin have written: 'On a per student basis, core funding has been reduced by one-third since 1995 in real terms. In addition, the maintenance and upgrading of the physical infrastructure for third-level teaching has virtually ground to a halt through lack of funding.' Rather than closing the gap with universities in other countries (they choose Scotland and Denmark for the purpose of comparison), they state that 'we are allowing it to widen by progressively eroding funding for core teaching'. They conclude their article by pointing to their fears for the future: 'Failure to invest now will place an entire generation of students and the future of this country at a serious disadvantage. To gamble with our future in this way is simply wrong' (Brady and Hegarty, 2008).

The outcome of all this investment has disappointed government. It is not surprising that Ireland's increasing spending on research has resulted in the country moving from twenty-second place on OECD rankings of higher education research and development (HERD) spending in 2000 to fourteenth place in 2006 (Forfás, 2008b). But Eurostat figures show that Ireland's increasing spending has not resulted in moving up the EU league table of R&D expenditure, measured as a percentage of GDP/GNP. Ireland's spend of 1.43 per cent of its GNI in 1996 increased to a spend of 1.53 per cent in 2006 putting Ireland in eleventh place among the EU27. This compares to an average EU spend of 1.84 per cent and is significantly behind the big spenders such as Sweden, Finland, Austria and Denmark and even lower than Slovenia and the Czech Republic. Furthermore, Ireland's rate of patent applications increased from just over 20 per million inhabitants in 1995 to just over 60 in 2000, but it has hovered at that level since while the average EU rate, about double the Irish rate, has continued to increase (CSO, 2008: Tables 2.3–2.6). As noted by Paus, attempting to move up the value-added chain through significant investment in R&D is a relatively new strategy for Ireland. And, as she puts it, 'the obstacles to success are formidable' (Paus, 2005: 126). Building the 'smart economy' is far from assured. In all of this expensive effort, there seems little willingness thoroughly to investigate the shortcomings of public policy and to design a policy more likely to succeed and more in keeping with the nature of the Irish economy. Small and medium-sized enterprises are poorly supported by state policy which still seems captivated by the needs of multinationals despite decades of warnings that such a policy focus is unwise for the long-term.

The service sector: Banking and construction

While public policy was focused on building a knowledge economy, a much more traditional sector of the economy was entering into crisis, namely the construction industry. Having become the main engine of economic growth in the Irish economy by the mid-2000s (see Chapter 2), concern began to be expressed about the increasing dependence on construction and on personal consumption (O'Malley and McCarthy, 2006), while attention was also being drawn to the role of the banks in fuelling the construction boom. As Tansey wrote in early 2008, 'Irish financial institutions have placed most of their lending eggs in the property basket. Of the total stock of loans outstanding to the private sector as of March 2008, more than €3 out of every €5 represented property-related lending.' Since Irish financial institutions had made 'an exceptionally large bet on the Irish property sector', he predicted: 'If it proves to be a beaten docket, the whole economy is in trouble' (Tansey, 2008b: 6). Within months, his worst fears were seen as coming true.

Once the crisis broke in September 2008 and the Irish government offered to guarantee deposits in Irish banks, major uncertainty has since dogged the sector as investors have little knowledge of the true extent of their exposure to risk from the collapse of construction. By January 2009, the share price of the two largest Irish banks were a tiny fraction of what they had been at their height just two years previously – Bank of Ireland's shares were worth 34 cents compared to €18.65 in February 2007 while AIB's share price was down to 60 cents against a high of €23.95 in January 2007. The government was forced to nationalise Ireland's third largest bank, Anglo-Irish Bank, in January 2009 as the collapse of its share price accelerated amid rumours of the withdrawal of large-scale deposits. The bank's share price was a mere 20 cents compared to a high of €17 in May 2007. Exacerbating its woes were revelations of large secret personal loans by the bank to its chairman, Sean FitzPatrick, over eight years that were kept off the bank's balance sheet. These amounted to €122 million in 2007 and €84 million in 2008. Furthermore, the bank had lent €451 million to ten longstanding clients in July 2007 to take a ten per cent share in the bank. These disclosures not only destroyed the reputation of Anglo-Irish Bank but by extension severely damaged the international reputation of the Irish banking sector. And the worst was not over: in February 2009 the government announced a €7 billion recapitalisation of Bank of Ireland and AIB (€3.5bn each) to guarantee their future stability; pre-tax losses by Anglo-Irish of €4.1 billion in the six months to March 2009 forced the government to announce a further injection of €4 billion into that bank while in May AIB admitted it faced a €4.3 billion charge on bad debts, exceeding the worst case scenario it had outlined just two months previously. By mid-2009, the scale of the damage to the Irish banking sector was still unclear.

The level of Irish banks' indebtedness to the property sector is indicated by the fact that, by mid-2009 when the extent of the huge liabilities facing the banks were at last being admitted, it was being reliably estimated that the top 50 property borrowers accounted for loans from five of the most important Irish banks that totalled between €40 and €50 billion, with fewer than ten of these accounting for loans of more than €1 billion each. These estimates were made in the context of the information being furnished by the banks to the 'bad bank' set up by the Irish government in April 2009 to take over and manage the non-performing loans held by Irish banks. Overall, the National Asset Management Agency (Nama) as it is called, is expected to take over an €80 to €90 billion loan portfolio, making it the third largest Irish bank (Carswell, 2009b). If a substantial proportion of these loans have to be written off, Nama will have to take over the assets on which they are secured, becoming perhaps the state's largest owner of land and buildings. Yet the government's decision to establish Nama remained controversial, particularly among academic economists. In a rare show of unity, 20 such leading economists wrote a joint article arguing that Nama 'represents only a partial solution to our problems and one that is unlikely to protect the taxpayer'. Instead they argue for a nationalisation of the leading banks as a temporary measure. They state:

> We consider that nationalisation will better protect taxpayers' interests, produce a more efficient and longer lasting solution to our banking problems, be more transparent in relation to pricing of distressed assets, and be far more likely to produce a banking system free from the toxic reputation that our current financial institutions have deservedly earned.
>
> (Whelan et al., 2009)

Nothing indicates the gravity of the crisis facing the Irish banking sector as much as a call by mainstream economists to nationalise the leading banks, something they themselves acknowledge. Central to their concern is the fear that the government may be seriously underestimating the losses facing the major banks and, as it plans to purchase these loans, it is crucial that it make as accurate a valuation as possible of the assets held by the banks to back these loans. As they write: 'With €90 billion in loans to be purchased, the consequences to the taxpayer of overpaying for bad assets by 10 to 30 per cent are truly appalling' (ibid.). With ranges of 15–50 per cent being cited by analysts as appropriate for discounts on these loans, the task of achieving an accurate valuation is going to be extremely challenging. The future solvency of the Irish state depends on them getting it as right as possible.

The scale of the crisis facing the banking sector is worthy of consideration not only because of the crucial role banking plays in the health of any economy but also because international financial services had become a leading sector of the Irish economy as industry declined in the early 2000s. Dublin's International Financial Services Centre (IFSC) constitutes a central hub for service exports, the value of which grew from €3.8bn in 2000 to €21bn in 2007. Established in 1987 in a move by Irish state authorities to avail of opportunities for job growth opened up by changes in the international financial services industry, the IFSC was initially established in the run-down docklands area of Dublin but from 1999 these locational requirements were largely eliminated. From the beginning, a regulatory framework was put in place to avoid it from becoming a tax haven and to ensure that companies had more than a phantom or brass plate presence. In 1999, IFSC companies were brought within the same corporation tax rate as all industries operating in Ireland. By 2004, there were 443 international financial services firms operating in Dublin along with 700 other IFSC-licensed firms acting through third-party intermediaries; over 80 per cent of these were non-Irish firms. In 2008, 296,000 people were employed in financial and other business services in Ireland (this figure relates to total employment in the sector and is not limited to the IFSC), more than all those employed in production industries (excluding construction). However, the sector was badly hit by the international financial crisis since it had established itself as a major centre for hedge fund servicing and for securitisation, both of them seriously damaged by international developments. Profits were down €1.2bn in 2008 over the previous year and the sector's contribution to tax revenues had fallen from €1.2bn in 2007 to €0.85bn in 2008. The reputation of the IFSC has also been damaged internationally, particularly in Germany and in the UK where it is seen as aggressively attracting firms as it offers them the possibility of paying lower taxes (Reddan, 2009).

Despite its success, concerns have been expressed about the benefits to the wider economy from the IFSC. White writes that it represents 'an enclave economy' and quotes Murray-Brown that it is 'almost like a separate country' (White, 2005: 401, 391). There are four grounds for concern. Firstly, while it attracts high levels of FDI, 'these direct investments are matched roughly by outward flows of portfolio investments and therefore have a limited impact on the productive potential of the [Irish] economy' (ibid.: 392). Secondly, as Breathnach puts it, 'the main areas of activity engaged in by these firms tend to be in routine sectors such as fund administration, asset financing and corporate treasury management, although there is also considerable active involvement in insurance and banking. However, the original aim of establishing an active trading floor in financial instruments has not been realised' (Breathnach, 2007a: 152). Back-office activities in four niche areas are responsible for most of the employment – fund administration, corporate treasury, corporate banking and insurance. This has implications for the nature of employment at the IFSC. White found a 'high rate of turnover among ISFC staff' due to the 'unchallenging and routine nature of this work, along with limited opportunities for advancement' (White, 2005: 395, 396). Thirdly, while IFSC firms use a lot of services provided by others, these linkages are most frequently with firms outside Ireland than within it. White writes that 'locally based linkages remain sparse and limited to several key ancillary services like law and accounting' and even, within these, links are with a very small number of Irish firms (ibid.: 397). Finally, there are concerns about the competitive pressures facing the industry as countries like Hungary and Estonia create similarly low-tax regimes. Buffeted therefore by the global financial crisis and by the domestic banking and construction crisis, Ireland's financial services sector faces major challenges.

Box 8.2   O'Brien on a 'fitting epitaph for the Celtic Tiger'

'The swagger of the Celtic Tiger has wilted in the face of staggering regulatory, corporate and political incompetence. Through the boom the population was encouraged to engage in a collective act of self-deception. Unsustainable property valuations created a speculative economy. The International Financial Services Centre became the symbol for some of the worst excesses of financialisation, a process that refers to the transformation of industrial managerial capitalism to speculative gambling.

'As the crisis intensified [in] September [2008], the Government took the unprecedented decision to provide an unlimited guarantee of all banking deposits. The move was designed to protect an increasingly strained domestic banking sector whose reckless lending has been instrumental in intensifying the scale of the crisis. As minister for finance, Brian Cowen amended the Finance Act to provide tax-free status to CFDs [contract for difference]. It reflects the power of interest groups to dictate policy and comes after similar scandals involving lax oversight of international banks and the reinsurance industry.

'The rash of banking failures reflects the deleterious combination of boardroom hubris, defective operational risk management systems and uninformed regulatory confidence. It could not have happened but for the inculcation of an ideological worldview that privileged innovation over security. It retained cogency despite increasing evidence that undermined the practical and normative value of such an approach. This generated in turn a new (but defective) risk paradigm informed by naivety and ignorance. While this model was most extreme in the US, its rationale was inculcated across the globe, particularly in Ireland.
'While it may be inopportune to engage in structural reform in the midst of a crisis, the advantages of ceding control to a self-serving, self-policing marketplace model have been falsified. Ireland has gone from poster child of globalisation to the symbol of corporate, regulatory and political failure. It is a fitting epitaph for the Celtic Tiger.'

Justin O'Brien, professor of corporate governance,
Canberra (2009)

The public sector

Compared to other models of extreme free-market capitalism, Ireland has not engaged in a sweeping sell-off of state companies and even at the height of the Celtic Tiger boom maintained an extensive state sector. This again seems to contradict the designation of Ireland as a neoliberal model and so warrants examination. In the mid-2000s a number of major companies were still in state ownership, including the national bus and train company CIÉ, the electricity generating company ESB, the company commercialising peat products Bord na Móna, the postal service An Post and the state forestry company Coillte. At the end of the 2000s the state still had a 25 per cent share in the former state airline, Aer Lingus. Where privatisation did take place, it was piecemeal and in response more to commercial pressures than to the ideological motivation that led to wide-scale sell-offs of state companies in the 1980s and 1990s in many parts of the world. Thus a trickle of sales took place throughout the Celtic Tiger period with a peak in 2001 when three state banks (the Agricultural Credit Corporation, the Industrial Credit Corporation and the Trustee Savings Bank) were sold on the open market and the Irish National Petroleum Corporation was sold. Over the course of the 1990s, the Irish Sugar Company had been floated on the stock market in 1991, the Irish Life insurance company in 1991–3 and the loss-making Irish Steel was sold to the Indian company ISPAT for IR£1, which went on to close the company in 2001.

Of all these privatisations, it was that of the state telecommunications company, Eircom, that has been most controversial. When sold, it was the largest company in Ireland employing 26,255 people in 1980s and 13,552 a decade later as a result of restructuring and modernisation under state control; this made it a much more competitive and profit-making company. In 1996, 20 per cent of it was sold to telecoms consortium KPN/Telia and 14.9 per cent was held by the Employee Share Ownership Trust (ESOT). The 50.1 per cent of the shares still held by the state were sold to the public and to institutions in July 1999 for €4.191 billion, valuing the company at €8.4 billion. Touted as an exercise in popular capitalism at the time, 575,000 members of the public bought shares but most had lost one-third of their investment when the company was bought out by US venture capitalists a little over two years later and taken off the stock exchange. While the sale generated exceptional gains for the Exchequer, Sweeney argues that it was not good for the country as the company was being progressively broken up and sold off. He writes that the failure of the privatised company 'to deliver the infrastructure which was needed in a modern economy and to offer prices which help Ireland remain internationally competitive was even more important than the losses incurred by investors' (Sweeney, 2004: 96). One consequence has been the failure to invest in upgrading the state's broadband infrastructure in which Ireland has lagged badly behind other countries throughout the 2000s.

Ireland's experience of privatisation is revealing of the Irish style of neo-liberalism. For what it reveals is the non-ideological nature of Irish politics and, indeed, of the Irish model. This has grown more through pragmatic experimentalism than according to any master plan and often reflects the interests and worldview of particular ministers rather than a clear collective plan by government. For example, the role of Mary O'Rourke, the Minister for Public Enterprise at the time of the sale of Eircom has been highlighted.

It was she who decided that shares should be sold to the public and told the Communications Workers' Union annual conference in 1999: 'It is my firm intention that there should be a significant tranche of the shares available to the citizens. This is a personal objective of mine' (quoted in Sweeney, 2004: 71). While she had plans for the sale of more state companies, what is most striking about the case of Eircom is the failure of the state to learn lessons from it and fine-tune its policy on privatisations accordingly. As O'Toole stated, she never acknowledged the 'complete failure of her strategy for Eircom, let alone reflected on its meaning for future privatisations' (quoted in Sweeney, 2004: 72). As the Irish state faces a far more serious and systemic collapse in 2009, there are few signs that the lessons of the policy failures that have helped cause it are being learnt and actions taken to address the weaknesses they reveal. For example, Casey writes that when the private Irish banks were losing deposits as the banking crisis struck in late 2008, most of this money was being deposited in the state-owned Post Office savings bank. However, by giving a blanket guarantee to deposits in the private banks, the government 'put a stop to the kind of funding it so badly needed' (Casey, 2009c: 10). This illustrates what Sweeney calls 'the current hostile attitude to public enterprise' on the part of the state's two largest parties, and instances where state companies were refused permission to undertake commercial investments that had every prospect of good returns, revealing the failure of the Irish state to see these companies as an asset that could be used proactively 'to add more value, to generate more high-quality jobs, to grow and become indigenously owned multinational firms' (Sweeney, 2004: 160). This is another aspect of neoliberalism Irish-style.

Pharmaceuticals: The social costs of success

As the Celtic Tiger collapsed, one success story stood out, the pharmaceutical industry. Accounting for almost 16 per cent of industrial exports and some five per cent of manufacturing employment, the sector showed a steady growth from the early 1980s and this continued in the 2000s even as employment in other manufacturing sectors contracted; furthermore, it is one of the highest-skill sectors within Irish manufacturing industry. In their study of the sector, van Egeraat and Barry find employment growth over the Celtic Tiger period occurring in the higher-value-generating sub-sectors (like active ingredients) while Irish plants have assumed a greater role in launch activities. Therefore the level of value creation in Ireland has substantially increased. Over this period, the market share of Irish pharmaceutical exports has grown substantially accounting for over six per cent of world pharmaceutical exports in 2006. However, as with other leading growth sectors of the Irish economy, the pharmaceutical industry is overwhelmingly foreign-owned. In 2003, the subsidiaries of foreign multinationals accounted for 93 per cent of employment in the sector while Irish-owned firms were small and only seven employed over 50 staff. Furthermore, it has been argued that a large share of the value of exports is not added in Ireland; since gross value added in the sector is more than double the EU15 average and one-and-a-half times that in the UK, van Egeraat and Barry estimate that Ireland's large trade surplus in pharmaceuticals is inflated by transfer pricing as corporations declare in Ireland profits made elsewhere in order to reduce their tax liability. They report that profit outflows from the foreign-owned sector are very substantial. They conclude: 'Thus, although much value may appear to be created in Ireland, a large share of this value is not *captured* in Ireland' (van Egeraat and Barry, 2009: 29; emphasis in original).

Yet the continuing economic success of this sector comes at a serious social cost according to some scholars. O'Donovan traces a trajectory of 'regulatory capture' by the industry in Ireland as a result of the establishment by the state of the Irish Medicines Board in 1995 as a licensing authority, assuming functions previously performed by the Department of Health but funded by the pharmaceutical industry. She shows how the agreement between the Department and the drug companies ensures generous prices for the companies (up to 15 per cent in excess of UK prices) and allows marketing practices that are essentially self-regulating, handing more and more control to the companies to define the health messages that reach the consumer and allowing 'pharmacocentric conceptions of health and well-being' to become commonplace (O'Donovan, 2008: 79). She concludes that 'efforts to promote pharma-unfriendly policies foundered, such as control of public expenditure on medicines through generic substitution and effective price controls, not to mention the nationalisation of drug manufacturing. What has emerged is a regulatory regime favoured by the industry, particularly in respect of its corporatist, industry-funded and self-regulatory aspects' (ibid.: 81). Evidence that this affects the practice of medicine in Ireland is provided by Bradley. A professor of general practice, he writes that the industry has 'a very major involvement in the provision of postgraduate educational and continuing professional development in Ireland' (Bradley, 2008: 125), and concludes that 'medicine is a more explicitly commercial enterprise in Ireland than is the case in many other European countries' (ibid.: 129). Lynch, a general practitioner, finds 'the deep entanglement between the pharmaceutical industry and the medical profession is a major cause for concern' (Lynch, 2008: 150). He writes that doctors rely on the industry for information about drugs, that potential addiction problems with these drugs are not being recognised nor addressed and that the specialist medical press, heavily dependent on the companies for advertising, does not report on incidences of adverse side effects. He concludes: 'Given the considerable medical enthusiasm which exists for prescribing antidepressant drugs, I find it quite disconcerting that one rarely hears a doctor outline (either in public or to patients) what I would call the real facts about the effectiveness of these drugs' (ibid.: 147). A final consequence of the power of the pharmaceutical industry is their influence over university research priorities. Glavanis-Grantham finds that the state's R&D spending and infrastructure 'are indicative of a state facilitating corporate interests to a high level' (Glavanis-Grantham, 2008: 97) and she traces the extensive involvement of multinational pharmaceutical companies as significant funders of academic activities in University College Cork (UCC) (since there is a major concentration of multinational pharmaceutical investment in the Cork region). This raises the need, as she herself writes, to examine 'the ways in which the pharmaceutical industry has come to influence health priorities and scientific research' in Ireland (ibid.: 100). The normalisation of the power of commercial pharmaceutical companies over health messages in Ireland is illustrated by a glossy publication distributed to participants at a series of health debates at UCC in spring 2009, co-hosted by *The Irish Times* and Pfizer Healthcare Ireland, a leading pharmaceutical multinational. Using well-known public figures such as rugby players, academics, actors, celebrities and the Minister of Health, the publication associates Pfizer with a range of public initiatives on health promotion and prevention. One of the initiatives reported is a 'Pfizer White Paper on Cardiovascular Health', appropriating the language of a public health publication to label a commercial publication (Pfizer, 2009).

Conclusions

This chapter has examined the interrelationship between state, market and society, showing how the state has played an active role in fostering a particular type of market economy in Ireland, highly dependent on high levels of FDI and ever attentive to the needs of these foreign corporations, even at the cost of endangering the health of its citizens. While public policy sets itself the objective of weaning itself off this dependence and fostering a more innovative indigenous sector, the evidence points to major difficulties in achieving this objective, partly due to the legacies of past policy options and to the institutional power of IDA Ireland over state development policy. The narrow horizons of economic policy are illustrated by the failure of the state to do anything to curb the speculative housing bubble and the reckless lending by the banks which fuelled it, resulting in a profound systemic crisis at the heart of the economy. While all this is happening, the state has failed to appreciate the potential of the shrinking state sector as a way of addressing some of the profound weaknesses of economic development. Finally, the outcomes for society have been illustrated by the case of the pharmaceutical industry. What this chapter has shown, therefore, are the contours of neoliberalism Irish-style, a model in which public authority favours market players, particularly major corporate players, and has actively used state power over the course of the Celtic Tiger boom to give ever greater freedom of action to these players, with disastrous consequences for sectors like construction and banking. The consequences for society of these interrelationships between state and market is the subject of the next chapter.

9
Society: Vulnerability and Control

> Our chaotic health service and our grossly understaffed education system, together with the many serious inadequacies of our social services, reflect very badly upon a political system that has massively maldistributed the huge resources we have created. The harsh truth is we have allowed far too much of our new wealth to be creamed off by a few influential people, at the expense of the public services our people are entitled to.
>
> Garret FitzGerald (2008b: 16)

The approach taken in this book to analysing the Celtic Tiger holds that it is social outcomes that constitute the ultimate objective of the state–market relationship. In other words, economic growth is not seen as an end in itself but as the means to a better society. Furthermore, it holds that the ways in which the state and the market interrelate profoundly affect the social outcomes achieved. This chapter therefore turns to society in order to examine how the state–market relationship that constituted the Celtic Tiger impacted on society. Society is understood here in two distinct ways and each is examined in turn. The first is society as social structure, namely the fundamental ways in which the state–market relationship constitutes the structures of society and thereby influences greatly the quality of life available to people who live in that society. The second sense of society is society as an actor, what we often call civil society. This refers to the ways in which people come together in groups to influence power in society; these social groups and movements can exercise an influence on the way the state and the market interrelate but they in turn are also constrained and shaped by that interrelationship, as became only too obvious in the late Celtic Tiger period as we shall see below. Examining what has happened to society – as understood in these two senses – over the course of the Celtic Tiger is the subject of this chapter.

The chapter begins by introducing the concept of vulnerability as it is argued that this expresses well the impact that the deference of the state to the market, as traced in the previous two chapters, has on society. Vulnerability is used here to capture the central insight of Karl Polanyi, as outlined in Chapter 6, about the destructive impact on society caused by the freeing of the market from controls that seek to ensure it serves the social good. The chapter therefore begins by outlining the concept of vulnerability and its links to globalisation. It then goes on to show how Irish society has grown more vulnerable over the course of the Celtic Tiger, a vulnerability dramatically illustrated by the social impacts of the collapse of late 2008 and 2009. Since environmental vulnerability is one of the principal ways in which society is today being made more vulnerable, the next section traces how this applied to the Ireland of the Celtic Tiger. Section three turns to society as an actor, examining how this has been shaped by the state's project of favouring market forces. The section following that highlights the role of social partnership in co-opting and controlling society, since social partnership is widely seen (as outlined in Chapter 2) as a central feature of the Irish model. The chapter ends by drawing conclusions about Irish society under the Celtic Tiger and the legacies it has left in its wake.

Vulnerability

The concept of vulnerability has come to be used as a way of capturing the distinctive impacts that globalisation is having on society (see Kirby, 2006). It can be defined as 'a state of high exposure to certain risks and uncertainties, in combination with a reduced ability to protect or defend oneself against those risks and uncertainties and cope with their negative consequences' (UN, 2003: 14). This definition then focuses attention both on increased risk and on the weakening of those mechanisms that help protect from risk such as, for example, a robust welfare system. Vulnerability therefore undermines and erodes resilience. Since vulnerability is coming into use in the social sciences in order to identify the ways globalisation is having an impact on society, it would seem an appropriate concept to employ for a country like Ireland which was held to be a showcase of globalisation (Smith, 2005). Vulnerability is also useful as it gives contemporary expression to the destructive impacts on society that Polanyi identified were the consequences of the nineteenth-century experiment when the state imposed the laws of the self-regulating market on society. These are again being seen in our times as constitutive features of the contemporary form of globalisation. Polanyi recognised that one of the 'baffling paradoxes' of the new industrial society in Britain was 'the incomprehensible fact that poverty seemed to go with plenty', as the new industries resulted in a rise in wages but the new society created was also marked by an 'increase in pauperism' (Polanyi, 2001: 89). This contrast between private wealth and social penury has been also noted in the Ireland of the Celtic Tiger (see Box 9.1), thus inviting consideration of why it is that the creation of such wealth as happened over the course of the Irish boom so poorly served society.

Box 9.1 FitzGerald on 'pathetic inadequacy' of public services

Writing in early 2008, the former Taoiseach, Dr Garret FitzGerald, drew attention to a startling contrast in contemporary Ireland. As the country became one of the richest in Europe in terms of output and income per head, he wrote that 'by contrast, our public services remain far behind those of many less prosperous European neighbours'. He went on: 'Why is it that, with a level of income higher than that of 22 of the 27 EU states, our public services fail to look after children in need or to care for the ill and the old; fail to make any serious attempt to rehabilitate our prisoners; and fail to ensure access to clean water – not to speak of failing to provide efficient competitive public transport, just to mention a few of our more obvious public service deficiencies?

'After all, over the past half century our political leaders were remarkably successful in securing much faster economic growth than anywhere else in Europe, moving Ireland from the poorest of the dozen countries in the northern part of Western Europe to becoming one of the richest. Given this success, why have our governments failed so miserably to deploy the vast resources thus created in such a way as to give us the kind of public services we can clearly afford and desperately need?

'One reason for this failure is certainly that during the past three decades many politicians have caved in to pressure from a minority of better-off people to maximise their private purchasing power by eliminating local taxation on households and also by giving massive tax exemptions to wealthy people seeking a high return from investment in construction. These two anti-social processes have undermined the public interest through erosion of tax revenues in ways that did not happen during the first half-century of independence. Next, while clearly some economic gains did accrue from social partnership in the 1990s, most notably in the form of the moderation of pay increases, the cosy relationship this created with two powerful vested interests, the trade unions and business, has worked to erode the public interest.

'The contrast between our new-found wealth and the pathetic inadequacy of [health] and other public services is frankly disgraceful. We deserve better from our system of government, which has a clear duty to so organise its affairs as to enable our citizens to benefit from the kind of health services that citizens of France and Sweden, to give but two examples, enjoy.'

Dr Garret FitzGerald, Taoiseach 1981–7 (2008a)

These considerations in the Ireland of the Celtic Tiger echo international debates about inequality and poverty in the era of globalisation (see Held and Kaya, 2007; Kwame Sundaram (K.S.) and Baudot, 2007). The impact of the liberalisation of markets on poverty and inequality is therefore one manifestation of increasing vulnerability. Other major vulnerabilities that characterise society today and that have grown ever more obvious are the vulnerability of our financial systems and of our environment. Instead of building social and personal resilience, the global financial system has instead come to transmit huge risks and erode coping mechanisms in societies throughout the world, most especially those in which the market was most extensively liberalised (see Gamble, 2009). With the publication of major reports in 2007 by the Intergovernmental Panel on Climate Change (IPCC), a global scientific and political consensus was finally reached on the profoundly destructive natural forces being unleashed by the high levels of carbon dioxide being released by human activities into the atmosphere, with ever more devastating social consequences. In these ways, therefore, the intense interconnections that constitute globalisation are acting to transmit risk and erode coping mechanisms in our world (see UNDP, 2007).

While all these forms of vulnerability are evident in Ireland, they are expressions of a more fundamental vulnerability, namely the vulnerability of the Irish model itself. In its 2003 tri-annual strategy report on Ireland's economic and social policy, the state's National Economic and Social Council (NESC) drew attention to a range of economic and social vulnerabilities that threaten its success. Some of these derive from its small size and peripheral location but others derive from its 'type of economic development' (NESC, 2003: 133). As a small and open economy very dependent on high levels of inward investment, the NESC saw Ireland as being very vulnerable to changes in the international system and to 'extensive decline' through the out-migration of both people and enterprises (ibid.: 54). Furthermore, its very openness makes it difficult to coordinate the actions of employers, unions and government; the NESC highlights the tensions that exist between the constant and rapid adaptation of policy, laws, regulatory regimes and structures on the one hand, and the need for a predictable long-term economic strategy and policy framework on the other. In this situation, 'policy errors, such as pro-cyclical fiscal policy, will be punished severely, because of the importance of competitiveness' (54). These economic characteristics 'contain undoubted social vulnerabilities', said the NESC: 'Economic openness creates the possibility of extensive decline, which can create unemployment, poverty and emigration' (133). The social vulnerabilities include inequalities in opportunities, increased inequality in earnings and incomes, the emergence of 'two-tier' social services, and 'expensive and slow progress on some key infrastructural developments' (151). The NESC recognised that what it called 'an internationalised economy' is only socially acceptable 'if a few key aspects of personal and social well-being – housing, education, health services, transport, enough income to live with dignity and, nowadays, training and life-long learning – are secured for everybody'. It adds that these are 'major challenges that must be met if Ireland is to secure its long-run social and economic well-being' (150). Read in the light of the collapse of 2008 and 2009, these can be seen as prophetic words; unfortunately, they went unheeded by political leaders and policymakers. What they point to is the vulnerability of the Irish model itself with its high level of dependence on global flows and its weak mechanisms to build resilience. The NESC recognised that vulnerabilities arise both from international market pressures and from state inadequacy, but it failed to realise that the latter is a consequence of how Ireland perceives its success in the former. In other words, central to the Irish model is a low-tax regime (which weakens state capacity) as this is seen as a central means to attract the high levels of foreign investment that have been the engine of growth for the economy. The vulnerabilities that the NESC recognises, therefore, are not accidental side effects but central structural features of the model. This alone explains the disgraceful contrast between wealth and penury criticised by FitzGerald (Box 9.1). The next two sections examine the vulnerable outcomes that result.

A Vulnerable Society

Chapter 3 has already outlined trends in poverty and inequality over the course of the Celtic Tiger as well as the inequalities that characterise key aspects of Irish society – its health, education and taxation systems, housing, regional disparities and gender inequalities. Chapter 7 has described Ireland's 'anorexic welfare state' (Box 7.1) and the weak ability of the Irish state to reduce poverty. These, therefore, highlight the vulnerabilities of the Irish political economy – both the generalisation of risk, particularly for those who bear the brunt of poverty, and the erosion of the capacity of the welfare state and its institutions to act as a strong coping mechanism. Here, attention is paid to the extent to which Irish society has grown more vulnerable over the course of the Celtic Tiger, engaging with claims made by ESRI researchers, both on social mobility and on economic vulnerability.

In 2007, Whelan and Layte updated their work on social mobility. In earlier work (Layte and Whelan, 2000) they had examined the transformation of the Irish class structure between 1973 and 1994 and they found a clear trend over time towards increased upward and long-range mobility reflecting 'the economic transformation from an agrarian and petty bourgeois society to a modern industrial, and indeed, post-industrial society' and they observed 'a striking increase in upward mobility and a proportionate decline in downward mobility' (Layte and Whelan, 2000: 104–5). Bringing the picture up to 2002, they find 'a general upgrading of positions in the labour market' (Whelan and Layte, 2007: 73) and, most significantly, they find that the rate at which men from working-class groups were moving into the professional and managerial class doubled between 1973 and 2000. However, an increase in upward mobility for some women is balanced by an equal increase in downward mobility for others. They conclude that 'the overall level of upward mobility in Irish society has increased substantially since the early 1970s and that this trend has been maintained in the recent period of accelerated growth' (ibid.: 79). However, while offering welcome evidence of a certain broadening of social mobility, they also confirm that structures of privilege remain entrenched in Irish society so that 'the ability of those from more favoured class origins to maintain their positions across generations clearly suggests that these groups possess advantages that they use to good effect in getting their children the most coveted jobs' (80). Thus, 'the direct inheritance of property or other forms of capital continues to play a significant role' (81) and they conclude that 'inequality of opportunity parallels inequality of material conditions' (80). What is most revealing about this picture of upward social mobility is the recognition that it relies almost completely on market forces for its realisation. The authors admit that the Irish state 'has not prioritised equity as an objective' and has made 'no concerted attempt to equalise incomes through taxation and redistribution' (68). This, then, is best characterised as a situation of marked vulnerability – social mobility is heavily dependent on what happens in the market while the ability of the state to underpin processes of social change through taxation and redistribution – the strengthening of coping mechanisms – is severely weakened. The risks of depending so totally on the market for social change are illustrated by the depth and severity of the collapse of 2008–9.

Furthermore, the picture of change in Ireland's social structures presented in the rather static periodic snapshots undertaken by Whelan and Layte fails to capture the larger dynamics that are reshaping these social structures. This has been well identified by Ó Riain: 'Underneath the façade of a seamless shift toward a postindustrial, professionalized labour force lies a seething politics – a noisy clash of two middle classes, each growing ever more distant from the low-paid service workers who rarely take their place on the political stage' (Ó Riain, 2004: 140). One of these is the technical-professional class 'driven primarily by business services, high-tech manufacturing and finance, commerce, and insurance' while the other derives from the growth of professional jobs in the social services sector (ibid.). The first of these depends on the success of the private sector and is suffering the brunt of the collapse of the Celtic Tiger while the second is largely the result of the expansion of jobs in the public sector over the course of the boom. The third group alluded to by Ó Riain has emerged as a result of the liberalisation of employment, particularly in the lower-paid part of the services sector (especially in the tourism and entertainment industries which saw major growth over the course of the boom and in which many positions are taken by immigrant workers); the existence of this group also helps explain the high level of relative poverty even as unemployment declined over the course of the Celtic Tiger. The depth of the division between public and private sector workers was illustrated by employers' leaders' use of a discourse hostile to the public sector (especially employment and pay levels) from the beginning of the economic collapse (see O'Sullivan, 2008: 13). The positive picture of the upgrading of Ireland's occupational and social structure needs to be tempered therefore by two other characteristics. The first of these is the growth in social polarisation (as documented by Breathnach, 2007b) and, as highlighted by Whelan and Layte, the entrenched structures of privilege and inequality that remain highly influential in determining life chances in Ireland; the second is the emergence of significant levels of vulnerability, not only among lower-paid or lower-skilled workers but indeed in many sectors of private sector employment. This is consistent with the conclusion drawn by Tasc that a characteristic of Ireland's changing occupational structure, especially in times of recession, is that 'those who are 'comfortably off' may share precarious employment with the 'working poor'' (Tasc, 2009: 6).

Recognising the limitations of using income poverty as a sufficient indicator of economic well-being during a period of boom, Whelan, Nolan and Maitre introduced the concept of 'economic vulnerability' to 'identify a class of economically vulnerable individuals and establish the extent to which overall levels and profiles of vulnerability have varied over time' (Whelan et al., 2006: 94). This helped move the debate on social well-being beyond what had become very familiar debates in the Irish social sciences on consistent versus relative poverty, and instead 'to incorporate concern with the dynamic and multidimensional character of deprivation and social exclusion' (Whelan et al., 2007: 90). This work bases its concept of economic vulnerability on three measures – economic exclusion, basic deprivation and subjective economic strain. Economic exclusion is measured by how many fall below 50, 60 or 70 per cent of average disposable income; basic deprivation by the authors' previous work on deprivation indicators (see Whelan et al., 2003) and subjective economic strain by being a member of a household reporting strain in making ends meet. The objective is not simply to identify those experiencing a specific deprivation at a particular time but to identify those vulnerable to such deprivation (Whelan et al., 2006: 95, 96). This work derives an 80:10:10 division of the population between the four-fifths who can be called reasonably secure and well-off and the remaining one-fifth who are vulnerable. However, they further divide this 20 per cent into two almost equal groups: one is made up of those who simultaneously experience low income and material deprivation, what the ESRI has for long identified as those in 'consistent poverty', and a further one-tenth who, while avoiding such poverty, continue to experience a heightened risk of income poverty, material deprivation and economic stress. They therefore identify 'a set of tiered levels of deprivation' though the levels and depth of this 'are a great deal more modest than suggested by radical critics' (Whelan et al., 2007: 103). Unfortunately, the methodology the authors use to assemble their evidence itself unnecessarily limits the extent of economic strain to be found in today's Ireland as it limits itself to identifying an economically vulnerable group in Ireland, distinguishable from the rest of the population, and measuring how large it is. Yet, as other analysts of vulnerability make clear, it is not limited to specific groups but can affect all in society (UN, 2003: 15). The ESRI authors acknowledge that vulnerability affects sectors of the population other than the vulnerable group it identifies; for example 12 per cent of the so-called 'non-vulnerable' group experience difficulty in making ends meet, while 15 per cent have difficulty in terms of housing costs (Whelan et al., 2007: 96, 98). This points therefore to the fact that a significant percentage of those classed as being 'non-vulnerable' are in fact exposed to potentially serious vulnerabilities, thus undermining the neat 80:10:10 division presented. Furthermore, the parsimonious methodology used by the authors could not capture other possible dimensions of vulnerability, for example the vulnerability of people to a collapse in house prices or employment, both of which have greatly increased following the collapse of the Celtic Tiger. While being methodologically rigorous, the work of Whelan, Nolan and Maitre adopts far too narrow a definition of vulnerability to capture the full range of vulnerabilities facing the Irish model and, through that, Irish society and its citizens. Indeed, the persistent and deepening problem of marginalisation and blocked mobility within the overall upgrading of Ireland's social class structure at the height of the boom, and the speed and depth of the collapse of the economy, points to the value of a fuller use of the concept of vulnerability to describe Irish society at the end of the Celtic Tiger.

Environment

As has already been stated, changes in the environment resulting from the release of greenhouse gases into the atmosphere are a major cause of social vulnerability in today's world. The environment has become a source of greatly increased risk of social damage though, of course, the coping mechanisms of some countries, regions, groups and individuals enable some to withstand these risks better than others. In the case of Ireland, at the height of the boom the state's Environmental Protection Agency (EPA) warned that economic growth was 'causing an acceleration of pressures on the environment' (Stapleton et al., 2000: xi). Among the concerns raised was the growth in the emissions of greenhouse gases which had shown a sustained growth over the 1990s. Furthermore, the EPA stated that 'Ireland's record in achieving emissions reductions as part of negotiated international agreement is not good compared with most European countries' (Stapleton et al., 2000: 39). By 2008, the EPA was reporting that Ireland's greenhouse gas emissions had increased steadily from 55.5 million tonnes to 70.7 million between 1990 and 2001 though they had then decreased slightly to 69.8 million in 2006. As the EPA stated, 'This represents just under 17 tonnes per capita, the second highest in the EU' (EPA, 2008: 30). The agriculture (27.7 per cent), energy (22.3 percent) and transport (19.7 per cent) sectors of the economy were the major sources of emissions with the industrial and commercial sector accounting for 17.2 per cent and the residential sector 10.4 per cent. The increase in car traffic alone between 1990 and 2006 accounted for a 170 per cent increase in CO_2 emissions while the heavy reliance of the energy sector on carbon-intensive fuels for generating electricity increased emissions by 53 per cent from that sector up to 2001, though energy-efficiency measures helped reduce that in the subsequent period.

Turning to the future, just before the collapse in the economy in late 2008, the EPA predicted that Ireland faced major challenges in meeting its annual target of 62.8 million tonnes of carbon emissions over the period 2008–12 under the Kyoto Protocol, stating that on the most optimistic predictions the country would exceed its annual target by 1.4 million tonnes (ibid.: 36–7). This would require the purchase of further emissions credits under the EU Emissions Trading Scheme (ETS). It furthermore stated that the EU target for Ireland in the post-Kyoto period is calculated as 37.9 million tonnes per annum but it could be even tighter if international targets are set that require EU reductions of 30 per cent by 2020. With emissions from agriculture, energy and transport predicted by the EPA to rise to 29 per cent, 27 per cent and 22 per cent, respectively, the agency stated: 'The magnitude of the challenge facing Ireland in trying to achieve these new targets should not be underestimated' (38). A positive consequence of the collapse in the economy was that estimates of Ireland's greenhouse gas emissions began to be revised downwards. The ESRI estimated a fall of five per cent on the earlier predictions with the biggest reductions in transport and manufacturing (McGee, 2009a). Using a number of different scenarios, one of which took the severity of the economic recession into account, the EPA estimated that Ireland's emissions could fall as low as 58.4 million tonnes per annum by 2012, well below its Kyoto target (EPA, 2009: 15). However, this not only estimates the impact of the recession but also presumes that policy measures will be implemented in full and will have the maximum effect predicted.

While Ireland's ability to meet ever stricter emissions targets in future is uncertain, what is not uncertain is the growing vulnerability of society and the ecosystem to the impacts of climate change and greenhouse gas emissions. The EPA predicts that the country's climate has warmed by 0.42 degrees Celsius per decade since 1980, a rate about twice as fast as the rest of the world, and it states that Ireland 'will continue to warm with possible increases of 3 to 4 degrees Celsius towards the end of the century' (EPA, 2008: 30). When it is realised that experts regard it as essential that global temperatures not be allowed to rise by more than two degrees Celsius above pre-industrial era levels if we are to avoid catastrophic climate change (see UNDP, 2007: 7), and that the average global increase since the advent of the industrial era was 0.7 degrees Celsius (UNDP. 2007: 26), then the situation in Ireland is grave indeed. The EPA is predicting more intense storms and rainfall events, an increased likelihood and magnitude of river and coastal flooding and increased storm surges, water shortages in the east of the country in the summers and negative impacts on water quality. It also predicts changes in the distribution of species with the possible extinction of vulnerable species such as the Arctic char, and an increased frequency of wild fires and pest infestation. What is noteworthy in the case of Ireland is the carbon-intensity of its economic growth. If it meets its Kyoto targets this will be in large part due to its economic collapse. It is another sign of the social vulnerability that has resulted from the Irish model.

A quiescent civil society

If the impacts of the Irish model have made society more vulnerable, this raises the question of the role of civil society. As stated in Chapter 6, Polanyi found a 'double movement' emerged from the spontaneous reaction of society to the destructive impact of market forces: if the first movement was the imposition of the rules of the market on society, the double movement refers to the ways in which society sought to put controls again on the market so that it served the good of society rather than society being subservient to the needs of the market (Polanyi, 2001). So why, during the boom years in Ireland, did civil society not react to the impact on society and attempt to impose more controls? To answer this question requires examining the role of civil society, particularly within social partnership. This debate is surveyed here and the role of social partnership in moulding civil society is examined in the next section.

While it is widely used, the term 'civil society' has, in Edwards's words, 'become a notoriously slippery concept, used to justify radically different ideological agendas, supported by deeply ambiguous evidence, and suffused with many questionable assumptions' (Edwards, 2004: vi). One can identify at least three very different understandings of the term in wide use today – civil society as the space of associations free of state control, a view consistent with neoliberal attempts to downsize the state and outsource its service provision; civil society as the space to challenge the state and market, motivating many social movements and NGO activity and civil society as a terrain of anti-state activity, such as terrorist groups and criminal networks of many kinds. In her mapping of Irish civil society, Daly makes the point that much of the focus in Ireland is on what is called the community and voluntary (C&V) sector, a rather ill-defined term that includes the more traditional sector of voluntary action often motivated by notions of charity and the more recent emergence since the 1970s of a strong community development sector inspired by notions of community empowerment (Daly, 2007). While social movements such as the women's movement and, of course, the trade union movement, have made a major impact on Irish society, the years of the Celtic Tiger saw the state draw the C&V sector into an institutionalised relationship thereby constituting it as *the* key sector of activist civil society. As a result, Daly can write: 'The analysis of voluntary and community organisations is key to understanding civil society in the Republic of Ireland' (Daly, 2007: 162). This is not to neglect the fact that, at times, organisations and movements outside the sector have played a significant role. A good example is the emergence of various civil society groups, both on the left and the right of the political spectrum, to lead the campaign for a 'No' vote in the first Irish referendum on the Lisbon Treaty in June 2008 (see Laffan and O'Mahony, 2008: 107–22). These included the Peace and Neutrality Alliance (PANA), the conservative Catholic group Cóir, the left-wing People's Movement and People before Profit Alliance, and the neoliberal Libertas with its shadowy links to the US military–industrial complex. Despite the fact that all political parties except for Sinn Féin (and the Green Party which was divided but whose leaders actively supported the 'Yes' side) were campaigning for the Treaty, joined by the main trade unions, farmers' organisations and employers' groups, these civil society groups managed to persuade the electorate that the Treaty was to be rejected on grounds that it might lead to the introduction of abortion, that it might erode workers' rights, that it might draw Ireland into military alliances or that it might result in EU tax harmonisation. However, though they emerge as strong voices at moments like the Lisbon referendum, most of these groups have little regular or visible presence on the stage of Irish civil society which remains dominated by the C&V sector.

The C&V sector in Ireland has emerged out of two very different traditions of social activism. One dates backs to the emergence in the nineteenth century of a large religious-based sector providing health care, education and other social services; this was dominated by the Catholic Church which by the time of independence in 1922 had become a parallel welfare state to that of the state itself, one the state was only too happy to leave to Church control. It was the establishment of the first pilot projects to combat poverty with EU funding in 1975 that spurred the emergence of a strong community sector, with a much more political vision than that of the voluntary sector. Though the social radicalism manifested in that first pilot programme led to the government shutting it down in 1981, it left a range of groups and organisations working in poor rural and urban areas. Amid the severe recession of the early 1980s, these had an active voice in critiquing state policy and in mounting campaigns such as the National Campaign for Welfare Reform. The establishment of the Combat Poverty Agency by the state in 1986 helped in establishing state links with such groups and programmes began to be developed to fund the work of the community groups, most notably the Community Development Programme (CDP) (Powell and Geoghegan, 2004: 81–100).

As the economy came out of recession in the late 1980s and moved into boom in the mid-1990s, more and more funds, both from the Irish state and through various EU programmes, were directed to the C&V sector. In 1996, they were invited to become social partners in the various partnership bodies, alongside the state, the employers, the trade unions and the farmers. The ever closer relationship between these groups and the state, both through reliance on state funding and through membership of a wide range of partnership bodies, elevated the importance of the sector, professionalising its activities, allowing it employ trained and accredited community and youth workers, and giving it a voice at the heart of policymaking fora.

Initially, this was viewed by some in the sector as a new form of participative democracy which opened important opportunities to influence public policy and achieve the goals it espoused (Crowley, 1998). However, the experience of being held in a tight embrace by the state since has come to be seen in much more critical and even negative terms (see Box 9.2). Recent research has thrown light on how state–civil society relationships have evolved over the Celtic Tiger period (see Ó Broin and Kirby, 2009). This shows a state that, particularly since 2002, has been ever more determined to use its power to make civil society subservient, limiting it to a service provision role, and severely restricting its ability to critique policy and lobby for social change. Four dimensions have been identified.

State control

Though Irish state–civil society relationships have over the decades gone through 'many evolutions, changes of course, u-turns, inconsistencies and adjustments' (Harvey, 2009: 27), over the Celtic Tiger period this relationship came to be ever more characterised by state control. A policy document on the role of civil society had been promised by the state since the 1970s; when published in 2000 as a White Paper *Supporting Voluntary Activity* (Government of Ireland, 2000), it endorsed the right of civil society organisations to have independence and freedom of action, and to be able to speak out on issues that concerned them. However, soon afterwards it became evident that policy was moving in the opposite direction, as a services paradigm began to dominate what the state wanted of civil society. As Harvey puts it, 'that the Irish state fears a civil society that might dare try, in its words, to "persuade" speaks volumes of its multiple insecurities' (Harvey, 2009: 32–3). Geoghegan and Powell place this strategy in the context of 'the hegemonic discourse of social partnership' over the past two decades to which alternative approaches such as local development initiatives and civil society are marginalised (Geoghegan and Powell, 2009: 98).

'Vindictive' funding

It is through funding that the state seeks to achieve its aims for the C&V sector. Murphy identifies a politicisation of the funding regime for the sector's organisations and a discernible shift in funding to organisations that provide services (Murphy, 2009). Furthermore, Harvey shows how the state's desire to control the sector was first demonstrated in funding cutbacks and in unilateral changes to well-established funding arrangements, and he comments that the sector was 'taken aback by the manner and vindictiveness' of these actions (Harvey, 2009: 29). The growth in state funding for the C&V sector over the past two decades and the ever greater dependence of the sector on such funding comes therefore at a great cost to the sector and to the quality of Irish democracy.

Service provision as objective

Observers identify the thrust of the Irish state's policy towards civil society as being one to move it from concerns with redistributive justice and social change towards the provision of services, usually in some kind of partnership with the state. Geoghegan and Powell describe the process as the 'reinvention of community development as consumerist welfare provision rather than developmental active citizenship'. They conclude that the managerialist logic of social service provision orients active citizenship away from political activism and points it towards 'more socially conservative conceptions of active citizenship that emphasise "self-reliance"', thereby reasserting the pre-eminence of the state in the social partnership policy paradigm (Geoghegan and Powell, 2009: 106).

Obfuscating ideology

Accompanying this process of tightening control has been a legitimising ideology that contradicts the state's actions. This found expression in the deliberations of the Taskforce on Active Citizenship. Cronin writes that these have hidden any understanding of the unequal distribution of power in Irish society so that what is presented is a highly individualised and idealised picture of the power individuals have (Cronin, 2009). Murphy makes a similar point when she writes of the failure of the state's discourse on social capital to address power inequalities between communities. As a result, what the Taskforce presents are 'sets of symptoms with no identifiable causes' (Cronin, 2009: 67); by refusing to provide a critical context for the understanding of the operations of the market economy, it deals with problems it can neither understand nor resolve.

The policy of the Irish state towards social partnership therefore helps explain how a well-organised and active civil society can be brought to heel and have its power to advocate for greater social justice and equality severely restrained. In this way, the potential of civil society to influence the state–market relationship through advocating for better quality social provision and more robust redistributive mechanisms has been greatly weakened, if not eliminated altogether. The growing determination of the Irish state to achieve such a quiescent civil society can only be understood in the context

Box 9.2 Crowley on 'diminishing capacity for dissent'

In a paper given to a seminar on 'Enabling Dissent' in Dublin in May 2009, the former chief executive of the Equality Authority, who resigned in protest at major cutbacks in funding for his organisation in late 2008, reflected on the diminishing space for dissent in Irish civil society. 'This space for dissent available to the community sector had already been diminished through an overt, organised and aggressive agenda of control pursued by the state. The state has sought to marginalise dissent through the control of ideas, control of funding to the sector and control of the statutory-community sector policy dialogue.

'The state has celebrated its commitment to equality at home and abroad. It is, however, a most limited form of equality that it puts forward – concerned with fairness and individual opportunity rather than outcomes and real change for groups experiencing inequality. Yet this limited ambition becomes established as the standard to be defended. The state has advanced themes of active citizenship and social capital to support cohesive and content communities. These however are themes divorced from the reality of inequalities of status, power and resources experienced by these communities. These themes involve a rhetoric that promotes connectedness and voluntary endeavour but ignores enduring contexts of inequality and disadvantage. This rhetoric then comes to define what might be appropriate goals for the work of the community sector.

'The dependence of the community sector on state funding has allowed the state to determine a role of service provision for the sector to the exclusion of advocacy roles. This is achieved through the activities for which funding is made available and through restrictive criteria attached to this funding that limit or even prohibit the funded organisation from engaging in advocacy or dissent. This is a growing bureaucratic burden that accompanies this funding. Administration, planning, evaluation, and accountability to the state drain the resources and energy of the funded organisation and limit the flexibility required for dissent and advocacy. Threats have also been deployed to limit dissent. Most recently organisations involved in the Equality and Rights Alliance, the campaign to restore the budgets of the Equality Authority and the Irish Human Rights Commission, had their funding threatened due to their involvement in the campaign.

'Social partnership at national and local level has become the dominant means of policy engagement between the community sector and the state. Social partnership has become an increasingly controlled environment. Non-adversarial partnership is required. Policy dialogue is deemed to be problem solving – and problem solving in the absence of any so-called ideological baggage. This limited partnership is offered but influence is increasingly limited. While policy gains can be identified from social partnership at national level in earlier times the current experience of this policy engagement is one of frustration. Recession has also provided cover for dismantling parts of this community sector. Significant funding cuts have already been made. Organisations have been forced to close, to downsize and to restructure. This, inevitably, diminishes any capacity for dissent.'

Niall Crowley, ex-CEO of the Equality Authority (2009)

of the state's commitment to providing the conditions for continuing to attract high levels of foreign investment. As Geoghegan and Powell have written: 'What is emerging is a form of welfare where the ideology of neo-liberal and communitarian civil society, of community, eclipses the idea of a politically active civil society, binding social actors together in the name of the national project of "partnership", that is, to make Ireland attractive for international investment' (Geoghegan and Powell, 2009: 108–9). It must be seen therefore as another, and sinister, aspect of the Irish model.

Social partnership

For many observers outside Ireland, the involvement of the C&V sector in social partnership appeared to contradict any claim that the state was trying to control civil society and silence its voice. As an active partner with other interest groups in the formulation of key areas of economic and social policy, the sector would appear to have had ample possibilities of influencing that policy. The emergence of social partnership in 1987 seemed to move Irish policymaking in a more social democratic direction, with the state mediating a trade-off between the interests of capital and labour and with a coordination of economic and social policy; the involvement of the C&V sector since 1996 was a unique Irish broadening of the process. Yet Taylor finds that 'almost perversely, these institutionalised forms of intermediation appear to have become a vehicle for imposing a neo-liberal political agenda' (Taylor, 2005: 14). Examining the contents of the tri-annual agreements signed between the social partners, Taylor identifies in the transition from the *Programme for Economic and Social Progress* (1990–3) to the *Programme for Competitiveness and Work* (1994–6) 'a subtle, but none the less crucial, shift towards a more conservative economic outlook, one that effectively abandoned any serious pretension to the social democratic ethos that may have permeated elements of earlier agreements' (ibid.: 41–2). This is consistent with the conclusion of Roche and Cradden that 'social partnership in Ireland since 1987 can best be understood in terms of the theory of competitive corporatism' (Roche and Cradden, 2003: 87), namely the enhancement of national competitiveness and the flexibilisation of the conditions for labour. So why was the influence of the trade unions and the C&V sector on these agreements so weak and, once they realised how little influence they were having, why have they stayed with the process?

In her work on social partnership, Hardiman has helped answer these questions. She sees it essentially as a form of 'flexible network governance ... in which issues can be moved onto or off the agenda, moved up or down in priority, moved into the legislative agenda, or identified as a concern within a longer-term framework of policy development' and thus constitutes 'an important network of policy formation and influence' (Hardiman, 2006: 346–7, 349). Yet she also highlights the fact that 'any prospect of a real trade-off between disposable income and improvement in social services is, for the most part, marginal to the negotiations' (ibid.: 359); ultimately the initiative rests with government, and social partnership agreements never limit the government's budgetary freedom. Furthermore, she finds that 'the input of organisations representing the most disadvantaged is likely to be treated as a "residual category", confined to securing whatever is left over after the established interests have had their say' (Hardiman, 1998: 141). For example, in April 2002 the Community Platform – representing 26 organisations working with the poor, the marginalised and women – left partnership negotiations in protest at government actions which, in their view, had 'rolled back the equality and rights agenda' (Hardiman, 2006: 362). Their protest failed to change the agreement being negotiated and those that remained outside partnership were shunned by government and had their funding cut.

The determination of the state to discipline groups who left social partnership is therefore one reason why so few have done so. For most, though privately critical of how little the process offered them, the balance of advantage lay in staying in rather than getting out. Surveying union members, Doherty finds strong support that partnership has been beneficial in terms of pay and the wider economic climate (Doherty, 2007). Similarly, in his analysis of the role of the Irish National Organisation for the Unemployed (INOU) in social partnership, Larragy concludes that the organisation joined 'because that was "where the action was" at the time, and because other methods yielded little success'. INOU leaders together with those of other C&V groups 'take credit for moderating the policies adopted by Irish governments in the 1990s on unemployment and for defending the position of unemployed people on social welfare' thereby avoiding its more thorough neoliberalisation (Larragy, 2006: 393, 395). It has also been found that social partnership was seen as 'the means of establishing a new pattern of state-financed local social care activity [in rural Ireland] that still continues' (Varley and Curtin, 2006: 430, 438). Enough was achieved therefore to allow most groups convince their members that they should continue to participate. However, it is also acknowledged that these outcomes have been achieved at the cost of becoming more dependent on the state. Doherty found that both union officials at shop-floor level and members had become extremely concerned at the circumscribing of union power that had resulted from immersion in partnership (Doherty, ibid.), and some unions did withdraw, especially those like Mandate which organise low-paid workers. While social partnership agreements effectively prohibit strikes, the large increase in disputes going to arbitration towards the end of the Celtic Tiger period was seen by close observers as shoring up trouble for the union leadership in the event of an economic downturn. The reluctance of union leaders following the economic collapse in 2008 to agree to a new partnership deal involving pay cuts and levies on workers is one sign of this. Larragy finds that the degree of influence of the C&V sector within partnership 'lessened in recent years and it may not easily regain the degree of influence that it had while unemployment and fiscal crises were major issues' so that it 'has had to adjust to a less prominent role' (Larragy, 2006: 395).

It is not surprising therefore that frustration has grown within the C&V sector about the dilemmas posed by social partnership. Meade reports that the sector 'has become pre-occupied with the business of the state. This business is conducted in forums that have been manufactured by the state in order to generate outcomes that, despite the best intentions of the community and voluntary sector, are predictably consistent with the state's economic agenda' (Meade, 2005: 350). Groups have had to abide by agreements and outcomes with 'no direct right to either influence or disavow them' (357) and rely on 'qualified financial support' (359). She concludes that the sector sees its function in social partnership as being 'primarily a defensive one [as] it shields the poor, not by improving their social and economic circumstances, but by protecting them against further immiseration'. She reports 'a palpable sense of frustration among members of the sector who have come to doubt the effectiveness of their own participation in the process and yet who are at a loss to identify alternative approaches to political mobilisation' (364).

From this examination, social partnership emerges therefore as one of the central means through which the state locked both the C&V sector and the trade unions into the power structures that underpinned the Celtic Tiger boom. As Ó Broin has concluded: 'In essence, the state has engaged in a process of bureaucratising potential vehicles for dissent' (Ó Broin, 2009: 123). In doing this, he worries that it has thereby sidelined politics, echoing a persistent criticism that, by giving a key role to unelected state officials and officials of various interest groups, social partnership has undermined the role of elected parliamentarians in the making of public policy (Ó Cinnéide, 1998). Examining these criticisms, Teague and Donaghey draw a distinction between the 'output dimension of democratic legitimation in

Ireland', namely the success in achieving economic and social goals, and the 'input dimension', namely its facilitation of various means to give citizens a greater role in the formation and delivery of public policies (Teague and Donaghey, 2009: 66). They conclude that social partnership has been very successful in the output dimension but has produced rather mixed results in the input dimension since the efforts to develop forms of deliberative democracy 'have hardly been impressive' and have been 'decidedly lacklustre' (ibid.: 65). They therefore conclude that 'social partnership and representative democracy have combined together in a symbiotic manner which has ensured that neither one has triumphed, but each has made a strong contribution' to economic success (66). The collapse of the Celtic Tiger however must temper such conclusions. Why did social partnership not succeed in addressing the unsustainable bubble which public policy did so much to inflate? And, as it met its first real test, analysts were far from certain just how robust it would be to make a contribution to economic and social recovery (Wall, 2009: 17). At best, it can be said that social partnership served well the institutionalisation of the Irish model; what is more debatable is just how good it has been for the longer-term health of Irish democracy and Irish society.

Conclusions

This chapter has surveyed both the social outcomes of the Celtic Tiger and the role of civil society in exercising a voice on behalf particularly of the marginalised in society. It has been concluded that the Celtic Tiger boom increased the vulnerability of Irish society, bearing out the insights of Karl Polanyi on the social impacts of the self-regulating market. Turning to the role of civil society, the chapter has traced the growing tendency of the state to control those sectors of civil society, such as the C&V sector and the trade unions which were most likely to critique the impacts of the Irish growth model. This marginalising of dissent has served Irish society very badly, as is only too obvious in the swift and sudden collapse of economic growth. This chapter has therefore established the outcomes that result from the particular relationship of state and market that constitutes the Irish model, namely the subservience of the state to the needs of market actors, especially global corporate actors. As has been argued, economic growth is never an end in itself but is rather a means to an end – this chapter therefore offers the fundamental criterion on which to judge the Irish growth model.

Part IV Has the Irish Model a Future?

10
Options

> The politics of recession often leads to the questioning of
> current orthodoxies and a ruthless reassessment of former
> beliefs and assumptions. The discrediting of a dominant set
> of assumptions creates new opportunities and new narra-
> tives. They do not always win through. The old order does
> not give up without a fight, since powerful interests have
> become associated with it and they resist change, and main-
> tain that there is no reason why things should not go on in
> the old way. But new interests, as well as those interests sub-
> ordinated within the old regime and forced to accommo-
> date to it, now seize the initiative to press their case. If the
> crisis is deep enough and prolonged enough then the result
> can be a period of turbulence in ideology and in politics, in
> which a range of outcomes becomes possible.
>
> Andrew Gamble (2009: 98)

Part III in each of its three chapters outlined the core elements of what has
become known as the Irish model, a model that has entered into a profound
crisis. This final chapter assesses the options now facing Ireland amid the
steps being taken to manage the crisis. While some may be quick to see
this as the end of the Irish model, the quote with which this chapter opens
reminds us that such an outcome is by no means assured and that a range of
options are possible at a moment like this. The most that can be said is that
the crisis opens a space of questioning and struggles, a discrediting of what
was largely accepted as legitimate by most citizens while it seemed to deliver
economic growth and employment opportunities. It is, then, a moment of
new possibilities but who is going to seize these possibilities and for what
requires careful analysis. This is the subject of this chapter.

This book has up to this point devoted virtually no attention to politics. This is not because politics is not central to the creation of a political
economy model; rather the emphasis so far has been upon identifying and

analysing the Irish political economy model as this has been remarkably lacking both in academic analyses and in public discourse in Ireland. Too much attention to politics can often miss the wider structural context in which this politics operates and far too rarely challenges. A moment of crisis like the present brings this structural context into question and shifts attention back to politics as citizens look to their political leaders to 'fix' it. Assessing what is likely to happen to the Irish model therefore requires examining carefully the arena of politics and the potential both of the political forces that are contending in that arena but also of the structures and culture of the arena itself which have their own distinctive features in every state. The chapter begins by examining the core features of the Irish model as they have been identified over the previous chapters, showing how the crisis of the present is a crisis of this model rather than having other causes. The following section turns to politics, analysing the nature of the Irish political and party systems and the political culture that dominates within them, and linking these to the features of the Irish model that have been identified. The chapter goes on to map the alternatives that can be seen at the present conjuncture – the dominant forces seeking to salvage as much as possible of the Irish model and the emergence of an alternative narrative of the crisis and how it might be addressed. Whether this is laying the foundations of a new political economy model is examined, as are the prospects for such a model to replace the current model that is in crisis. Separate attention is devoted to the wider international contexts that impact on domestic politics and the prospects for a political economy model, namely globalisation, climate change and the European Union. The final section draws conclusions about the Irish model and its likely fate.

The 'Irish model'

While widely used, the concept of a political economy model or a model of development can often be quite vague. Before describing the features of the Irish model therefore, the concept of what constitutes a model requires clarification. The first thing to realise is that models are usually recognised only after they emerge rather than being the result of careful planning. Among the most successful models we have known since the Second World War are the Nordic social democratic model and the East Asian developmental model. Yet, of course, there have been many other models such as the primary commodity exporting model that dominated in most 'developing' countries up until the 1980s or the communist model (or 'state capitalism' if one prefers) that ruled almost half of humanity at one point in the twentieth century. Whether we regard them as successful in terms of their economic and social outcomes or not, what all these have in common are two features. The first is the productive model of resource generation, what we can call the regime of capital accumulation, whether this is in the hands of the private sector or of the state. The second is the regime of distribution, how the resources generated are socially distributed. Both these key features rely centrally on the relationship of state and market and for this reason are called a political economy model. A stable model rests on what Rapley has called 'an implied contract that binds elites and masses in bonds of mutual obligation' (Rapley, 2004: 6–7).

The term Celtic Tiger was first applied to Ireland by the British economist, Kevin Gardiner, head of global equity strategy at the investment banking unit of HSBC bank in 1994 as he compared Irish growth rates with those in the East Asian tiger economies (Gardiner, 1994). The title immediately stuck and was taken up nationally and internationally as the label for Ireland's success. However, the bases of the Irish success and those in the East Asian cases were shown by O'Hearn to be very different, with the state playing a much more directive role in the latter cases whereas it was much more market-friendly in the Irish case (O'Hearn, 1998). Accepting O'Hearn's comparison, O'Sullivan has written that it is rather surprising that the term Celtic Tiger has stuck as 'the image of a bull is a more fitting one for Ireland's economy than a tiger' (O'Sullivan, 2006: 81). If Ireland was a tiger, then, it was a new sort of tiger and this was what interested policymakers and observers abroad, particularly in regions like central and eastern Europe and Latin America which had shared many of Ireland's development problems and wanted to learn how these seemed to have been so dramatically overcome. Viewed from a distance, they saw the state playing an active role in winning high levels of foreign investment in cutting-edge high-tech sectors and thereby upgrading the industrial and services economy, the coordination of policymaking between the main stakeholders through social partnership, and the spectacular increase in living standards and employment that resulted. This appeared to contradict the dominant neo-liberal model being promoted by agencies like the World Bank and the IMF and offer a new form of state-led road to successful development, but one able to manoeuvre deftly amid the pressures and threats of globalisation. They wanted to learn more about the 'Irish model' and Irish policymakers and academics were much in demand to explain what constituted it. As Casey has written: 'When Ireland was booming we had a more important voice in international fora. At meetings in the EU whenever structural reform was being discussed, the Irish delegation would usually be asked to explain the flexibility of our labour market or the beneficial effects of low taxation. How had we done what the rest of Europe – still in the throes of Eurosclerosis – could not do? ... It was heady stuff. Instead of being ignored as we were in the 1970s and 1980s, we were now the talking point and an oracle to be consulted' (Casey, 2009a: 13).

Yet the model that from a distance seemed so successful, turned out to be much more ambiguous on closer examination. The previous three chapters have documented the key features of the Irish model. The first relates to the model of capital accumulation, examined in Chapter 8. This emphasised the fact that the motor of growth in the Irish economy did not come from capabilities developed within that economy but rather was by and large an extension of the success of the US economy since it depended on the growth and innovation generated largely by US multinationals attracted to Ireland. Bradley was quoted as stating that Ireland inverted the normal process of development – instead of generating a wealth-building strategy for the Irish nation, the state simply adapted to the needs of the firms in the global corporate environment. The same reflexive dependence on multinationals was shown to exist in the one area of state policy that is seeking to build innovative capacity in Ireland, namely state spending on R&D. While this may have some successes, it fails to build resilient capacity in the Irish economy and perpetuates the vulnerabilities that are partly responsible for the deep recession in which Ireland now finds itself. This, then, is the first core feature of the Irish model – its regime of capital accumulation is largely a foreign one as the capital is accumulated by foreign firms and substantial amounts of it are repatriated out of Ireland.

The second feature concerns the role of the state and was examined in Chapter 7. This looked at the capability and effectiveness of the Irish state in the sphere of welfare and of regulation, and concluded that it tended to seek low-cost solutions that weakened its effectiveness to achieve the goals it set itself. Outlining the debate between proponents of Ireland as a developmental state or as a competition state, it concluded that while pockets of developmentalism have been evident in the Irish state, the overriding logic that can be identified in the uneven nature of its actions is one that gives priority to the maximisation of competitiveness and profitability over investment in the welfare of society. While the state has remained a central actor in Ireland's development, what it has shaped is a deeply dualistic economy and a weak welfare state. This is the second core feature of the Irish model – the role played by the state has configured both the regime of capital accumulation and the regime of distribution in such ways that they respond much more to the needs of corporate capital rather than to the needs of its own citizens.

The third feature of the Irish model concerns social outcomes and these were examined in Chapter 9. While the increased living standards and improved employment opportunities generated by the Irish model have improved the lives of many, less attention has been focused on the increases in relative poverty and in inequality that characterised the boom years in Ireland or on the failures to invest adequately in quality social services, especially for the most marginalised. The argument was made that what characterises the social outcomes of the Irish model is an increase in vulnerability evident in the depth of the recession that so quickly hit the economy and people's living standards, in the damage to the environment of Ireland's growth model, and in the control exercised over civil society so that critical voices were silenced and ignored. This identifies a third core feature of the Irish model that results from the first two already identified – people's livelihoods and quality of life became far too dependent on the sustainability of a model that was itself highly vulnerable. In these ways therefore the very positive picture of the Irish model that gained widespread acceptance while the Irish economy was booming needs severe modification to take account of its more ambiguous or negative features. As has been emphasised throughout, these weaknesses are not accidental failures of the model that could be corrected but are essential features of a growth model highly dependent on foreign investment and on a low-tax environment.

The final issue to be discussed relates to the causes of the economic collapse. Are these the direct consequence of the structural features of the model that are here identified or, as the Irish government's economic adviser Alan Ahearne has suggested, are they caused by a particular problem in the banking and construction sector which masks the continuing strength of other parts of the economy? Ahearne has argued that by mid-2009, Ireland was showing much more resilience in its export performance than were other European countries and that the Irish workforce was much more agile as it was willing to accept wage cuts that were resisted in other countries. This was already helping to restore competitiveness which had the potential to even keep Irish incomes above European levels (McGee, 2009b: 11). What this account misses is that the growing reliance of the Irish economy on construction, which grew from four per cent of GDP in the 1990s to 13 per cent in 2009, reflected not just the poor judgement of bankers who fuelled this construction boom but the central role played by property developers in the domestic economy and also the failure of the economy to generate an alternative and more productive engine of growth following the collapse of the dotcom bubble. It therefore reflects structural weaknesses of the economy that were not overcome with all the resources generated by the boom: indeed government policies that helped fuel the housing boom actively diverted economic resources from more productive investment, especially in small and medium-sized enterprises (SMEs) (Adshead and Robinson, 2009: 14). Why, then, might we expect these structural features of the Irish economy to be overcome simply by the magic of cutting costs when the state lacks the resources to invest in stimulating a more innovative domestic economy? If Irish exports are resilient at the height of the collapse, it reflects the strength of the pharmaceutical sector rather than any wider resilience in the economy. The willingness of workers to accept wage cuts touches on the distributional challenges that the Irish state has largely failed to address in times of boom. The success of any generalised attempt to reduce living standards will depend to a great extent on whether this is seen to hit hardest those on high incomes and with high levels of wealth; what has fuelled public anger as the state imposes new levies on workers' incomes is that the same state is seen to be bailing out bankers and property developers with huge subventions. Ahearne's optimism about Irish workers' willingness to accept wage cuts displays a remarkable naiveté about the volatility of such distributional issues.

The principal weaknesses of the Irish model relate to its core features – its highly dependent regime of capital accumulation and its very weak regime of distribution. These reflect long-standing weaknesses of the Irish state that, of course, persist as it struggles to contain a huge economic and social crisis. These weaknesses are linked to elements of the political and party system usually not understood by observers outside the country. These are the subjects of the next section.

Populist politics Irish-style

Ireland has an electoral system and political parties that are distinctive, particularly when compared to most other European countries. The origins of the party system lie in the emergence of a single Irish nationalist party in the nineteenth century; this won the great majority of Irish parliamentary seats in the Westminster parliament from the 1870s onwards where at certain periods it held the balance of power between the Conservatives and the Liberals. Following the 1916 Rising and the upsurge in sympathy for the rebels when their leaders were executed by the British, the Sinn Féin party rose to prominence and in the historical 1918 general election replaced the Irish parliamentary party going on to establish an independent Irish parliament, Dáil Éireann in January 1919 that provided political leadership during the War of Independence (1919–21). Sinn Féin drew support from across the class spectrum since it embodied popular demands for political autonomy for Ireland. Following independence, it split along lines that were not based on class but on more radical versus more moderate versions of the constitutional status of the new state – the acceptance of dominion status by the majority in the Dáil who accepted the Treaty offered by the British government and its rejection by a large minority who held out for the mythical 'republic' for which they had fought. The more moderate formed the Cumann na nGaedheal party in 1923 which ran the state up to 1932. Fianna Fáil (FF), a more radical party in nationalist terms (standing for complete independence, the Irish Republic, and therefore known as republicans) was formed in 1926 out of the group defeated in the civil war when they split from Sinn Féin due to frustration with the abstentionist stance of the latter (refusing to take seats in Dáil Éireann since they regarded it as illegitimate). Led by Eamonn de Valera, FF went on to dominate political life in the Irish state after first gaining power in 1932.[1] Cumann na nGaedheal renamed itself Fine Gael (FG) in 1933 and has formed the principal opposition party since then. The Labour Party (LP), even though it is one of Ireland's oldest parties being formed in 1912 during a period of labour militancy, was sidelined during the struggle for independence when nationalist issues took precedence over class issues and Labour agreed to stand aside in the 1918 election to allow a clear choice to the electorate on the question of national independence. In this party system dominated by two large parties, Labour remained a much smaller party, gaining around 10–12 per cent of the vote in most elections – for this reason the Irish party system was traditionally known as a 'two and a half party system'. Smaller parties have come and gone with none lasting for much more than 20 years. An example is the Progressive Democrats (PDs), formed in 1985 out of a split from FF on the basis of honesty and probity in public life and liberal values (both economic and social). It remained a very small party (gaining around five per cent of the national vote) but exercised an influence way beyond its electoral support due to the key ideological role it played in coalition with FF until it lost six of its eight seats in the 2007 general election, including the party leader's, and subsequently disbanded. Ireland's party system has therefore been dominated by FF and it has only been possible to dislodge it from power by a coalition of FG and Labour (with some smaller parties added in on some occasions). FF has only ever been out of power for one parliamentary period at a time; as a consequence it has tended to regard itself as the natural party of government.

While the dominance of FF appears similar to the dominance of the Social Democrats in some European party systems, particularly the Nordic ones, it differs greatly in ideological terms. For, even though clear class bases can be identified for Irish political parties, political culture and discourse has been largely non-ideological, appealing to national interests over class ones. At times FF has portrayed itself as the party of the rural and urban working class and therefore Ireland's natural labour party, but this is always subservient to its vision of itself as a national movement. FG has been more clearly a middle-class party representing large farmers and the urban bourgeoisie and professionals but again has tended to present itself as a national party. In this political culture and with many workers voting for FF, Labour has tended to emphasise how it is different from FF rather than present a strong, class-based alternative. As Mair sums up:

> In sum, Irish party politics grew out of a culture which had emphasised solidarity, cohesion, and homogeneity. This culture was then consciously sustained by Fianna Fáil, which saw itself as a party that represented the interests of the Irish people as a whole, and that decried any attempt to turn sections of this people against others. And, finally, Labour in its own modest and cautious way, acquiesced in this same vision of politics, rarely mobilising, and never sustaining an effective alternative politics. In such a context, no major voice sought to persuade a class alignment.
>
> (Mair, 1992: 409)

Mair finds 'many echoes' of FF's focus on national unity 'in some of the more extreme populist rhetoric employed in the developing economies of

Latin America' (ibid.: 406). But FF's success does more than echo the rhetoric of Latin American populist parties. For, like them, its success lies in having espoused a project of national development through state-led industrialisation and through the extension of welfare measures, as rightly emphasised by Dunphy in his ground-breaking study of the party (Dunphy, 1995). In doing this, it has reinforced a strong dependence of wide sectors of Irish civil society on the party (industrialists, property developers, agro-business interests as well as small farmers, rural labourers and public sector workers). As a result, Jacobsen identifies 'a high degree of deference ... a high propensity by non-elites to defer to policy prescriptions' (Jacobsen, 1994: 95). He also links this to the dominant political reflex of the Irish state, namely a populist response towards co-opting dissent. Thus he says that a level of high deference is based on the diffusion of material benefits to other groups allowing elites to defuse popular protest through concessionary measures (Jacobsen, 1997: 105–7). Furthermore, the clientelistic nature of such politics tends to incorporate organisations of civil society in a vertical way, weakening their autonomy and reducing their understanding of politics to a struggle to gain benefits from the state. Peillon has described how this form of politics tends to give priority to vertical links with those in power as against horizontal links out of which collective interests could be formulated and promoted. Through it, the state can exercise control over society, offering selective access by interest groups to central power (Peillon, 1992: 22). In this way, FF rule corresponds well to Jorge Castañeda's definition of populism: 'a compromise between limited political will to impose reform from above, and limited capacity to fight for reform from below' (Castañeda, 1994: 46). FF's populist success forced opposition parties to try to emulate them but with little long-term success; populism suffuses Ireland's political culture (see Box 10.1).

Box 10.1 Ireland's 'politics of easy options'

Following Ireland's defeat of the EU Lisbon treaty in a referendum in June 2008, well-known commentator and journalist Fintan O'Toole wrote a column in which he likened Irish political culture to that of the trickster.

'[O]ur approach to Lisbon is a very old fantasy, embodied in the trickster. In folk tales, the trickster is a weak figure, an ordinary peasant, who gets one over on the strong – the king, the lords, the bishop – by evading and inventing, by ducking and weaving. He embodies the wish-fulfilment of the weak. You can't shape the world, you can only poke it in the eye. ... We inherited this trickster mentality from our colonial past, but we've had a very hard job leaving it behind.

'In political terms, tricksterism translates, at the personal level, into stroke politics and at the collective level into populism. The stroke – the concept, in this sense, is uniquely Irish – is all about pulling a fast one. It assumes that the system is rotten and will always be so, and uses this assumption to justify the raising of low cunning to the level of high art. The point is not to reform or change the system, but to exploit its weaknesses.

'Populism is this mentality writ large. … The aim is to avoid explicit choice, to have something for everyone in the audience, to let everybody know that you're on their side, even when those sides are at opposite ends of the spectrum. Decisiveness, in this way of configuring politics, is the ultimate sin. The Irish solution to the abortion problem – none of that filth here but, sure why not go to England? – is the ultimate manifestation of genius.

'This political tricksterism, this art of ducking and diving, of endless evasion, is forgivable in the weak. It expresses a view of the world that has helped to get the oppressed through their miserable days for much of human history. But at what point does a society grow up and realise that it's not weak anymore? Could we have reached that point now, where we're actually willing to live with the consequences of the way we've voted rather than looking for someone to save us by concocting a phoney plan C?'

Fintan O'Toole (2008)

The Irish electoral system has reinforced these tendencies. Though Ireland is not unusual in having Proportional Representation (PR), its system of the Single Transferable Vote (STV) is only also found in Malta and Tasmania. This gives voters the possibility of transferring their single vote in order of preference to as many candidates as they wish in multi-seat constituencies. Thus, if their first preference candidate is not elected or does not require their vote because she or he has already passed the quota to be elected, the vote is not wasted and is passed on until it elects someone (see Sinnott, 1999 for an analysis of the system). The consequence of this system is to pit candidates of the same party against one another for votes in their local area, thereby minimising an emphasis on what they have in common with other candidates from their own party (namely party policies) and instead emphasising their effectiveness in representing constituents' interests. Once elected, such a localist view of their role tends to dominate and less emphasis is usually put on their role as legislators so that, as Collins and O'Shea put it, 'in Ireland personalism is at the heart of politics' (Collins and O'Shea, 2003: 105). A report by an all-party parliamentary committee described its consequences as follows for individual TDs (members of parliament are known as deputies in Ireland): 'excessive constituency workloads; an absence of encouragement to parties to nominate socially representative slates; internecine local rivalries, leading to a high turnover of deputies and the discouragement of some high quality candidates' (quoted in Collins and O'Shea, 2003: 104).

From this political system therefore has emerged a policy system 'dominated by the culture of short-term pragmatic politics' (Murphy, 2006: 152). Because politicians have little interest in long-term policy planning, policy tends to be developed 'in an ad hoc and fragmented fashion' (ibid.: 125) and this has resulted in a 'consensus-driven, blame-avoidance, no-losers political culture' which helps explain the success of social partnership and the failure to generate more robust debate on political economy options (ibid.: 242). This political system and culture have also had a major impact on the nature and operations of the Irish state making it very good at problem solving but very bad at long-term decisive planning. The consequences are obvious in the failure to develop more robust mechanisms of redistribution or of market regulation, and in the erosion of the taxation system at the height of the Celtic Tiger boom. This is the state and the political system that now has to deal with its worst economic and social crisis for at least 50 years, and which could well turn out to be the worst since independence.

Mapping alternatives

In his account of the present crisis, Andrew Gamble stresses the importance of ideas. He writes that 'it matters which explanation of the crisis becomes dominant, because that will shape the political response. Interpretations of the crisis become part of the politics of the crisis.' While the crisis will ultimately be resolved through politics 'one of the main aspects is the battle over how the crisis is to be understood, because that determines what can be done, and what should be done, and who has the legitimacy to do it' (Gamble, 2009: 141, 143). In examining the politics of the crisis in Ireland, therefore, we begin with the battle of ideas that has finally emerged after the long period of the Celtic Tiger boom when politics was dominated by a myopic and self-congratulatory consensus. A clear division is emerging into two broad approaches and, for the first time ever in the independent Irish state, this can broadly be characterised as a right–left division, though there are of course differences within these broad approaches.

The first can be called the mainstream approach as it is proposed by the current governing coalition of FF and the Green Party as well as by most economists; though it seeks to distance itself from the actions of the government, the position of the largest opposition party, FG, is broadly in line with this approach. It is characterised by a number of core elements:

- Unlike most Western governments, the dominant view in Ireland is that the crisis must be addressed through severe cuts in public spending and increases in taxation. Following the collapse in the state's Exchequer returns in late 2008 and early 2009, two emergency Budgets were brought in (October 2008 and April 2009) both of which increased taxes on income and implemented a series of cuts in public spending. The government has admitted the need to broaden the tax base and increase the amount it raises through taxation and is expected to introduce a property tax and a carbon tax as well as possibly further increases in income tax. A body of experts was established to examine all state spending and recommend cuts. It is explicitly argued by the government's economic adviser that a stimulus package like that implemented by most other Western governments would not be wise as the benefits would largely leak out of the economy in the form of increased imports.

- The dominant view concentrates on the issue of competitiveness: since costs increased so much in Ireland during the Celtic Tiger boom, it is held that these must be reduced if Ireland is to return to a competitive position in its main export markets.
- The crisis in the banking system is being dealt with through wide-ranging state backing for deposits in Irish banks and through state injection of capital into some of the main banks. One bank, Anglo-Irish Bank, had to be nationalised but the government is resisting calls for the nationalisation of other major banks and instead is establishing a 'bad bank', the National Assets Management Agency (Nama) to take their bad debts from the banks and manage these. As outlined in Chapter 8, some mainstream economists, who otherwise support the government's approach, argue that the two large Irish banks, Bank of Ireland and AIB, should be nationalised on a temporary basis.
- While there is an acknowledgement of the need for more robust regulation of the market and proposals for a new regulatory system for the financial services sector, the agenda of state reform is dominated by the need to save money with no consideration of how this will affect the functions of the state. The main opposition party, FG, places even more emphasis on the potential for savings from a reduction in state spending and personnel than does the FF–Green government.
- Due to the presence of the Green Party in government, there is a mildly Green tinge to the mainstream proposals for recovery which include, as outlined in Chapter 8, investment in renewable sources of energy, in the insulation of homes and in lower carbon emissions from transport, both private and public.
- The final element that characterises the mainstream approach is a firm commitment to holding tax on corporate profits to the current level of 12.5 per cent. It is remarkable that, when taxes in general are being increased, there is no public debate on the need to raise more taxes from the many corporations making very substantial profits in Ireland. This betrays a belief that Ireland can return to its highly FDI-dependent model of development (see Box 8.1).

An alternative view of the crisis and what needs to be done to address it is emerging from a number of sources among them the Irish Congress of Trade Unions (ICTU), the Labour party, the left-wing think tank Tasc and the Community Platform of 28 national networks and organisations within the community and voluntary sector. While there are differences of emphasis, the following elements characterise this alternative approach:

- While acknowledging the gravity of the crisis, the alternative view rejects the deflationary approach and instead seeks state stimulus and support in certain key ways. Labelled the 'social solidarity approach' by the economic adviser to ICTU, Paul Sweeney (Sweeney, 2009: 15), it rejects what it sees as the unfair burdens being imposed on workers while those who benefited most from the boom are not seen to be contributing to recovery. It therefore emphasises the need for income from all sources, capital as well as labour, to be taxed at the same levels, and for a new 48 per cent income tax rate for higher earners. The Labour Party is proposing a National Skills Campaign to re-skill the workforce. ICTU proposes a National Recovery Bond as a way of increasing Exchequer income and wants spending of such income to go on improving public services such as education and transport. Overall, this alternative approach fears that depressing demand in the economy is going to postpone rather than aid recovery. It points out that retail sales in Ireland have been falling at an annual rate of eight per cent as compared to the EU average of 1–2 per cent (ICTU, 2009: 7).
- The alternative approach views competitiveness as requiring more than cutting costs; it also requires that credit is flowing in the economy and so places more emphasis on getting a functioning banking system operating again. The Labour party has proposed the establishment of a Banking Commission to monitor the operation of Irish banks and, since it fears the government's 'bad bank' approach is mired in legal uncertainty, it proposes a temporary nationalisation of the banking system to reconstitute a functioning banking system as quickly as possible. ICTU asks for 'a largely enforceable obligation [on the banks] to provide support for innovation and development in the economy' (ICTU, 2009: 4). The claim that wage costs are high in Ireland is also challenged; Sweeney has assembled data showing the cost of employing an average worker in Ireland is twenty-second on a list of the world's 30 richest countries (Sweeney, 2009: 15). Instead the alternative approach points to the strength of the euro and high charges for utilities such as energy as being the real reasons for loss of competitiveness.
- The alternative approach places much more emphasis on the role of the state in aiding recovery. Labour has a pro-active plan for public service reform with a focus on improving the management and scrutiny of public expenditure. ICTU speaks of 'the critical importance of strategic

state intervention in the economy' showing how the privatisation of the telecommunications company, Eircom, resulted in higher prices and the failure to undertake key infrastructural investments. Labour proposes a revitalisation of the company either through nationalisation or a strategic alliance with another European telecommunications company. A central demand of the trade unions in discussions with the state has been for a €1bn Job Creation and Protection Plan to seek to ensure that redundancy is a last resort. It proposes job rotations, short-term working, a social employment programme, changes in employment law and a more focused, strategic approach to training. Union leaders ask that the government 'treat the jobs crisis as at least being equal in magnitude and scale to the banking crisis' (Begg, 2009: 13).

- There are also points of agreement between both approaches. The alternative approach agrees with the need for property and carbon taxes and with the importance of investment in Green activities. Labour speaks of laying the foundations of a new competitive advantage based on 'smart, eco-growth' (Labour, 2009: 2).
- Overall, the alternative approach sees the need for a much more radical break with the past. Sweeney has written that 'the solution must go far deeper than simply addressing the public finances. ... We require a fundamental realignment of our economy and society' (Sweeney, 2009: 15). ICTU is also willing to address the issue of corporation tax and has called for a modest increase. Labour calls for an end to 'crony capitalism' and a new code of practice for corporate governance.

While these alternatives are focused on the measures necessary to reactivate the economy, the current crisis has also opened a more active debate on the need for fundamental reforms to the political and administrative systems. For example, the Political Studies Association of Ireland (PSAI), the professional grouping of political studies academics, convened a conference on reform of the political system in June 2009 and has begun a campaign for such reform. Among the ideas proposed was the need for greater policy oversight through exposing policies 'to a thorough interrogation by a diverse range of interested parties and experts' (O'Malley, 2009: 12), and the creation of a register of lobbyists to prevent undue influence 'including abuse of dominant financial positions of some interest groups' (Murphy, 2009: 14). A former government Minister, Gemma Hussey, has asked if the political system is 'suitable for Ireland of the 21st century'. From her own experience as a TD (member of the Dáil), she concludes that much of the work of elected politicians is neither suitable nor productive and she hopes that Ireland will emerge out of the present crisis with 'a lean and efficient legislature which will be equipped to face future challenges' (Hussey, 2009: 11). For some, what is needed is nothing less than a re-founding of the Irish political system, a 'second republic' (Box 10.2).

Box 10.2 O'Sullivan on the need for a 'second republic'

'The credit crisis has highlighted the lack of serious strategic thinking on the part of the political and policy-making classes, not just in the past six months but in a habitual way. By and large the skills and incentives of our political class draw them toward small, local issues and leave them unprepared for "bigger picture" ones. The political havoc sown by the smaller political parties during the EU treaty debate [on the Lisbon treaty referendum] was a warning signal of where the abilities and motivation of the mainstream political class lay.

'There is also a sense that the moral paradigm shift that took place in Irish politics from the late 1970s onwards has now caught up with us. Moral courage, accountability and leadership are in short supply. As a framework for reform we should begin to think of a "second republic". While this sounds theoretical, the practical implications are increasingly clear.

'Here are a few proposals: a small Dáil that focuses on "big picture" national and international issues; a presidency with more power and resources is also necessary; elevate local politics to the provincial from county level, and attract better qualified and more accountable local politicians.

'We must also institute an unambiguous legal framework to oversee political corruption, and to govern the interaction between commerce and the State. Upgrading the technical skills of politicians and policy-makers is also very important. Both groups need a deeper grounding in technical areas like economics, sciences and management, for example. Something along the lines of a "Grand École" is an option here, together with co-operation with international universities and institutions such as the OECD.

'Ireland's economic policy-making framework needs a complete remaking. This must be done with the guidance of international economists and institutions such as the ECB [European Central Bank]. It may well be that functions like regulation and governance need to be "outsourced" to multinational bodies.

'With the historically significant Easter period as a backdrop [a reference to the 1916 Easter Rising], the way we think about the economic, social and political issues facing Ireland in a post-credit crisis world needs to be revolutionary rather than the tame fumbling we are used to.'

Michael O'Sullivan,
Irish banker (2009)

If developing an understanding of the crisis is a necessary starting point, which of the alternatives is going to inform policy and who is going to carry through the necessary reforms? These questions touch the heart of the politics of the crisis, and of the potential for fundamental change that it opens up. But, as Gamble states, while the nature of the crisis might seem to play into the hands of the left as it illustrates the need for stronger state regulation of the market, the lessons of history teach us that it is the right that has been the beneficiary of major economic crises in the 1930s and 1970s. In Ireland, the anger of citizens has understandably been directed at the parties in government. FF support in the local and European elections of June 2009 fell to around 24 per cent, its lowest support since it was founded, and it was reduced to the second largest party in the state for the first time since 1932. FG became the state's largest party in local government for the first time. Similarly, the Green Party, which had thought itself to be better insulated from the crisis since it only went into government in 2007 and has not been tainted by its close association with property developers and bankers as has FF, was virtually eliminated from local government in the June 2009 elections and is fearful of its future as a small party. Though the main beneficiary of the shifts in electoral support has been the centre-right FG, some commentators have been pointing to the fact that a combination of the three progressive parties in Irish electoral politics – Labour, the Greens and Sinn Féin – would, based on opinion polls since the crisis broke in late summer 2008, make them the largest single grouping over each of the large more conservative parties. However, despite sharing many common elements in their analysis of the current crisis, an alliance of these three parties poses major difficulties. What all this illustrates, however, is the potential for a fundamental re-alignment of the Irish party system, with FF losing its position as the natural party of government. Were FF to be so displaced, it might erode the dominance of the populist political culture that has so characterised Irish politics, blurring options and avoiding hard choices (Box 10.1). The prospects for an alternative approach to dealing with the current crisis depends on whether FG emerges as the greater beneficiary or whether Labour does. Labour has the benefit of a much more popular leader in the person of Eamon Gilmore but its base of support is only around half that of FG. All of this illustrates the volatility of the present moment and the difficulty of knowing just how radically the shape of electoral politics is going to change; which of the two alternative approaches continues to dominate policy will depend on this.

For the first time since independence, the alternative approaches to the present crisis show the outlines of the options facing the Irish people. The mainstream approach seeks to return to the principal elements of the Irish model, highly dependent on FDI and highly unequal in its distribution of the benefits of the productive economy, favouring global and local elites over those most marginalised and disadvantaged. The one addition is a new and belated awareness of the need for a certain 'greening' of this model to make it more environmentally sustainable. The alternative, though still in the very early stages of being shaped, carries the prospect of a new political economy model emerging; this would require a much more innovative and entrepreneurial state, with the capacity to shape the market so that it better serves the objective of an equitable and sustainable productive economy, with robust mechanisms of redistribution and with a taxation system sufficient to resource a capable state. It would entail a shift of power in Irish society, not only politically but socially as well. Thus, politics and political economy are intimately related.

Yet Ireland's future is not going to be shaped by its own actions alone. As has already been outlined in Chapter 2, the Celtic Tiger model emerged due to Ireland's ability to avail of a more benign international environment, both associated with the forces we label globalisation and with possibilities that came from membership of the EU. If anything, these international forces have now turned much more negative and challenging for Ireland. To these we now turn.

Globalisation

Much has been made of Ireland's ability to ride the waves of globalisation and turn them to its advantage. However, the present crisis poses major question marks about globalisation itself as countries respond to the crisis by giving state support to their banks and other sectors of their economies, and seeming to favour the national over the international. Writing from the World Economic Forum in Davos in February 2009, Rachman identified a continuing support for the liberal economic order at the level of ideas but acknowledged that 'while the ideas that underpinned globalisation remain firmly in place, events are moving in the opposite direction'. By this he meant that world leaders are being pulled in two directions – intellectually they want to keep trade and investment flowing but politically they are under pressure to respond to angry and frightened voters who want their jobs and livelihoods protected (Rachman, 2009: 13). For a country like Ireland, so dependent on the liberal trading and investment order, this constitutes something of a warning signal. At the moment, it may not be possible to envisage a breakdown of that order in any fundamental way, but it does make political leaders more determined to ensure that the benefits are distributed as widely as possible and that some countries are not allowed to undercut others.

This is the point that is most threatening to the Irish model, built as it was on attracting high levels of foreign investment through low taxes on corporate profits. When the Celtic Tiger boomed while its neighbours struggled with anaemic growth rates, leaders in Britain, France and Germany became ever more critical of the impact of Ireland's low-tax regime on their economies, attracting some of their companies to set up in Ireland thereby avoiding tax, and winning foreign investment that otherwise might have gone to them. Once the crisis struck, such leaders were not slow in expressing their wish that Ireland would now have to increase its levels of corporation tax. Senior German officials have publicly stated that increasing corporation tax would be a condition for Ireland receiving German economic assistance. As one was quoted on this issue: 'Sometimes there is a need for a prod from outside. Sometimes countries recognise from themselves that things they have done in the past are not always sustainable in a crisis' (Scally, 2009: 1). In a lecture in Dublin, an advisor to the European Commission, Prof. Maria Joao Rodrigues made a similar point when she emphasised that Ireland's use of competitive tax policies was in conflict with the concept of European solidarity (Keena, 2009b: 20). It looks ever more likely therefore that Ireland's ability to resist EU moves towards tax harmonisation will be greatly weakened in the present crisis. This will pose a major challenge to Ireland's growth model.

Climate change

The second issue that is fundamentally changing the international context is climate change. As outlined in Chapter 9, the Celtic Tiger paid little attention to environment with the result that Ireland has been warming at an alarmingly high rate. It took the consensus generated by the four reports of the Intergovernmental Panel on Climate Change in 2007 to bring the issue to the centre of the political agenda, helped in the case of Ireland by the entry of the Green party into government for the first time in mid-2007. Yet as soon as the financial crisis struck a year later, the twin threats of peak oil and climate change seemed to become less immediate. What cannot be forgotten is that countries like Ireland are going to face a major challenge of reducing carbon emissions by at least 20 per cent over the coming decade; to achieve this it is clear that there can be no return to the previous form of growth. The optimists present this as an economic opportunity to invest in clean energies and in retrofitting the housing stock, and there undoubtedly is some potential in these forms of investment. Yet climate change and peak oil pose a deeper challenge to the growth economy itself. Put simply, as environmentalists state it, we cannot have infinite growth in a finite world. So, even if Ireland managed to recreate the conditions for a return to the high growth of the boom years, the destructive impacts this is having on resource depletion, on biodiversity and habitats, on the melting of the ice caps and the rise of sea levels, as well as on greenhouse gas emissions, make growth itself unsustainable (Daly, 1996). The implications for the role of the state in establishing the institutions and lifestyle changes necessary for a sustainable future are identified by Gamble:

> The implications for the global economy are immense, since these changes would require a gradual but persistent redistribution of wealth

and power within national societies and within the global economy, and the use of state power at both national and global level to fashion a very different kind of economy and society, in which types of organisation, the nature of work and individual lifestyles would all be transformed.

(Gamble, 2009: 162)

Ireland is of course not alone in facing these immense challenges but the Irish model, with its extremely market-friendly state, its low tax base and its inability to plan for a more successful society all make it ill-prepared for dealing with them. However, if it wants to ignore them it is not going to be allowed do so as the European Union has made it clear that it is taking a leadership role on climate change.

The EU

Ireland joined the European Union (the European Economic Community as it was then) on 1 January 1973. The role of the EU in helping create the conditions for the Irish model and the Celtic Tiger boom has been outlined in Chapter 2. Broadly speaking, these are two. Firstly, membership of the EU provided the reason why so many US multinationals were attracted to establish in Ireland, namely access to the European market; secondly, from the late 1980s, Ireland won high levels of structural funds that allowed it to invest in human resources, in upgrading the country's infrastructure and in aids to the private sector. Indeed, Adshead and Robinson see this inflow of EU funds as having allowed Ireland avoid the hard choices facing any latecomer to development, namely the choice between investment and consumption. They write that, in Ireland 'the role of traditional developmental state was displaced on to the European Union, which channelled investment into infrastructural projects without the need for the Irish state to curtail consumption to finance developments to underpin general economic growth'. As a result, 'international economic liberalisation enabled the Irish state to "free ride" on the benefit of globalisation (in the form of access to global financial markets and to foreign direct investment)' (Adshead and Robinson, 2009: 18).

These free rides are now over. Not only is Ireland about to move from being a net beneficiary to becoming a net contributor to the Union, but the goodwill towards Ireland that had characterised its membership was severely undermined by the 'No' vote in the 2008 Lisbon treaty referendum. This was perceived throughout Europe, and particularly among the new central and eastern European members, as indicating a lack of willingness to share the fruits of its success with poorer member states. Irish diplomats immediately moved to limit the damage but there was a general recognition that a lot of damage had been done to Ireland's reputation. Amid its own severe recession, therefore, Ireland has far less goodwill among its fellow members on which to trade. Instead it faces critical questions of having squandered its boom. It is therefore very clear that there is no return to the conditions that helped create the Irish model.

Whither the Irish model?

Ireland faces a crisis of huge proportions. Not only is the depth of its economic downturn quite unique by the standards of developed countries in the post–World War II world, but it faces the challenge of emerging from it without the ability to devalue, a mechanism widely used by states to boost exports and competitiveness in a way that impacts uniformly across the domestic economy and society. Instead, the Irish state faces years of implementing major cutbacks, each of which will further fuel public anger, and the challenge (which it has never successfully addressed in its history) of trying to impose such cuts in a way that is seen to hit the rich and powerful as well as the average earner and the marginalised. Opting so far not to implement a stimulus package, 'could prove to be the worst own goal in our history' in the words of former chief economist of the Central Bank, Michael Casey. 'If economic activity falls further, so will revenue, and the Government will find itself chasing a target from which it is constantly moving away' (Casey, 2009c: 10).

Amid such uncertainty, it would be foolhardy to make predictions. But, as this chapter has argued, there is every reason to believe that it decisively marks the end of the Irish model. As a model, it reflected not only the lucky correlation of international conditions that allowed Ireland hitch a free ride on a largely US boom, but it also seemed to offer an easy route out of long-term developmental weaknesses for a political system lacking the ability to analyse accurately the major challenges facing it and to plan decisively to address them. It is not that the Irish state is inactive; rather it is characterised by a general scattergun approach to distributing public goods based on the hope that some of them might prove beneficial and by far too close and closed a relationship with elite vested interests (property developers, financiers, the legal and medical profession, to name the principal ones). All this reflects a state dominated and controlled for far too long by one political party, FF.

If there is to be no return to the Irish model as it developed over the course of the boom, what is far less sure is that this deep crisis will be the opportunity to redress the enormous political, social and economic weaknesses that gave rise to it. It is far too early to say. A precondition will be the emergence of new political forces linked to wider social interests among small and medium enterprises, in the universities, in organised civil society, and elsewhere that could give leadership and mobilise talents and capacities for a re-founding of the Irish state. Even if this daunting task could be undertaken with some coherence and vision, such a state then faces an immense task of helping develop a more sustainable economy in a much more volatile world order. It would require a very different Irish model to achieve that, one characterised by solidarity, a real awareness of the scale of the challenges, greater self-reliance and independence of spirit, and bucket-loads of creativity. Since independence, Ireland has tended to imitate others' public policies, particularly those of Britain. Though the Celtic Tiger appeared to mark a new level of innovation in public policy, the collapse raises real questions as to how much of this was based on a rather overblown rhetoric that hid a lot of fundamental continuity in the power structures of Irish society. Now, at long last, is the time for a decisive break with the politics and political economy that brought Ireland to collapse; the time has come for a new beginning.

Notes

1 Before the Tiger

1. Ireland is seen by some commentators as more akin to a regional economy within Europe (see Barry, 2002; Tomaney, 1995: 109). However, this throws no light on its development path.
2. In surveying this debate, Jacobson (1989) explores whether terms like late industrialising countries (LICs) or semi-industrialized countries (SICs) may not be more appropriate to the Irish case but does not opt for one over the others (172–4). For the purposes of this study, the term NIC, which is widely used in international literature, is a satisfactory categorisation.
3. Equivalence scales are different means used to adjust the income of each household to reflect its size and composition, allowing for the fact that adults have greater needs than children and for the sharing of household costs.
4. Nolan's results are not strictly comparable to the estimates produced by Lyons since they are based on the household unit rather than on the individual.

2 Assessing the Boom

1. Whereas GNP deducts factor income flowing out of the country and adds such income received from abroad, GNI in addition adds subsidies received from abroad and deducts taxes paid abroad. Since EU subsidies have been a significant source of income in Ireland, GNI is regarded as the more comprehensive measure of income available to Irish residents particularly since the late 1980s. For example, over the decade 1996–2005, Ireland's GNI declined from 90 per cent of its GDP to 85 per cent.
2. The social partnership agreements were as follows: *Programme for National Recovery* (1987–90), *Programme for Economic and Social Progress* (1991–3), *Programme for Competitiveness and Work* (1994–6), *Partnership 2000* (1997–2000), *Programme for Prosperity and Fairness* (2000–2), *Sustaining Progress* (2003–5) and *Towards 2016* (2006–16).

3 Best of Times?

1. The authors add that some of this may be due to a greater willingness by very high earners to declare their income than previously was the case, due to more efficient administration by the tax authorities and their high-profile investigations into tax evasion.
2. The use of GDP rather than GNP here may be a factor in Ireland's worsening position including as it does substantial profits repatriated by foreign multinationals operating in Ireland and the practice of transfer pricing.
3. The seven counties along the western seaboard are Donegal, Leitrim, Sligo, Roscommon, Galway, Mayo and Clare. They contain some of the poorest regions in Ireland.

4   Dominant Readings

1. At the end of his article on classical growth models in *The New Palgrave*, Harris (1987: 448) concludes that 'The theory of growth of capitalist economies continues to be one of the most fascinating and still unresolved areas of economic theory'.
2. For an overview of international attempts to develop alternative measures of social development to GDP/GNP, see Scott et al. (1996: Chapter 5).
3. For a unique attempt to develop an Index of Social Progress (ISP) for Ireland, see Clark and Kavanagh (1996).
4. For example, in acknowledging that the Swedish approach is strongly influenced by Sen's theory of functionings and capability, they simply dismiss this by saying that these concepts 'are not of direct assistance here because the aim was to measure *inequality* in the distribution of the individual's command over resources ... not poverty' (Nolan and Whelan, 1996: 183). This entirely overlooks the fact that such an approach might uncover the nature and extent of social deprivation in a fuller and more adequate way than does their approach.
5. For example, locating the motivation for crime 'in the patterns of exclusion and disadvantage created by the operation of the class structure and in the experience of offenders with the institutions of social control in Ireland' (McCullagh, 1996: 53).
6. The reference is to Declan Kiberd, *Inventing Ireland: The Literature of the Modern Nation*, Jonathan Cape, London, 1995.
7. Of 25 footnotes to his 53-page closing chapter in *Europe: The Irish Experience* (2000) which he edited, seven refer to O'Toole.

5   Critical Readings

1. O'Hearn (n.d.: 7, 8) describes the differences as follows: 'Core regions specialise in capital-intensive products, using skilled and relatively high-wage labour. Peripheral regions specialise in labour-intensive products, using unskilled and low-wage labour. Semi-peripheral regions mix both types of production. This is associated with a hierarchy of incomes between rich, moderately poor, and poor regions. A few countries move between zones, giving the appearance of mobility, but the hierarchy remains.'
2. Munck specifies the causal connection between external dependence and internal uneven development as follows: 'The disparities in productivity caused by foreign investment lead to inter-sectoral imbalances, a widening of income differentials and a growing marginalization of the population outside the dynamic sector. The local dominant class (or 'dependent bourgeoisie') is increasingly incapable, under these conditions, of creating an autonomous capitalist path of development. The development which does take place is thus in association with the dominant economies, in particular the transnational corporations. The links of dependence are thus strengthened while, at the same time, the state tends to exclude growing sections of society from participation in the benefits of development. The dependent nation state is thus not sovereign in either economic or political terms, a state of affairs dictated equally by internal forces as much as by external ones' (Munck, 1993: 3).
3. The reference is to André Gunder Frank, a father of dependency theory (see Kirby, 1997: 54–7).

4. Bradley writes: 'The most extraordinary assertion of the dependency theory concerns the claim of "decapitalisation" as TNCs "drain" capital out of the host country. But surely what is going on here is that TNCs invest in building and operating factories in (say) Ireland, but ship their profits out. Thus there is a net gain in the stock of physical plant and equipment in Ireland, a continuous injection of income through the wage bill and other purchases of intermediate inputs sourced in Ireland, and a retention of at least a fraction of the profit stream, with the balance being repatriated. A possible down-side is the potential that a TNC may "crowd out" domestic activity by abuse of its global market access or through driving up the price of labour in sheltered sectors (what economists call the "Dutch" disease). However, compared with the alternative – i.e., no TNC in Ireland – the gains are massive" (Bradley, 1997: 8).

6 Elaborating Theory

1. Giddens mentions such theoretical perspectives as ethnomethodology, various forms of symbolic interactionism, neo-Weberianism, phenomenology, structuralism, hermeneutics and critical theory (Giddens, 1996: 66).
2. The 'growth with equity' literature is largely concerned with the developing world. However, the hypothesis which dominated the literature for two decades (the Kuznets curve) was based on the experience of three developed countries at an earlier phase of their development (Britain, the US and Germany), and some scholars use databases which include so-called 'developed countries' (for example, Bornschier et al. (1978), Nielsen and Alderson (1995), Alesina and Perotti (1997), Birdsall and Londoño (1997) and Ahluwalia (1976)). The first four of these include Ireland.
3. I understand this to mean not the aspiration towards a unified theoretical framework but rather a social science within which disciplinary and theoretical boundaries do not have the result of fragmenting enquiry into separate and exclusive disciplines each with theoretical schools that have little to say to one another. Instead, in the light of Giddens' views of the changing self-understanding of the social sciences, I conceive of a unified historical social science as one characterised by a concern for larger issues of long-term social change and, while inevitably containing a wide range of specialist areas of study, the ability to draw on the insights and methods of a multiplicity of disciplines and approaches in order to offer a deeper understanding of social reality. A plurality of theoretical approaches would still characterise such a unified social science, though hopefully there would be more dialogue between them than is currently the case. This would require an acknowledgement that no theoretical approach has a monopoly of explanatory power.

10 Options

1. FF has governed in the years 1932–47, 1951–54, 1957–73, 1977–81, a brief six-month government from late 1981 to early 1982, 1987–94 and 1997–date. It governed on its own up to 1989 when it entered a coalition for the first time with the small Progressive Democrat party until 1992. From 1992 to 1994 it was in coalition with the Labour Party. Since returning to office in 1997, it was in coalition with the PDs from 1997 to 2007 and, following the 2007 general election, the Green Party joined this coalition.

Bibliography

A. T. Kearney/Foreign Policy (2001): 'Measuring Globalization', in *Foreign Policy*, January/February 2001, pp. 56–65.

—— (2002): 'Globalization's Last Hurrah?', in *Foreign Policy*, January/February 2002, pp. 38–51.

—— (2003): 'Measuring Globalization: Who's Up, Who's Down?', in *Foreign Policy*, January/February 2003, pp. 60–72.

—— (2004): 'Measuring Globalization: Economic Reversals, Forward Momentum', in *Foreign Policy*, March/April 2004, pp. 54–69.

—— (2005): 'Measuring Globalization: The Global Top 20', in *Foreign Policy*, May/June 2005, pp. 52–60.

—— (2006): 'The Globalization Index', in *Foreign Policy*, November/December 2006, pp. 74–81.

—— (2007): 'The Globalization Index', in *Foreign Policy*, November/December 2007, pp. 68–76.

Adelman, Irma and Cynthia Taft Morris (1973): *Economic Growth and Social Equity in Developing Countries*, Stanford Conn.: Stanford University Press.

Adshead, Maura and Neil Robinson (2009): 'Late development and State developmentalism – never the twain? Towards a political economy of "post–Celtic Tiger" Ireland', paper given to the Political Studies Association annual conference, University of Manchester, 7–9 April 2009.

Adshead, Maura, Peadar Kirby and Michelle Millar, eds (2008): *Contesting the State: Lessons from the Irish case*, Manchester: Manchester University Press.

Ahluwalia, Montek S. (1976): 'Inequality, Poverty and Development', in *Journal of Development Economics*, Vol. 3, pp. 307–42.

Alesina, Alberto and Roberto Perotti (1997): 'The Politics of Growth: A Survey', in Villy Bergstrom, ed.: *Government and Growth*, Oxford: Clarendon Press, pp. 11–60.

Allen, Kieran (1999): 'The Celtic Tiger, Inequality and Social Partnership', in *Administration*, Vol. 47, No. 2, pp. 31–55.

—— (2000): *The Celtic Tiger: The Myth of Social Partnership in Ireland*, Manchester: Manchester University Press.

—— (2007): *The Corporate Takeover of Ireland*, Dublin: Irish Academic Press.

Amsden, Alice (1989): *Asia's Next Giant: South Korea and Late Industrialization*, Oxford: Oxford University Press.

Archer, Peter (2001): 'Public Spending on Education, Inequality and Poverty', in Sara Cantillon, Carmel Corrigan, Peadar Kirby and Joan O'Flynn, eds: *Rich and Poor: Perspectives on Tackling Inequality in Ireland*, Dublin: Oak Tree Press in association with the Combat Poverty Agency, pp. 197–234.

Atkinson, Anthony B., Lee Rainwater and Timothy M. Smeeding (1995): *Income Distribution in OECD Countries: Evidence from the Luxembourg Income Study*, Paris: OECD.

Barber, William J. (1991): *A History of Economic Thought*, Harmondsworth: Penguin.

Barr, Nicholas (1998): *The Economics of the Welfare State*, Oxford: Oxford University Press.

Barrett, Alan, Ide Kearney and Jean Goggin (2009): *Quarterly Economic Commentary*, spring 2009, Dublin: ESRI.

Barry, Frank (1991): 'Industrialisation Strategies for Developing Countries: Lessons from the Irish Experience', in *Development Policy Review*, Vol. 9, pp. 85–98.

—— (1999): 'Irish Growth in Historical and Theoretical Perspective', in Frank Barry, ed.: *Understanding Ireland's Economic Growth*, Basingstoke: Macmillan, pp. 25–44.

—— (2002): 'The Celtic Tiger Era: Delayed Convergence or Regional Boom?', in Daniel McCoy, David Duffy, Adele Bergin, John Eakins, Jonathan Hore and Conall MacCoille: *Quarterly Economic Commentary*, summer 2002, Dublin: ESRI, pp. 84–91.

—— (2006): 'Future Irish Growth: Opportunities, Catalysts, Constraints', in Alan Barrett, Ide Kearney, Shane Garrett and Yvonne McCarthy: *Quarterly Economic Commentary*, winter 2005, Dublin: ESRI, pp. 34–58.

Barry, Frank and Aoife Hannan (1995): 'Multinationals and Indigenous Employment: An "Irish Disease"?', in *The Economic and Social Review*, Vol. 27, No. 1, pp. 21–32.

Barry, Frank and Nick Crafts (1999): 'Some Comparative Aspects of Ireland's Economic Transformation', in *Irish Banking Review*, autumn, pp. 39–51.

Barry, Frank, Aoife Hannan and Eric A. Strobl (1999): 'The Real Convergence of the Irish Economy and the Sectoral Distribution of Employment Growth', in Frank Barry, ed.: *Understanding Ireland's Economic Growth*, Basingstoke: Macmillan, pp. 13–24.

Barry, Ursula (2008): 'Changing Economic and Social Worlds of Irish Women', in Ursula Barry, ed.: *Where are we now? New feminist perspectives on women in contemporary Ireland*, Dublin: Tasc with New Island, pp. 1–29.

Bartley, Brendan and Rob Kitchen, eds (2007): *Understanding Contemporary Ireland*, London: Pluto Press.

Begg, David (2008): 'Dangers of worshipping false god of self-regulating markets', in *The Irish Times*, 3 October 2008, p. 14.

—— (2009): 'Support scheme key to tackling jobs crisis', in *The Irish Times*, 2 July 2009, p. 13.

Birchfield, Vicki (1999): 'Contesting the Hegemony of Market Ideology: Gramsci's "good sense" and Polanyi's "double movement"' in *Review of International Political Economy*, Vol. 6, No. 1, pp. 27–54.

Birdsall, Nancy and Juan Luis Landoño (1997): 'Asset Inequality Does Matter: Lessons from Latin America', OCE Working Paper, Washington DC: Inter-American Development Bank.

Birdsall, Nancy, David Ross and Richard Sabot (1995): 'Inequality and Growth Reconsidered: Lessons from East Asia', in *The World Bank Economic Review*, Vol. 9, No. 3, pp. 477-508.

Booth, David, ed. (1994): *Rethinking Social Development: Theory, Research and Practice*, Harlow: Longman.

Bornschier, Volker, Christopher Chase-Dunn and Richard Rubinson (1978): 'Cross-national Evidence of the Effects of Foreign Investment and Aid on Economic Growth and Inequality: A Survey of Findings and a Reanalysis', in *American Journal of Sociology*, Vol. 84, No. 3, pp. 651–83.

Boylan, Thomas A. (2002): 'From stabilisation to economic growth: The contribution of macroeconomic policy', in George Taylor, ed.: *Issues in Irish Public Policy*, Dublin: Irish Academic Press, pp. 9–27.

Boyle, Nigel (2005): *FÁS and Active Labour Market Policy 1985–2004*, Dublin: The Policy Institute at Trinity College.

Bradley, Colin (2008): 'The Medical Profession and the Pharmaceutical Industry: Entwined, Entangled or Ensnared?' in Orla O'Donovan and Kathy Glavanis-Grantham, eds: *Power, Politics and Pharmaceuticals*, Cork: Cork University Press, pp. 117–34.

Bradley, Finbarr and James J. Kennelly (2008): *Capitalising on Culture, Competing on Difference: Innovation, Learning and Sense of Place in a Globalising Ireland*, Dublin: Blackhall Publishing.

Bradley, John (1997): 'Tigers, Tiggers and Tortoises: Changing Faces of the Irish Development Experience', paper to conference on Poverty Amid Plenty: Development Strategies Reconsidered, Dublin, February 1997.

―― (2000): 'The Irish Economy in Comparative Perspective', in Brian Nolan, Philip J. O'Connell and Christopher T. Whelan, eds: *Bust to Boom? The Irish Experience of Growth and Inequality*, Dublin, Institute of Public Administration, pp. 4–16.

―― (2002): 'The Computer Sector in Irish Manufacturing: Past Triumphs, Present Strains, Future Challenges', in *Journal of the Statistical and Social Inquiry Society of Ireland*, Vol. XXXI, pp. 26–73.

Bradley, John, Karl Whelan and Jonathan Wright (1993): *Stabilization and Growth in the EC Periphery: A Study of the Irish Economy*, Aldershot: Avebury.

Brady, Hugh and John Hegarty (2008): 'We must invest now in our universities or pay later', in *The Irish Times*, 18 March 2008, p. 11.

Breathnach, Proinnsias (1985): 'Rural Industrialization in the West of Ireland', in Michael J. Healey and Brian W. Ilbery, eds: *The Industrialization of the Countryside*, Norwich: Short Run Press, pp. 173–95.

―― (2007a): 'The services sector', in Brendan Bartley and Rob Kitchin, eds: *Understanding Contemporary Ireland*, London: Pluto Press, pp. 146–57.

―― (2007b): 'Occupational change and social polarisation in Ireland: Further evidence', in *Irish Journal of Sociology*, Vol. 16, No. 1, 2007, pp. 22–42.

Breen, Richard, Damian F. Hannan, David B. Rottman and Christopher T. Whelan (1990): *Understanding Contemporary Ireland: State, Class and Development in the Republic of Ireland*, Dublin: Gill & Macmillan.

Brennan, Niamh (2008): 'Reputation of Ireland Inc is under spotlight after resignations', in *The Irish Times*, 20 December 2008, p. 19.

Browne, Frank X. and Donal McGettigan (1993): 'Another Look at the Causes of Irish Underemployment', Technical Paper 1/RT/93, Dublin: Central Bank of Ireland.

Bruno, Michael, Martin Ravallion and Lyn Squire (1996): 'Equity and Growth in Developing Countries: Old and New Perspectives on the Policy Issues', Policy research Working Paper 1563, Washington, DC: The World Bank.

Burke, Sara (2008): 'Unequal in Life and Death: Women's health – gender and inequality in the Irish health system', in Ursula Barry, ed.: *Where are we now? New feminist perspectives on women in contemporary Ireland*, Dublin: Tasc with New Island, pp. 53–81.

―― (2009): *Irish Apartheid: Healthcare Inequality in Ireland*, Dublin: New Island.

Burke-Kennedy, Eoin (2009): 'Plunge in May tourist figures bodes ill for tourism sector', in *The Irish Times*, 15 July 2009, p. 3.

Cahill, Noel and Francis O'Toole (1998): 'Taxation Policy', in Seán Healy and Brigid Reynolds, eds: *Social Policy in Ireland: Principles, Practice and Problems*, Dublin: Oak Tree Press, pp. 221–37.

Callan, Tim and Brian Nolan (1992): 'Distributional Aspects of Ireland's Fiscal Adjustment', in *The Economic and Social Review*, Vol. 23, No. 3, pp. 319–42.

Callan, Tim, Mary Keeney, Brian Nolan and Bertrand Maitre (2004): *Why is Relative Income Poverty so High in Ireland?*, Policy Research Series No. 53, Dublin: Economic and Social Research Institute.

Callan, Tim, Richard Layte, Brian Nolan, Dorothy Watson, Christopher T. Whelan, James Williams and Bertrand Maitre (1999): *Monitoring Poverty Trends*, Dublin: ESRI, the Department of Social, Community and Family Affairs and Combat Poverty Agency.

Campos, José Edgardo and Hilton L. Root (1996): *The Key to the Asian Miracle: Making Shared Growth Credible*, Washington, DC: The Brookings Institution.

Carroll, Steven (2007): 'Study links debt with ill health in women', in *The Irish Times*, 11 October 2007, p. 6.

Carswell, Simon (2009a): 'Reforms spell end of light-touch era', in *The Irish Times*, 19 June 2009, *Business This Week* supplement, p. 5.

—— (2009b): 'Banks asked to give names of top 100 developer customers', in *The Irish Times*, 10 June 2009, p. 18.

Casey, Michael (2009a): 'Boom growth came too easy – now we'll have to graft', in *The Irish Times*, 8 May 2009, p. 13.

—— (2009b): 'Entering New Territory', in *Top 1000 Companies*, a supplement published with *The Irish Times*, 12 June 2009, pp. 5–6.

—— (2009c): 'Economics', in *Innovation*, May 2009, p. 10.

Castañeda, Jorge G. (1994): *Utopia Unarmed: The Latin American Left after the Cold War*, New York: Vintage Books.

Cerny, Philip G., Georg Menz and Susanne Soederberg (2005): 'Different Roads to Globalization: Neoliberalism, the Competition State, and Politics in a More Open World' in Susanne Soederberg, Georg Menz and Philip G. Cerny, eds: *Internalizing Globalization: The Rise of Neoliberalism and the Decline of National Varieties of Capitalism*, Basingstoke: Palgrave Macmillan, pp. 1–30.

Chenery, Hollis, Montek S. Ahluwalia, Clive L. G. Bell, John H. Duloy and Richard Jolly (1974): *Redistribution with Growth*, Oxford: Oxford University Press.

Clancy, Patrick, Sheelagh Drudy, Kathleen Lynch and Liam O'Dowd, eds (1995): *Irish Society: Sociological Perspectives*, Dublin: Institute of Public Administration.

Clark, Charles M. A. and Catherine Kavanagh (1996): 'Progress, Values and Economic Indicators', in Brigid Reynolds and Seán Healy, eds: *Progress, Values and Public Policy*, Dublin: CORI, pp. 60–92.

Clinch, Peter, Frank Convery and Brendan Walsh (2002): *After the Celtic Tiger: Challenges Ahead*, Dublin: The O'Brien Press.

Cobb, Clifford, Ted Halstead and Jonathan Rowe (1995): 'If the GDP is up, why is America down?', in *The Atlantic Monthly*, October 1995, pp. 59–78.

Collins, Micheál L. and Catherine Kavanagh (2006): 'The changing patterns of income distribution and inequality in Ireland, 1973–2004', in Seán Healy, Brigid Reynolds and Micheál Collins, eds: *Social Policy in Ireland: Principles, Practice and Problems*, second edition, Dublin: The Liffey Press, pp. 149–69.

Collins, Neil (2007): 'The public service and regulatory reform', in Neil Collins, Terry Cradden and Patrick Butler, eds: *Modernising Irish Government: The Politics of Administrative Reform*, Dublin: Gill & Macmillan, pp. 115–36.

Collins, Neil and Mary O'Shea (2003): 'Clientelism: Facilitating rights and favours', in Maura Adshead and Michelle Millar, eds: *Public Administration and Public Policy in Ireland: Theory and Methods*, London: Routledge, pp. 88–107.

Collins, Patrick and Seamus Grimes (n.d.): 'Ireland's foreign-owned technology sector: From branch plants to control centers?', unpublished paper, Centre for Innovation and Structural Change (CISC), Department of Geography, National University of Ireland, Galway.

Collins, Stephen (2009): 'New tax system to cover €16bn gap "needed"', in *The Irish Times*, 2 April 2009, p. 11.

Connolly, Eileen (2007): *The Institutionalisation of Anti-Poverty and Social Exclusion Policy in Irish Social Partnership*, Research Working Paper 07/01, Dublin: Combat Poverty Agency.

Cousins, Mel (1995): *The Irish Welfare System: Law and Social Policy*, Blackrock, Co. Dublin: The Round Hall Press.

—— (2005): *Explaining the Irish Welfare State*, Lewiston, NY: The Edwin Mellen Press.

Cox, Robert W. (1995): 'Critical Political Economy', in Bjorn Hettne, ed.: *International Political Economy: Understanding Global Disorder*, London: Zed Books, pp. 31–45.

—— (1996a): 'Social Forces, States and World Order: Beyond International Relations Theory', in Robert W. Cox with Timothy J. Sinclair: *Approaches to World Order*, Cambridge: Cambridge University Press, pp. 85–123.

—— (1996b): 'Globalization, Multilateralism and Democracy', in Robert W. Cox with Timothy J. Sinclair: *Approaches to World Order*, Cambridge: Cambridge University Press, pp. 524–36.

Cox, Robert W. with Michael G. Schechter (2002): *The Political Economy of a Plural World: Critical Reflections on Power, Morals and Civilization*, London: Routledge.

Crane, George T. and Abla Amawi (1997): 'Introduction: Theories of International Political Economy', in George T. Crane and Abla Amawi, eds: *The Theoretical Evolution of International Political Economy: A Reader*, Oxford: Oxford University Press, second edition, pp. 3–34.

Cronin, Michael (1998): 'Gulliver's Isles', in *Graph*, Vol. 3, No. 1, pp. 4–5.

—— (2009): 'Active citizenship and its discontents', in Deiric Ó Broin and Peadar Kirby, eds: *Power, Dissent and Democracy: Civil society and the state in Ireland*, Dublin: A & A Farmer, pp. 62–77.

Crotty, Raymond D. (1966): *Irish Agricultural Production: Its Volume and Structure*, Cork: Cork University Press.

—— (1979): 'Capitalist Colonialism and Peripheralisation: the Irish Case', in Dudley Seers, Bernard Schaffer and Marja-Lijse Kiljunen, eds: *Underdeveloped Europe: Studies in Core–Periphery Relations*, Hemel Hempstead: Harvester Wheatsheaf, pp. 225–35.

—— (1986): *Ireland in Crisis: a Study of Capitalist Colonial Undevelopment*, Dingle: Brandon.

Crotty, Raymond D. (2001): *When Histories Collide: The Development and Impact of Individualistic Capitalism*, Lanham, MD: AltaMira Press, a division of Rowman & Littlefield Publishers.

Crowley, Niall (1998): 'Partnership 2000: Empowerment or Co-option?', in Peadar Kirby and David Jacobson, eds: *In the Shadow of the Tiger: New Approaches to Combating Social Exclusion*, Dublin: DCU Press, pp. 69–80.

Crowley, Niall (2009): 'Marginalising Dissent on Equality Issues', paper given at seminar on 'Enabling Dissent', Dublin, 20 May 2009.

CSO (2000): *That Was Then, This Is Now: Change in Ireland, 1949–1999*, Dublin: CSO.

—— (2003): *Measuring Ireland's Progress 2003*, Volume 1, Dublin: Central Statistics Office.

—— (2006): *EU Survey on Income and Living Conditions (EU-SILC)*, Dublin: Central Statistics Office.

—— (2008a): *EU Survey on Income and Living Conditions (EU-SILC)*, Dublin: Central Statistics Office.

—— (2008b): *Measuring Ireland's Progress 2007*, Dublin: Central Statistics Office.

Cullen, Elizabeth (2006): 'Growth and the Celtic Cancer: Unprecedented Growth but for Whose Benefit?' in Tom O'Connor and Mike Murphy, eds: *Social Care in Ireland*, CIT Press, pp. 141–60.

Curtin, Chris, Trutz Haase and Hilary Tovey, eds (1996): *Poverty in Rural Ireland: A Political Economy Perspective*, Dublin: Oak Tree Press in association with the Combat Poverty Agency.

Daly, Herman E. (1996): *Beyond Growth: The Economics of Sustainable Development*, Boston: Beacon Press.

Daly, Mary (1992): *Industrial Development and Irish National Identity, 1922–1939*, Dublin: Gill & Macmillan.

—— (1997): *The Spirit of Earnest Inquiry: The Statistical and Social Inquiry Society of Ireland, 1847–1997*, Dublin: Statistical and Social Inquiry Society of Ireland.

Daly, Siobhan (2007): 'Mapping civil society in the Republic of Ireland', in *Community Development Journal*, Vol. 43, No. 2, pp. 157–76.

Doherty, Michael (2007): *Does the Union Still Make Us Strong? Irish Trade Union Membership in the Partnership Era*, PhD thesis, Trinity College, Dublin.

Donnellan, Eithne (2007): 'The long waiting times for outpatients have not gone away', in *The Irish Times*, 31 December 2007, p. 4.

Drudy, P. J. (2006): 'Housing in Ireland: Philosophy, Problems and Policies', in Sean Healy, Brigid Reynolds and Micheál Collins, eds: *Social Policy in Ireland: Principles, Practice and Problems*, Dublin: The Liffey Press, pp. 241–69.

Dukelow, Fiona (2004): 'The path towards a more "employment friendly" liberal regime?: Globalisation and the Irish social security system', paper presented at the Foundation for International Studies of Social Security Seminar (FISS), Stockholm, June 2004.

Dunphy, Richard (1995): *The Making of Fianna Fáil Power in Ireland, 1923–1948*, Oxford: Clarendon Press.

Economist (2005): 'Quality of Life Index', London: The Economist.

Edwards, Michael (2004): *Civil Society*, Cambridge: Polity Press.

EPA (2008): *Ireland's Environment 2008*, Wexford: Environmental Protection Agency.

—— (2009): 'Ireland's Greenhouse Gas Emission Projections 2008–2020', Wexford: EPA.

Erikson, Robert (1993): 'Descriptions of Inequality: The Swedish Approach to Welfare Research', in Martha Nussbaum and Amartya Sen, eds: *The Quality of Life*, Oxford: Clarendon Press, pp. 67–83.

Esping-Andersen, Gosta (1990): *The Three Worlds of Welfare Capitalism*, Cambridge: Polity.

European Commission (2009a): *Economic Forecast Spring 2009*, Brussels: European Commission.

—— (2009b): *Statistical Annex of the European Economy*, spring 2009, Brussels: European Commission.

Evans, Peter (1995): *Embedded Autonomy: States and Industrial Transformation*, Princeton, NJ: Princeton University Press.

Fahey, Tony (2007): 'How do we feel? Economic Boom and Happiness', in Tony Fahey, Helen Russell and Christopher T. Whelan, eds: *Best of Times? The Social Impact of the Celtic Tiger*, Dublin: Institute of Public Administration, pp. 11–26.

Fahey, Tony and Richard Layte (2007): 'Family and Sexuality', in Tony Fahey, Helen Russell and Christopher T. Whelan, eds: *Best of Times? The Social Impact of the Celtic Tiger*, Dublin: Institute of Public Administration, pp. 155–74.

Fahey, Tony, Brian Nolan and Bertrand Maitre (2004): *Housing, Poverty and Wealth in Ireland*, Dublin: Combat Poverty Agency and the Institute of Public Administration.

Fahey, Tony, Helen Russell and Emer Smyth (2000): 'Gender Equality, Fertility Decline and Labour Market Patterns among Women in Ireland', in Brian Nolan, Philip J. O'Connell and Christopher T. Whelan, eds: *Bust to Boom? The Irish Experience of Growth and Inequality*, Dublin: Institute of Public Administration, pp. 244–67.

214   *Celtic Tiger in Collapse*

Fahey, Tony, Helen Russell and Christopher T. Whelan, eds (2007): *Best of Times? The Social Impact of the Celtic Tiger*, Dublin: Institute of Public Administration.

Fell, John P. C. (1989): 'In Search of a Causal Relationship between Industrial Output and Employment in Ireland', Technical Paper 2RT/89, Dublin: Central Bank of Ireland.

Ferriter, Diarmaid (2005): *The Transformation of Ireland, 1900–2000*, London: Profile Books.

Fields, Gary S. (1989): 'Changes in Poverty and Inequality in Developing Countries', in *The World Bank Research Observer*, Vol. 4, No. 2, pp. 167–85.

Fink, Philipp (2004): *Purchased Development: The Irish Republic's Export-oriented Development Strategy*, with a Preface by Hartmut Elsenhans. Münster: Lit Verlag.

—— (2007): *Foreign Direct Investment and Development: The Cases of Hungary and Ireland*, PhD thesis, University of Leipzig.

—— (2009): *Late Development in Hungary and Ireland: From Rags to Riches?*, Baden-Baden: Nomos Verlagsgesellschaft.

Fitz Gerald, John (1998): 'The Way we Are: Education and the Celtic Tiger', in Brian Farrell, ed.: *Issues in Education: Changing Education, Changing Society*, Dublin: ASTI, pp. 35–44.

—— (2000): 'The story of Ireland's failure – and belated success', in Brian Nolan, Philip J. O'Connell and Christopher T. Whelan, eds: *Bust to Boom The Irish Experience of Growth and Inequality*, Dublin: Institute of Public Administration, pp. 27–57.

—— (2009): 'How Ireland can stage an economic recovery', in *The Irish Times*, 24 January 2009, p. 15.

FitzGerald, Garret (2007): 'Recent economic growth has unhealthy basis', in *The Irish Times*, 24 February 2007, p. 14.

—— (2008a): 'End of asset boom reveals foolishness of tax cuts', in *The Irish Times*, 11 October 2008, p. 14.

—— (2008b): 'Short-term pain should not blind us to bright future', in *The Irish Times*, 17 May 2008, p. 16.

—— (2008c): 'Public services make a shabby contrast with national wealth', in *The Irish Times*, 22 March 2008, p. 14.

Forfás (2006): *International Trade and Investment Report*, Dublin: Forfás.

—— (2008a): *Enterprise Statistics at a Glance, 2008*, Dublin: Forfás.

—— (2008b): *The Higher Education R & D Survey 2006 (HERD)*, Dublin: Forfás.

Foster, Roy F. (2007): *Luck and the Irish: A brief history of change, 1970–2000*, London: Penguin.

Frieden, Jeffry A. and David A. Lake (1995): 'Introduction: International Politics and International Economics', in Jeffry A. Frieden and David A. Lake, eds: *International Political Economy: Perspectives on Global Wealth and Power*, third edition, London: Routledge, pp. 1–16.

Gallagher, Liam A., Eleanor Doyle and Eoin O'Leary (2002): 'Creating the Celtic Tiger and sustaining economic growth: A business perspective', in Daniel McCoy, David Duffy, Jonathan Hore and Conall MacCoille: *Quarterly Economic Commentary*, spring 2002, pp. 63–81.

Gallen, Seamus (2005): *Background to the Irish Software Industry*, available at www.nsd. ie/htm/ssii/back.htm, accessed on 12 July 2007.

Gamble, Andrew (2009): *The Spectre and the Feast*, Basingstoke: Palgrave Macmillan.

Garavan, Mark (2009): 'Civil society and political argument: How to make sense when no-one is listening', in Deiric Ó Broin and Peadar Kirby, eds: *Power, Dissent and Democracy: Civil society and the state in Ireland*, Dublin: A & A Farmer, pp. 78–91.

Gardiner, Kevin (1994): 'The Irish Economy: A Celtic Tiger' in *MS Euroletter*, 31 August 1994.

Garvin, Tom (2005): *Preventing the Future: Why Ireland was so poor for so long?*, Dublin: Gill & Macmillan.

Geary, Patrick T. (1977): 'Wages, prices, incomes and wealth', in Norman J. Gibson and John E. Spencer, eds: *Economic Activity in Ireland: A Study of Two Economies*, Dublin: Gill & Macmillan, pp. 149–89.

Geoghegan, Martin and Fred Powell (2009): 'Community development, the Irish state and the contested meaning of civil society', in Deiric Ó Broin and Peadar Kirby, eds (2009): *Power, Dissent and Democracy: Civil society and the State in Ireland*, Dublin: A & A Farmar, pp. 95–110.

Giddens, Anthony (1987): *Social Theory and Modern Sociology*, Cambridge: Polity.

—— (1996): *In Defence of Sociology: Essays, Interpretations and Rejoinders*, Cambridge: Polity.

Ging, Debbie (2009): 'All-consuming images: New gender formations in post–Celtic Tiger Ireland', in Debbie Ging, Michael Cronin and Peadar Kirby, eds: *Transforming Ireland: Challenges, critiques, resources*, Manchester: Manchester University Press, pp. 52–70.

Ging, Debbie, Michael Cronin and Peadar Kirby, eds (2009): *Transforming Ireland: Challenges, Critiques, Resources*, Manchester: Manchester University Press.

Girvin, Brian (1989): *Between Two Worlds: Politics and Economy in Independent Ireland*, Dublin: Gill & Macmillan.

Glavanis-Grantham, Kathy (2008): 'Alliance for Progress or Unholy Alliance? The Transnational Pharmaceutical Industry, the State and the University in Ireland', in Orla O'Donovan and Kathy Glavanis-Grantham, eds: *Power, Politics and Pharmaceuticals*, Cork: Cork University Press, pp. 82–104.

Gottheil, Fred (2003): 'Ireland: what's Celtic about the Celtic Tiger?', in *The Quarterly Review of Economics and Finance*, Vol. 43, pp. 720–37.

Government of Ireland (2000): *Supporting Voluntary Activity: A White Paper on a Framework for Supporting Voluntary Activity and for Developing the Relationship between the State and the Community and Voluntary Sector*, Dublin: Stationery Office.

—— (2008): *Building Ireland's Smart Economy: A Framework for Sustainable Economic Renewal*, Dublin: Stationery Office.

Green New Deal Group (2008): *A Green New Deal: Joined-up policies to solve the triple crunch of the credit crisis, climate change and high oil prices*, London: New Economics Foundation.

Grimes, Seamus and Patrick Collins (2009): 'The contribution of the overseas ICT sector to expanding R & D investment in Ireland', in *Irish Geography*, Vol. 42, No. 1, March 2009, pp. 45–67.

Hardiman, Niamh (1998): 'Inequality and the Representation of Interests,' in William Crotty and David E. Schmitt, eds: *Ireland and the Politics of Change*, Harlow: Longman, pp. 122–43.

Hardiman, Niamh (2006): 'Politics and social partnership: Flexible network governance', in *The Economic and Social Review*, Vol. 37, No. 3, pp. 343–74.

Harris, Donald J. (1987): 'Classical Growth Models', in John Eatwell, Milgate Murray and Peter Newman: *The New Palgrave: A Dictionary of Economics*, Basingstoke: Macmillan, pp. 445–8.

Harvey, Brian (2009): 'Ireland and civil society: Reaching the limits of dissent', in Deiric Ó Broin and Peadar Kirby, eds: *Power, Dissent and Democracy: Civil society and the state in Ireland*, Dublin: A & A Farmar, pp. 25–33.

Hay, Colin and David Marsh (1999): 'Introduction: Towards a New (International) Political Economy?' in *New Political Economy*, Vol. 4, No. 1, pp. 5–22.

HEA (2008a): *Higher Education: Key Facts and Figures 07/08*, Dublin: Higher Education Authority.

—— (2008b): *Transformations: How Research is Changing Ireland*, Dublin: HEA.

Healy, John and Charles M. A. Clark (1998): 'Measurement and Understanding in Economics', in Seán Healy and Brigid Reynolds, eds: *Social Policy in Ireland: Principles, Practice and Problems*, Dublin: Oak Tree Press, pp. 85–102.

Held, David and Ayse Kaya, eds (2007): *Global Inequality*, Cambridge: Polity.

Hettne, Bjorn (1995): *Development Theory and the Three Worlds*, Harlow: Longman.

Hewitt-Dundas, Nola and Stephen Roper (2008): 'Ireland's Innovation Performance: 1991–2005', in Alan Barrett, Ide Kearney and Martin O'Brien, *Quarterly Economic Commentary*, Summer 2008, Dublin: ESRI, pp. 45–68.

Holland, Kitty (2008): 'Cocaine use five times higher in Irish teens', in *The Irish Times*, 24 May 2008, p. 10.

Hoogvelt, Ankie (1997): *Globalisation and the Postcolonial World: The New Political Economy of Development*, Basingstoke: Macmillan.

Hughes, Gerard (2005): 'Pension tax reliefs and equity', in Jim Stewart, ed.: *For Richer, For Poorer: An Investigation of the Irish Pension System*, Dublin: Tasc and New Island Books, pp. 129–49.

Hussey, Gemma (2009): 'Our political system is no long fit for purpose', in *The Irish Times*, 4 May 2009, p. 11.

ICTU (2008): *Economic Outlook 2008: Narrowing the Pay Gap in Ireland*, Dublin: ICTU.

—— (2009): *There is a Better, Fairer Way: Congress Plan for National Recovery*, Dublin: ICTU.

IMF (2009): 'Ireland: IMF Country Report No. 09/195', Washington, DC: International Monetary Fund.

Inayatullah, Naeem and David L. Blaney (1999): 'Towards an Ethnological IPE: Karl Polanyi's Double Critique of Capitalism', in *Millennium*, Vol. 28, No. 2, pp. 311–40.

Jacobsen, John Kurt (1994): *Chasing Progress in the Irish Republic*, Cambridge: Cambridge University Press.

—— (1997): 'Peripheral Postindustrialism: Ideology, High Technology and Development', in John Kurt Jacobsen: *Dead Reckonings: Ideas, Interests, and Politics in the 'Information Age'*, New Jersey: Humanities Press, pp. 82–122.

Jacobson, David (1989): 'Theorizing Irish Industrialization: The Case of the Motor Industry', in *Science & Society*, Vol. 53, No. 2, pp. 165–91.

Jarrett, Peter (1999): 'Review of Frank Barry's *Understanding Ireland's Economic Growth*' in *The Economic and Social Review*, Vol. 30, No. 2, pp. 197–201.

John, Andrew (1995): 'Primary Policy Objectives', in J. W. O'Hagan, ed.: *The Economy of Ireland: Policy and Performance of a Small European Country*, Dublin: Gill & Macmillan, pp. 50–85.

Johnson, Chalmers (1982): *MITI and the Japanese Miracle: The Growth of Industrial Policy, 1925–1975*, Stanford: Stanford University Press.

Jones, R. J. Barry (1988): 'Political Economy: Contending Perspectives on a Changing World' in R. J. Barry Jones, ed.: *The Worlds of Political Economy*, London: Pinter, pp. 1–26.

Jordan, Bill (1996): *A Theory of Poverty and Social Exclusion*, Cambridge: Polity.

Jordan, Declan and Eoin O'Leary (2008): 'Innovation is not academic', in *The Irish Times, Innovation* supplement, January 2008, p. 10.

Joyce, Laraine and Anthony McCashin (1982): *Poverty and Social Policy*, Dublin: Institute of Public Administration.

Kane, Eileen (1996): 'The Power of Paradigms: Social Science and Intellectual Contributions to Public Discourse in Ireland', in Liam O'Dowd, ed.: *On Intellectuals and Intellectual Life in Ireland*, Dublin: Institute of Irish Studies and RIA, pp. 132–55.

Keena, Colm (2009a): 'Revenue data understate contribution of lower and middle-income earners', in *The Irish Times, Business This Week* supplement, 20 March 2009, p. 3.

—— (2009b): 'Irish low-tax regime problematic – EU adviser', in *The Irish Times*, 12 May 2009, p. 20.

Kelleher, Cecily (2007): 'Health and modern Irish society: The mother and father of a dilemma', in Mel Cousins, ed.: *Welfare Policy and Poverty*, Dublin Combat Poverty Agency and Institute for Public Administration, pp. 201–28.

Kennedy, Kieran (1992a): The Context of Economic Development', in John H. Goldthorpe and Christopher T. Whelan, eds: *The Development of Industrial Society in Ireland*, Oxford: Oxford University Press, pp. 5–29.

—— (1992b): 'Real Convergence, the European Community and Ireland', paper given to the Statistical and Social Inquiry Society of Ireland.

—— (1993): *Facing the Unemployment Crisis in Ireland*, Cork: Cork University Press.

—— (1998): 'Irish Economy Transformed', in *Studies*, Vol. 87, January, pp. 33–42.

Kennedy, Kieran, Thomas Giblin and Deirdre McHugh (1988): *The Economic Development of Ireland in the Twentieth Century*, London: Routledge.

Kennedy, Stanislaus (2008): 'Budget must provide more funding to end homelessness', in *The Irish Times*, 25 September 2008, p. 15.

Kiberd, Declan (1995): *Inventing Ireland: The Literature of the Modern Nation*, London: Jonathan Cape.

King, Patrick (2006): *Locating the Decisions behind Irish Outward FDI: An Empirical Analysis of the Significance of Economic and Cultural Factors on Irish Investment Destinations*, M.Sc. in Strategic Management dissertation, Dublin: DIT.

Kirby, Peadar (1994): *Adjusting to Develop? The Impact of Neo-liberalism in Mexico*, Dublin: Oxfam.

—— (1997): *Poverty Amid Plenty: World and Irish Development Reconsidered*, Dublin: Trócaire and Gill & Macmillan.

—— (2000): 'Growth with Inequality: The International Political Economy of Ireland's Development in the 1990s', PhD thesis, London School of Economics.

—— (2002a): *The Celtic Tiger in Distress: Growth with Inequality in Ireland*, Basingstoke: Palgrave Macmillan.

—— (2002b): 'Contested Pedigrees of the Celtic Tiger', in Peadar Kirby, Luke Gibbons and Michael Cronin, eds: *Reinventing Ireland: Culture, Society and the Global Economy*, London: Pluto Press, pp. 21–37.

—— (2005): 'The Irish State and the Celtic Tiger: A "flexible developmental state" or a competition state?', in Graham Harrison, ed.: *Global Encounters: International Political Economy, Development and Globalisation*, Basingstoke: Palgrave Macmillan, pp. 74–94.

—— (2006): *Vulnerability and Violence: The Impact of Globalisation*, London: Pluto Press.

—— (2008a): 'The 'Best of Times' or besting the critics? The ESRI on the social impact of the Celtic Tiger', in *Administration*, Vol. 55, No. 3, 2008, pp. 171–90.

—— (2008b): *Explaining Ireland's Development: Economic Growth with Weakening Welfare*, Geneva: United Nations Research Institute for Social Development (UNRISD).

Kirby, Peadar and Mary Murphy (2008): 'Ireland as a "competition state"', in Maura Adshead, Peadar Kirby and Michelle Millar, eds: *Contesting the State: Lessons from the Irish case*, Manchester: Manchester University Press, pp. 120–42.

Krugman, Paul (2009): 'Erin Go Broke', in *The New York Times*, 20 April 2009.
—— (1994): *Peddling Prosperity*, New York: W. W. Norton.
—— (1997): 'Good News from Ireland: A Geographical Perspective', in Alan W. Gray, ed.: *International Perspectives on the Irish Economy*, Dublin: Indecon, pp. 38–53.
Kuhling, Carmen and Kieran Keohane (2007): *Cosmopolitan Ireland: Globalisation and Quality of Life*, London: Pluto Press.
Kurtz, Marcus (2001): 'State Developmentalism without a Developmental State: The Public Foundations of the "Free Market Miracle" in Chile', in *Latin American Politics and Society*, Vol. 43, No. 2, summer 2001, pp. 1–25.
Kuznets, Simon (1955): 'Economic Growth and Income Inequality', in *The American Economic Review*, Vol. 45, No. 1, March, pp. 1–28.
Kwame Sundaram (K. S.), Jomo and Jacques Baudot, eds (2007): *Flat World, Big Gaps: Economic Liberalization, Globalization, Poverty & Inequality*, London: Zed Books.
Labour (2009): 'Restoring confidence: Labour's proposals for economic recovery', Dublin: Labour.
Laffan, Brigid and Jane O'Mahony (2008): *Ireland and the European Union*, Basingstoke: Palgrave Macmillan.
Lally, Conor (2008): 'Republic's crime rate up 5% on last year', in *The Irish Times*, 31 October 2008, p. 7.
—— (2009): 'Ireland a more violent place, says Garda chief', in *The Irish Times*, 12 January 2009, p. 4.
Lane, Jan-Erik and Svante Ersson (1997): *Comparative Political Economy: A Developmental Approach*, London: Pinter.
Larragy, Joe (2006): 'Origins and significance of the community and voluntary pillar in Irish social partnership', in *The Economic and Social Review*, Vol. 37, No. 3, p. 375–98.
Latham, Robert (1997): 'Globalisation and Democratic Provisionism: Re-reading Polanyi', in *New Political Economy*, Vol. 2, No. 1, pp. 53–63.
Layte, Richard and Christopher T. Whelan (2000): 'The Rising Tide and Equality of Opportunity: the Changing Class Structure', in Brian Nolan, Philip J. O'Connell and Christopher T. Whelan, eds: *Bust to Boom? The Irish Experience of Growth and Inequality*, Dublin: IPA, pp. 90–108.
Lecaillon, Jacques, Felix Paukert, Christian Morrisson and Dimitri Germidis (1984): *Income Distribution and Economic Development: An Analytical Survey*, Geneva: ILO.
Leddin, Anthony (2008): 'How wage agreements eroded competitiveness', in *The Irish Times*, *Business This Week* supplement, 22 August 2008, p. 15.
Leddin, Anthony and Brendan Walsh (1997): 'Economic Stabilisation, Recovery and Growth: Ireland 1979–1996', Working Paper WP97/8, Department of Economics, Dublin: UCD.
Lee, Joseph J. (1989): *Ireland 1912–1985: Politics and Society*, Cambridge: Cambridge University Press.
—— (2008): 'From Empire to Europe: The Irish state 1922–73', in Maura Adshead, Peadar Kirby and Michelle Millar, eds: *Contesting the State: Lessons from the Irish Case*, Manchester: Manchester University Press, pp. 25–49.
Leftwich, Adrian, ed. (1996): *Democracy and Development*, Cambridge: Polity.
Leys, Colin (1996): 'The Crisis in "Development Theory"', in *New Political Economy*, Vol. 1, No. 1, pp. 41–58.
Lucy, Brian (2008): 'The Government that mistook a blueprint for a recovery plan', in *The Irish Times*, 20 December 2008, p. 15.

Lynch, Patrick (1998): 'Societal Change and Education: Investment in Education Revisited', in Brian Farrell, ed.: *Issues in Education: Changing Education, Changing Society*, Dublin: ASTI, pp. 9–16.

Lynch, Terry (2008): 'The Dominance of Drug-Based Mental Health Care in Ireland: A Personal Account of a General Practitioner Turned Psychotherapist', in Orla O'Donovan and Kathy Glavanis-Grantham, eds: *Power, Politics and Pharmaceuticals*, Cork: Cork University Press, pp. 135–50.

Lyons, Patrick M. (1972): 'The Distribution of Personal Wealth in Ireland', in Alan A. Tait and John A. Bristow, eds: *Ireland: Some Problems of a Developing Economy*, Dublin: Gill & Macmillan, pp. 159–85.

Mac Laughlin, Jim (1994a): *Ireland: The Emigrant Nursery and the World Economy*, Cork: Cork University Press.

—— (1994b): 'Emigration and the Peripheralization of Ireland in the Global Economy', in *Review*, Vol. 17, No. 2, pp. 243–73.

Mac Sharry, Ray and Padraic White (2000): *The Making of the Celtic Tiger: The Inside Story of Ireland's Boom Economy*, Cork: Mercier Press.

Madden, Caroline (2009a): 'Financial Assets of Irish households down by 42%', in *The Irish Times*, 17 June 2009, p. 19.

—— (2009b): 'Regulator "added to slump" by failing to curb property bubble', in *The Irish Times*, 26 May 2009, p. 1.

Maddison, Angus (1995): *Monitoring the World Economy 1820–1922*, Paris: OECD.

Maguire, John (1988): 'The Case for a New Social Order', in Miriam Hederman, ed. *The Clash of Ideas*, Dublin: Gill & Macmillan, pp. 61–88.

Mair, Peter (1992): 'Explaining the absence of class politics in Ireland', in John. H. Goldthorpe and Christopher T. Whelan, eds: *The Development of Industrial Society in Ireland*, Oxford: Oxford University Press, pp. 383–410.

Martinussen, John (1997): *Society, State and Market: A Guide to Competing Theories of Development*, London: Zed Books.

Matthews, Alan (1995): 'Agricultural Competitiveness and Rural Development', in John. W. O'Hagan, ed.: *The Economy of Ireland: Policy and Performance of a Small European Country*, Dublin: Gill & Macmillan, pp. 328–62.

McAleese, Dermot and Anthony Foley (1991): 'The Role of Overseas Industry in Industrial Development', in Anthony Foley and Dermot McAleese, eds: *Overseas Industry in Ireland*, Dublin: Gill & Macmillan, pp. 1–28.

McCullagh, Ciaran (1996): *Crime in Ireland: A Sociological Introduction*, Cork: Cork University Press.

McErlean, Eugene (2009): 'Regulator's general failure is to blame for carnage now afflicting Irish households', in *The Irish Times*, 13 May 2009, p. 20.

McGee, Harry (2009a): 'Recession to bring Ireland close to its CO_2 Kyoto target', in *The Irish Times*, 27 February 2009, p. 7.

—— (2009b): 'Exports will be vital part of economic recovery', in *The Irish Times*, 6 July 2009, p. 11.

McGinnity, Frances, Helen Russell and Emer Smyth (2007): 'Gender, Work-Life Balance and Quality of Life', in Tony Fahey, Helen Russell and Christopher T. Whelan, eds: *Best of Times? The Social Impact of the Celtic Tiger*, Dublin: Institute of Public Administration, pp. 199–215.

McGreevy, Ronan and Gerry Moriarty (2008): 'Number of recorded suicides increased 12% to 460 last year', in *The Irish Times*, 11 September 2008, p. 6.

McManus, John (2009): 'Patrick Neary's departure a repudiation of our approach to regulation', in *The Irish Times*, 12 January 2009, p. 18.

Meade, Rosie (2005): 'We hate it here, please let us stay! Irish social partnership and the community/voluntary sector's conflicted experiences of recognition', in *Critical Social Policy*, Vol. 25, No. 3, pp. 349–73.

Minihan, Mary (2008): 'Ireland fourth-worst in Europe for drug deaths', in *The Irish Times*, 7 November 2008, p. 6.

—— (2009): 'Report finds Irish teenagers have high drunkenness rate', in *The Irish Times*, 20 January 2009, p. 7.

Mishra, Ramish (1999): *Globalisation and the Welfare State*, London: Edward Elgar.

Mjøset, Lars (1992): *The Irish Economy in a Comparative Institutional Perspective*, Dublin: NESC.

Munck, Ronaldo (1993): *The Irish Economy: Results and Prospects*, London: Pluto.

Murphy, Antoin (1994): *The Irish Economy: Celtic Tiger or Tortoise?* Dublin: Money Markets International.

—— (1998): *The Celtic Tiger – The Great Misnomer*, Dublin: Money Markets International.

Murphy, Craig N. and Roger Tooze, eds (1991): *The New International Political Economy*, Boulder, CO: Lynne Rienner.

Murphy, Gary (2009): 'A register of lobbyists is about preventing undue influence', in *The Irish Times*, 7 July 2009, p. 14.

Murphy, Mary (2006): *Domestic Constraints on Globalisation: A case study of Irish Social Security 1986–2006*, unpublished PhD thesis, Dublin City University, 2006.

—— (2009): 'What impact might globalisation have on Irish civil society?', in Deiric Ó Broin and Peadar Kirby, eds: *Power, Dissent and Democracy: Civil society and the State in Ireland*, Dublin: A & A Farmar, pp. 34–47.

Murphy, Mary and Michelle Millar (2007): 'The NESC Developmental Welfare State: Opportunity or Threat?', in *Administration*, Vol. 55, No. 3, pp. 75–100.

Myrdal, Gunnar (1989): 'The Equality Issue in World Development', in *American Economic Review*, Vol. 76, No. 6, pp. 8–17.

NAPS (1997): *Sharing in Progress*, Dublin: The Stationery Office.

NCC (2008): *Discussion Paper on Wellbeing and Competitiveness*, Dublin: National Competitiveness Council.

—— (2009): *Statement on Education and Training*, Dublin: Forfás.

Nederveen Pieterse, Jan (1997): 'Equity and Growth Revisited: A Supply-Side Approach to Social Development', in *European Journal of Development Research*, Vol. 9, No. 1, pp. 128–49.

NESC (1993): *A Strategy for Competitiveness, Growth and Employment*, Dublin: National Economic and Social Council.

—— (1997): *Population Distribution and Economic Development: Trends and Policy*, Dublin: National Economic and Social Council.

—— (2003): *An Investment in Quality: Services, Inclusion and Enterprise*, Dublin: National Economic and Social Council.

—— (2005): *The Developmental Welfare State*, Dublin: National Economic and Social Council.

NESF (1997): *A Framework for Partnership: Enriching Strategic Consensus Through Participation*, Dublin: National Economic and Social Forum.

Nielson, Francois and Arthur S. Alderson (1995): 'Income Inequality, Development, and Dualism: Results from an Unbalanced Cross-National Panel', in *American Sociological Review*, Vol. 60, October, pp. 674–701.

Nolan, Brian (1977–8): 'The Personal Distribution of Income in the Republic of Ireland', in *Journal of the Statistical and Social Inquiry Society of Ireland*, Vol. XXIII, Part 5, pp. 91–161.

—— (1991): *The Wealth of Irish Households*, Dublin: Combat Poverty Agency.

—— (1998): 'Poverty Trends in Ireland: Sound-bites and Substance', in *Poverty Today*, No. 40, June/July, p. 16.

Nolan, Brian and Bertrand Maitre (2007): 'Economic Growth and Income Inequality: Setting the Context', in Tony Fahey, Helen Russell and Christopher T. Whelan, eds: *Best of Times? The Social Impact of the Celtic Tiger*, Dublin: Institute of Public Administration, pp. 27–41.

Nolan, Brian and Christopher T. Whelan (1996): *Resources, Deprivation and Poverty*, Oxford: Clarendon Press.

Nolan, Brian and Tim Callan, eds (1994): *Poverty and Policy in Ireland*, Dublin: Gill & Macmillan.

Nolan, Brian, Bertrand Maitre, Donal O'Neill and Olive Sweetman (2000): *The Distribution of Income in Ireland*, Dublin: Oak Tree Press, in association with the Combat Poverty Agency.

Nolan, Brian, Philip J. O'Connell and Christopher T. Whelan, eds (2000): *Bust to Boom? The Irish Experience of Growth and Inequality*, Dublin: IPA.

Norton, Desmond (1994): 'The Scope of Economics', in Desmond Norton, with Alan Mathews, Martin Kenneally, Patrick McNutt and Rory O'Donnell, eds: *Economics for an Open Economy: Ireland*, Dublin: Oak Tree Press, pp. 3–16.

Ó Broin, Deiric (2009): 'Institutionalising social partnership in Ireland', in Deiric Ó Broin and Peadar Kirby, eds (2009): *Power, Dissent and Democracy: Civil society and the State in Ireland*, Dublin: A & A Farmar, pp. 111–25.

Ó Broin, Deiric and Peadar Kirby, eds (2009): *Power, Dissent and Democracy: Civil Society and the State in Ireland*, Dublin: A & A Farmar.

Ó Cinnéide, Séamus (1972): 'The Extent of Poverty in Ireland', in *Social Studies*, Vol. 1, No. 4, pp. 381–400.

Ó Cinnéide, Séamus (1980): 'Poverty and Inequality in Ireland', in Vic George and Roger Lawson, eds: *Poverty and Inequality in Common Market Countries*, London: Routledge and Kegan Paul, pp. 124–60.

Ó Cinnéide, Séamus (1998): 'Democracy and the Constitution', in *Administration*, Vol. 46, No. 4, winter 1998–9, pp. 41–58.

Ó Gráda, Cormac (1994): *Ireland, a New Economic History 1780–1939*, Oxford: Clarendon Press.

—— (1997): *A Rocky Road: The Irish Economy since the 1920s*, Manchester: Manchester University Press.

Ó Riain, Seán (1998): 'Review of Denis O'Hearn's *Inside the Celtic Tiger*', in *Irish Journal of Sociology*, Vol. 8, pp. 130–3.

—— (2000): 'The Flexible Developmental State: Globalization, Information Technology, and the "Celtic Tiger"', in *Politics & Society*, Vol. 28, No. 2, pp. 157–93.

—— (2004): *The Politics of High-Tech Growth: Developmental Network States in the Global Economy*, Cambridge: Cambridge University Press.

—— (2008): 'Competing state projects in the contemporary Irish political economy', in Maura Adshead, Peadar Kirby and Michelle Millar, eds: *Contesting the State: Lessons from the Irish Case*, Manchester: Manchester University Press, pp. 165–85.

Ó Riain, Seán and Philip J. O'Connell (2000): 'The Role of the State in Growth and Welfare', in Brian Nolan, Philip J. O'Connell and Christopher T. Whelan, eds: *Bust to Boom? The Irish Experience of Growth and Inequality*, Dublin: IPA, pp. 310–39.

Ó Séaghdha, Barra (2002): 'The Celtic Tiger's Media Pundits', in Peadar Kirby, Luke Gibbons and Michael Cronin, eds: *Reinventing Ireland: Culture, Society and the Global Economy*, London: Pluto, pp. 143–59.

Ó Tuathaigh, Gearóid (1986): 'The Regional Dimension', in Kieran A. Kennedy, ed.: *Ireland in Transition*, Cork: Mercier, pp. 120–32.

O'Brien, Justin (2009): 'After hubris always comes catastrophe', in *The Irish Times*, 9 February 2009, p. 11.

O'Connell, Philip J. and Helen Russell (2007): 'Employment and the Quality of Work', in Tony Fahey, Helen Russell and Christopher T. Whelan, eds: *Best of Times? The Social Impact of the Celtic Tiger*, Dublin: IPA, pp. 43–66.

O'Connell, Philip J. and David B. Rottman (1992): 'The Irish Welfare State in Comparative Perspective', in John H. Goldthorpe and Christopher T. Whelan, eds: *The Development of Industrial Society in Ireland*, Oxford: Oxford University Press, pp. 205–39.

O'Connor, Orla and Mary Murphy (2008): 'Women and Social Welfare', in Ursula Barry, ed.: *Where are we now? New feminist perspectives on women in contemporary Ireland*, Dublin: Tasc with New Island, pp. 30–52.

O'Connor, Pat (2008): 'The Irish patriarchal state: Continuity and change', in Maura Adshead, Peadar Kirby and Michelle Millar, eds: *Contesting the State: Lessons from the Irish case*, Manchester: Manchester University Press, pp. 142–64.

O'Donnell, Ian (2007): 'Crime and its Consequences', in Tony Fahey, Helen Russell and Christopher T. Whelan, eds: *Best of Times? The Social Impact of the Celtic Tiger*, Dublin: IPA, pp. 245–64.

O'Donnell, Rory (1999): 'Reinventing Ireland: From Sovereignty to Partnership', Jean Monnet inaugural lecture, UCD, 29 April 1999.

—— (2000): 'The New Ireland in the New Europe,' in Rory O'Donnell, ed.: *Europe: The Irish Experience*, Dublin: Institute for European Affairs, pp. 161–214.

—— (2008): 'The partnership state: building the ship at sea', in Maura Adshead, Peadar Kirby and Michelle Millar, eds: *Contesting the State: Lessons from the Irish Case*, Manchester: Manchester University Press, pp. 73–99.

O'Donnell, Rory and Colm O'Reardon (1996): 'The Irish Experiment: the "Social Partnership" has yielded economic growth together with social progress', in *New Economy*, Vol. 3, No. 1, pp. 33–8.

O'Donnell, Rory and Damian Thomas (1998): 'Partnership and Policy-making' in Seán Healy and Brigid Reynolds, eds: *Social Policy in Ireland: Principles, Practice and Problems*, Dublin: Oak Tree Press, pp. 117–46.

O'Donoghue, Adrian (2009): 'Responding to the Recession: the challenge for Ireland's regions', in *Public Affairs Ireland*, March 2009, pp. 14–15.

O'Donoghue, Cathal (2003): 'Redistributive forces of the Irish tax-benefit system', in *Journal of the Statistical and Social Inquiry Society of Ireland*, Vol. XXXII, pp. 33–69.

O'Donovan, Orla (2008): 'The Emergence of Pharmaceutical Industry Regulation for Competition (aka Profit) in Ireland', in Orla O'Donovan and Kathy Glavanis-Grantham, eds: *Power, Politics and Pharmaceuticals*, Cork: Cork University Press, pp. 61–81.

O'Donovan, Orla and Kathy Glavanis-Grantham, eds (2008): *Power, Politics and Pharmaceuticals*, Cork: Cork University Press.

O'Dowd, Liam (1986): 'Beyond Industrial Society', in Patrick Clancy, Sheelagh Drudy, Kathleen Lynch and Liam O'Dowd, eds: *Ireland: A Sociological Profile*, Dublin: Institute of Public Administration, pp. 198–220.

—— (1995): 'Development or Dependency? State, Economy and Society in Northern Ireland', in Patrick Clancy, Sheelagh Drudy, Kathleen Lynch and Liam O'Dowd, eds: *Irish Society: Sociological Perspectives*, Dublin: Institute of Public Administration, pp. 132–77.

O'Hagan, John (1995): 'Employment and Unemployment', in John O'Hagan, ed.: *The Economy of Ireland: Policy and Performance of a Small European Country*, Dublin: Gill & Macmillan, pp. 228–64.

O'Hearn, Denis (1989): 'The Irish Case of Dependency: An Exception to the Exceptions?', in *American Sociological Review*, Vol. 54, No. 4, August, pp. 578–96.

—— (1993): 'Global Competition Europe and Irish Peripherality', in *The Economic and Social Review*, Vol. 24, No. 2, pp. 169–97.

—— (1995): 'Global Restructuring and the Irish Political Economy', in Patrick Clancy, Sheelagh Drudy, Kathleen Lynch and Liam O'Dowd, eds: *Irish Society: Sociological Perspectives*, Dublin: Institute of Public Administration, pp. 90–131.

—— (1998): *Inside the Celtic Tiger: The Irish Economy and the Asian Model*, London: Pluto.

—— (2000): 'Globalization, "New Tigers", and the End of the Developmental State? The case of the Celtic Tiger', in *Politics and Society*, Vol. 28, No. 1, pp. 67–92.

—— (2001): *The Atlantic Economy: Britain, the US and Ireland*, Manchester: Manchester University Press.

—— (n.d): *Putting Ireland in a Global Context*, Department of Sociology, University College Cork.

O'Leary, Jim (2009): 'Budget must focus on cutting structural deficit', in *The Irish Times, Business This Week* supplement, 3 April 2009, p. 6.

O'Malley, Eoin (1989): *Industry and Economic Development: The Challenge for the Latecomer*, Dublin: Gill & Macmillan.

—— (1992): 'Problems of Industrialisation in Ireland', in John H. Goldthorpe and Christopher T. Whelan, eds: *The Development of Industrial Society in Ireland*, Oxford: Oxford University Press, pp. 31–52.

—— (1998): 'The Revival of Irish Indigenous Industry 1987–1997', in T. J. Baker, David Duffy and Fergal Shortall, eds: *Quarterly Economic Commentary*, April 1998, Dublin: ESRI, pp. 35–60.

—— (2004): 'Competitive Performance in Irish Industry', in Daniel McCoy, David Duffy, Adele Bergin, Shane Garrett, Yvonne McCarthy: *Quarterly Economic Commentary*, winter 2004, pp. 66–101.

—— (2009): 'Policy oversight required', in *The Irish Times*, 26 June 2009, p. 12.

O'Malley, Eoin and McCarthy, Yvonne (2006): 'New Drivers of Growth? Sectoral Contributions to the Irish Economy', in Alan Barrett, Ide Kearney and Yvonne McCarthy, eds: *Quarterly Economic Commentary*, July 2006, Dublin: ESRI, pp. 35–62.

O'Rourke, Kevin (1995): 'Emigration and Living Standards in Ireland since the Famine', in *Journal of Population Economics*, Vol. 8, Part 4, pp. 407–21.

O'Shea, Eamon (1996): 'Rural Poverty and Social Services Provision', in Chris Curtin, Trutz Haase and Hilary Tovey, eds: *Poverty in Rural Ireland: A Political Economy Perspective*, Dublin: Oak Tree Press, pp. 211–45.

O'Shea, Eamon and Brendan Kennelly (1993): 'Poverty, Values and Public Policy', in Brigid Reynolds and Seán Healy, eds: *New Frontiers for Full Citizenship*, Dublin: CMRS, pp. 9–39.

—— (1995): 'Caring and Theories of Welfare Economics', Working Paper No. 7, Department of Economics, University College Galway.

—— (2002): 'The Welfare State in Ireland: Challenges and Opportunities', in George Taylor, ed.: *Issues in Irish Public Policy*, Dublin: Irish Academic Press, pp. 52–79.

O'Sullivan, Mary (2000): 'Industrial Development: A new beginning?', in John O'Hagan, ed.: *The Economy of Ireland: Policy and Performance of a European Region*, Dublin: Gill & Macmillan, pp. 260–85.

O'Sullivan, Michael (2009): 'We need a political system that encourages strategic thinking', in *The Irish Times*, 14 April 2009, p. 10.

—— (2006): *Ireland and the Global Question*, Cork: Cork University Press.

O'Sullivan, Pat (2006): *The Wealth of the Nation: How Ireland's wealthy will invest in the next decade*, Dublin: Bank of Ireland.

O'Sullivan, Turlough (2008): 'Ireland simply cannot afford luxury of our public service', in *The Irish Times*, 7 November 2008, p. 13.

O'Toole, Fintan (2008): 'Carlsberg politics of easy options is an ugly hangover', in *The Irish Times*, 24 June 2008, p. 13.

O'Toole, Francis (1997): *Tax and PRSI Reform from a Low-income Perspective*, Dublin: Combat Poverty Agency.

O'Toole, Francis and Noel Cahill (2006): 'Taxation policy and reform', in Seán Healy, Brigid Reynolds and Micheál Collins, eds: *Social Policy in Ireland: Principles, Practice and Problems*, second edition, Dublin: The Liffey Press, pp. 205–22.

OECD (1999): *Economic Surveys 1999, Ireland*, Paris: OECD.

—— (2006a): *Economic Surveys 2006, Ireland*, Paris: OECD.

—— (2006b): *Economic Outlook 79*, Paris: OECD.

Paus, Eva (2005): *Foreign Investment, Development and Globalization: Can Costa Rica become Ireland?*, New York: Palgrave Macmillan.

Peillon, Michel (1992): 'State and Society in the Republic of Ireland', in Patrick Clancy and Mary Kelly, eds: *Ireland and Poland: Comparative Perspectives*, Dublin: Department of Sociology, UCD, pp. 15–24.

Pfizer (2009): *Pfizer: Many hands make communities work*, Pfizer.

Pierson, Christopher (2004): *The Modern State*, London: Routledge.

Polanyi, Karl (2001): *The Great Transformation: The Political and Economic Origins of our Time*, Boston: Beacon Press, original 1944.

Powell, Fred and Martin Geoghegan (2004): *The Politics of Community Development*, Dublin: A & A Farmar.

Rachman, Gideon (2009): 'When globalisation goes into reverse', in *The Financial Times*, 3 February 2009, p. 13.

Ragin, Charles C. (1994): *Constructing Social Research*, Thousand Oaks, CA: Pine Forge.

Ramirez, Alejandro, Gustav Ranis and Frances Stewart (1997): 'Economic Growth and Human Development', unpublished document.

Rapley, John (2004): *Globalization and Inequality: Neoliberalism's Downward Spiral*, Boulder, CO: Lynne Rienner.

Reddan, Fiona (2009): 'IFSC banks on fresh approach', in *The Irish Times*, 8 June 2009, p. 15.

Rhodes, Frank H. T. and John R. Healy (2006): 'Investment in Knowledge: A Case Study of a Philanthropy's Partnership with Government', in *Administration*, Vol. 54, No. 2, 2006, pp. 63–84.

Robbins, Lionel (1995): 'The Significance of Economic Science', in Meghnad Desai, ed.: *LSE on Equality*, London: London School of Economics, pp. 250–66.

Roche, William K. and Terry Cradden (2003): 'Neo-corporatism and social partnership', in Maura Adshead and Michelle Millar, eds: *Public Administration and Public Policy in Ireland: Theory and Methods*, London: Routledge, pp. 69–87.

Rottman, David B., Damien F. Hannan, Niamh Hardiman and Miriam M. Wiley (1982): *The Distribution of Income in the Republic of Ireland: A Study in Social Class and Family-Cycle Inequalities*, Dublin: ESRI.

Ruggie, John Gerard (2003): 'Taking Embedded Liberalism Global: The Corporate Connection', in David Held and Mathias Koenig-Archibugi (eds), *Taming Globalisation: Frontiers of Governance* (Polity Press, 2003), pp. 93–129.

Sabel, Charles (1996): *Ireland: Local Partnerships and Social Innovation*, Paris: OECD.

Sachs, Jeffrey (1997): 'Ireland's Growth Strategy: Lessons for Economic Development', in Alan W. Gray ed.: *International Perspectives on the Irish Economy*, Dublin: Indecon, pp. 54–63.

Scally, Derek (2008): 'Have we gone over the edge?', in *The Irish Times, Innovation* supplement, December 2008, pp. 14–15.

—— (2009): 'Merkel says Germany may come to Ireland's aid', in *The Irish Times, Business This Week* supplement, 27 February 2009, p. 1.

Scharpf, Fritz W. (2000): 'The viability of advanced welfare states in the international economy: Vulnerabilities and options', in *Journal of European Public Policy*, Vol. 7, No. 2, 2000, pp. 190–228.

Scott, S., Brian Nolan and Tony Fahey (1996): *Formulating Environmental and Social Indicators for Sustainable Development*, Dublin: ESRI.

Sexton, J. J. (2007): 'Trends in Output, Employment and Productivity in Ireland, 1995–2005', in Forfás, ed.: *Perspectives on Irish Productivity*, Dublin: Forfás.

Sinnott, Richard (1999): 'The electoral system', in John Coakley and Michael Gallagher, eds: *Politics in the Republic of Ireland*, London: Routledge, third edition, pp. 99–126.

Skocpol, Theda (1985): 'Bringing the State Back In: Strategies of Analysis in Current Research', in Peter B. Evans, Dieter Reuschemeyer and Theda Skocpol, eds: *Bringing the State Back In*, Cambridge: Cambridge University Press, pp. 3–37.

Slattery, Laura (2008): 'Jobless will jump to 8% next year, says ESRI', in *The Irish Times*, 8 October 2008, p. 8.

Smeeding, Timothy and Brian Nolan (2004): *Ireland's Income Distribution in Comparative Perspective*, LIS Working Paper Series No. 395, December 2004, Luxembourg: LIS.

Smith, Nicola Jo-Anne (2005): *Showcasing globalisation? The political economy of the Irish Republic*, Manchester: Manchester University Press.

Smyth, Emer and Damien F. Hannan (2000): 'Education and Inequality', in Brian Nolan, Philip J. O'Connell and Christopher T. Whelan, eds: *Bust to Boom? The Irish Experience of Growth and Inequality*, Dublin: Institute of Public Administration, pp. 109–26.

Smyth, Jamie (2008): 'Irish pay more for childcare than most Europeans', in *The Irish Times*, 4 October 2008, p. 3.

Smyth, John J. and Thomas A. Boylan (1991): 'Industrialisation and the Contribution of Multinational Companies to Economic Development in County Mayo', in Tony Varley, Thomas A. Boylan and Michael P. Cuddy, eds: *Rural Crisis: Perspectives on Irish Rural Development*, Galway: Centre for Development Studies, University College Galway, pp. 156–71.

Sørensen, Georg (2007): 'Globalisation and Development: Ireland and Denmark in Comparative Perspective', Aarhus: Department of Political Science, University of Aarhus.

Stapleton, Larry, Mícheál Lehane and Paul Toner, eds (2000): *Ireland's Environment: A Millennium Report*, Wexford: Environmental Protection Agency.

Strange, Susan (1994): *States and Markets*, second edition, London: Pinter.

Sweeney, Paul (1999): *The Celtic Tiger: Ireland's Continuing Economic Miracle*, Dublin: Oak Tree Press.

—— (2004): *Selling Out? Privatisation in Ireland*, Dublin: Tasc at New Island.

—— (2009): 'What we need for recovery is a major Keynesian-style stimulus package', in *The Irish Times*, 31 January 2009, p. 15.

Tansey, Paul (1998): *Ireland at Work: Economic Growth and the Labour Market, 1987–1997*, Dublin: Oak Tree Press.

—— (2007) 'Roaring trade required', in *The Irish Times, Business This Week* supplement, 6 April 2007.

—— (2008a): 'ESRI puts faith in resilient economy', in *The Irish Times, Business This Week* supplement, 16 May 2008, p. 3.

—— (2008b): 'Too many eggs in property basket,' in *The Irish Times, Business This Week* supplement, 30 May 2008, p. 6.

Tasc (2009): 'The Solidarity Factor: Public Responses to Economic Inequality in Ireland', Dublin: Think Tank on Action for Social Change (TASC).

Taylor, George (2005): *Negotiated governance and public policy in Ireland*, Manchester: Manchester University Press.

Teague, Paul and Jimmy Donaghey (2009): 'Social Partnership and Democratic Legitimacy in Ireland', in *New Political Economy*, Vol. 14, No. 1, March 2009, pp. 49–69.

Tierney, John (2006): 'The importance of the local in a global context', in David Jacobson, Peadar Kirby and Deiric Ó Broin, eds: *Taming the Tiger: Social Exclusion in a Globalised Ireland*, Dublin: Tasc with New Island, pp. 59–73.

Timonen, Virpi (2003): *Irish Social Expenditure in a Comparative International Context*, Dublin: Combat Poverty Agency and Institute of Public Administration.

Tomaney, John (1995): 'Recent Developments in Irish Industrial Policy', in *European Planning Studies*, Vol. 3, No. 1, pp. 99–113.

UN (2003): *Report on the World Social Situation: Social Vulnerability: Sources and Challenges*, New York: United Nations Department of Economic and Social Affairs.

UNDP (1990): *Human Development Report 1990*, New York: Oxford University Press.

—— (2007): *Human Development Report 2007/2008: Fighting Climate Change: Human solidarity in a divided world*, Basingstoke: Palgrave Macmillan for the UNDP.

UNICEF (2008): *State of the World's Children 2009*, New York: UNICEF.

Van Egeraat, Chris and Frank Barry (2009): 'The Irish pharmaceutical industry over the boom period and beyond', in *Irish Geography*, Vol. 42, No. 1, March 2009, pp. 23–44.

Varley, Tony and Chris Curtin (2006): 'The Politics of Empowerment: Power, Populism and Partnership in Rural Ireland,' in *The Economic and Social Review*, Vol. 37, No. 3, pp. 423–46.

Wade, Robert (1990): *Governing the Market: Economic Theory and the Role of Government in East Asian Industrialization*, Princeton, NJ: Princeton University Press.

Wall, Martin (2009): 'Partnership by other means', in *The Irish Times*, 9 May 2009, p. 17.

Walsh, Brendan (1999): 'What's in Store for the Celtic Tiger?', in *Irish Banking Review*, spring, pp. 2–16.

—— (2004): 'The Transformation of the Irish Labour Market: 1980–2003', in *Journal of the Statistical and Social Inquiry Society of Ireland*, Vol. XXXIII, pp. 83–115.

Walsh, Jim (2007): 'Monitoring Poverty and Welfare Policy 1987–2007', in Mel Cousins, ed.: *Welfare Policy and Poverty*, Dublin: Combat Poverty Agency and Institute of Public Administration, pp. 13–57.

Walsh, Jim, Sarah Craig and Des McCafferty (1998): *Local Partnerships for Social Inclusion?*, Dublin: Oak Tree Press.

WDC (1999): 'Promoting Foreign Direct Investment in the West', Ballaghadereen: Western Development Commission.

Welch C. (1989): 'Utilitarianism', in John Eatwell, Murray Milgate and Peter Newman, eds: *The Invisible Hand*, Basingstoke: Macmillan, pp. 257–69.

Whelan, Christopher T., Brian Nolan and Bertrand Maitre (2007): '*Consistent Poverty and Economic Vulnerability*', in Tony Fahey, Helen Russell and Christopher T. Whelan, eds: *Best of Times? The Social Impact of the Celtic Tiger*, Dublin: Institute of Public Administration, pp. 87–103.

Whelan, Christopher T. and Richard Layte (2007): 'Opportunities for All in the New Ireland?', in Tony Fahey, Helen Russell and Christopher T. Whelan, eds: *Best of Times? The Social Impact of the Celtic Tiger*, Dublin: Institute of Public Administration, pp. 67–85.

Whelan, Christopher T., Brian Nolan and Bertrand Maitre (2006): 'Trends in Economic Vulnerability in the Republic of Ireland', in *The Economic and Social Review*, Vol. 37, No. 1, spring 2006, pp. 91–119.

Whelan, Christopher T., Richard Layte, Bertrand Maitre, Breda Gannon, Brian Nolan, Dorothy Watson and James Williams (2003): *Monitoring Poverty Trends in Ireland: Results from the 2001 Living in Ireland Survey*, Dublin: ESRI.

Whelan, Karl et al. (2009): 'Nationalising banks is the best option', in *The Irish Times*, 17 April 2009, p. 13.

White, Mark C. (2005): 'Assessing the role of the international financial services centre in Irish regional development', in *European Planning Studies*, Vol. 13, No. 3, pp. 387–405.

Wickham, Ann (1980): 'National Educational Systems and the International Context: The Case of Ireland', in *Comparative Education Review*, Vol. 6, No. 4, pp. 323–37.

Wickham, James (1983): 'The Politics of Dependent Capitalism: International Capital and the Nation State', in Austin Morgan and Bob Purdie, eds: *Ireland: Divided Nation, Divided Class*, London: Ink Links, pp. 53–73.

—— (1983): 'Dependence and State Structures: Foreign Firms and Industrial policy in the Republic of Ireland', in Otmar Holl, ed.: *Small States in Europe and Dependence*, Vienna: Austrian Institute for International Affairs, pp. 164–85.

Wilkinson, Richard and Kate Pickett (2009): *The Spirit Level: Why More Equal Societies Almost Always Do Better*, London: Allen Lane.

Wilkinson, Richard G. (1996): *Unhealthy Societies: The Afflictions of Inequality*, London: Routledge.

World Bank (1993): *The East Asian Miracle: Economic Growth and Public Policy*, New York: Oxford University Press.

—— (1994): *World Development Report 1994*, New York: Oxford University Press.

—— (2002): *World Development Indicators 2002*, The World Bank: Washington, DC.

Wren, Maev-Ann (2003): *Unhealthy State: Anatomy of a Sick Society*, Dublin: New Island.

—— (2006): 'A Healthier State' in Tom O'Connor and Mike Murphy, eds: *Social Care in Ireland: Theory, Policy and Practice*, Cork: CIT Press, pp. 101–11.

Index

Page references in *italic* refer to tables.